d72e79-uatrd

FREE Unlimited General FAA ExamPrep

Course URL: **https://actechbooks.skyprepapp.com/users/enrol?course_id=98926**

As owner of this book, you are entitled to an unlimited number of A&P General practice exams for a period of 6 months from the time you sign in. Each exam will be a simulation of your actual FAA test using a random selection of the sample question bank found in this book. Following each attempt you will receive detailed results including corrections, explanations, and references from the H-8083-30A-ATB of those questions answered incorrectly.

SkyPrep Online ExamPrep can be accessed from any internet connected device with a web browser. You will need to Email or Call us for your unique access code. Once you have entered the above URL or scanned the QR code, fill out the registration form and enter the unique code provided to access ExamPrep.

Please remember that your free subscription is valid for only 6 months from the day you sign in; so plan accordingly. If you need more practice time, additional 6 month blocks are available for purchase at www.actechbooks.com

If you require assistance enrolling in or using ExamPrep, please write to: techsupport@actechbooks.com

Thank you for purchasing this product, and we wish you the best success in your exams.

D1607220

AIRFRAME & POWERPLANT MECHANICS

GENERAL TEST GUIDE

Written, Oral & Practical FAA Exam Prep with Practical Test Standards

FOR USE WITH
FAA-H-8083-30A & FAA-H-8083-30A-ATB
Airframe & Powerplant Mechanics Handbook

2022 EDITION

Printed and Published by
Aircraft Technical Book Company
72413 US Hwy 40 - Tabernash, CO 80478-0270 USA
+1.970.726.5111
www.actechbooks.com

COMPLETE MATCHING AND INTEGRATED STUDY SET
FOR THE A&P STUDENT

Available in Print Format or as Bookmarked PDF eBooks at *www.actechbooks.com*

FAA-H-8083 ATB TEXTBOOKS
GENERAL - AIRFRAME - POWERPLANT
ATB editions correct nearly 300 errors found in original editions.

FAA-H-8083 ATB WORKBOOKS
GENERAL - AIRFRAME - POWERPLANT
Written to match and referenced to the 8083 textbooks
with Exercises, Chapter Exams, and more.

FAA-H-8083 ATB TEST GUIDES
GENERAL - AIRFRAME - POWERPLANT
Written to match and referenced to the 8083 textbooks
with Written, Oral And Practical questions.

AC43.13 1B/2B
Acceptable Methods
Aircraft Inspection and Repair

A&P LOGBOOK
Record your shop and work experience.
FAA and EASA compliant.

AIRCRAFT TECHNICAL BOOK COMPANY

+1.970.726.5111

www.actechbooks.com
Tabernash, Colorado USA

TABLE OF CONTENTS

ISBN: 978-1951275235

9 781951 275235

HOW TO USE THIS TEST GUIDE

This book is designed to help you pass your FAA knowledge test. But, even more important, it is designed to help reinforce your understanding of the subject which you have been studying in the classroom or with your textbooks and other tools. Rather than this being the first book you pick up, it should be the last. When you take that route, you will find the questions in this book both easy and an excellent reinforcement to your studies.

The process we suggest is: Learn first from the textbooks and your instructors. When you are comfortable with a subject, and can see problems from different sides, then it is time to prepare for the test. This Test Guide, if properly used, will serve as your proof that you know what you need to know or if a subject requires further study. If so, the explanation with each question may refresh your understanding, or the textbook reference given will point you to the right place for review.

WHERE THE QUESTIONS COME FROM:
In 2011, FAA made the decision to stop publishing actual test questions. Previous test guides, where one could memorize questions are no more. Questions in this and other current FAA test guides now contain only examples of the type of question you will see on your actual FAA test.

Questions in this book come from two sources. First are previous FAA written questions which remain relevant to the curricula covered in the FAA 8083 Handbooks. Second are new questions written by Aircraft Technical Book Company and its team of authors to cover topics in the 8083s (the FAA required curricula) for which previous FAA samples did not exist.

Should you "make sure" and buy other test guides as well? In one sense it can't hurt. After all, our question on any particular topic may have different wording or may approach that topic slightly differently than another's. However, all will be different from the actual test questions, and different too from those asked by an examiner, or more important; by an employer.

So your first job is to learn in the classroom, study the textbooks, and understand the subject. With that, all questions, no matter how they are written will be easy and obvious, so making your career in aerospace rich and rewarding. Remember, its not the quick way; its the right way.

Learning Statement Codes A&P Mechanic — General

Learning statement codes replace the old subject matter codes and are noted on the test report. They refer to measurable statements of knowledge that a student should be able to demonstrate following a defined element of training. The learning statement corresponding to the learning statement code on the test report can be located in the Learning Statement Reference Guide on the Web site.

AMG001	Ability To Draw/Sketch Repairs/Alterations
AMG002	Calculate Center Of Gravity
AMG003	Calculate Weight And Balance
AMG004	Determine Correct Data
AMG005	Determine Regulatory Requirement
AMG006	Interpret Drag Ratio From Charts
AMG007	Aerodynamic Fundamentals
AMG008	Air Density
AMG009	Aircraft Cleaning - Materials/Techniques
AMG010	Aircraft Component Markings
AMG011	Aircraft Control Cables - Install/Inspect/Repair/Service
AMG012	Aircraft Corrosion - Principles/Control/Prevention
AMG013	Aircraft Drawings - Detail/Assembly
AMG014	Aircraft Drawings/Blueprints - Lines/Symbols/Sketching
AMG015	Aircraft Electrical System - Install/Inspect/Repair/Service
AMG016	Aircraft Engines - Performance Charts
AMG017	Aircraft Hardware - Bolts/Nuts/Fasteners/Fittings/Valves
AMG018	Aircraft Instruments - Tachometer Indications/Dual Tachometers
AMG019	Aircraft Metals - Inspect/Test/Repair/Identify/Heat Treat
AMG020	Aircraft Metals - Types/Tools/Fasteners
AMG021	Aircraft Publications - Aircraft Listings
AMG022	Aircraft Records - Required/Destroyed
AMG023	Aircraft Repair - Major
AMG024	Airframe - Inspections
AMG025	Airworthiness Certificates - Validity/Requirements
AMG026	ATA Codes
AMG027	Basic Physics - Matter/Energy/Gas
AMG028	Data - Approved
AMG029	Dissymmetry
AMG030	Effects Of Frost/Snow On Airfoils
AMG031	Electrical System - Components/Operating Principles/Characteristics/Symbols
AMG032	Environmental Factors Affecting Maintenance Performance
AMG033	External Loading
AMG034	Flight Characteristics - Autorotation/Compressibility
AMG035	Flight Operations - Air Taxi
AMG036	Fluid Lines - Install/Inspect/Repair/Service
AMG037	Fluid Lines - Material/Coding
AMG038	Forces Acting On Aircraft - Angle Of Incidence
AMG039	Forces Acting On Aircraft - Yaw/Adverse Yaw
AMG040	Fuel - Types/Characteristics/Contamination/Fueling/Defueling/Dumping
AMG041	Fundamental Inspection Principles - Airframe/Engine
AMG042	Fundamental Material Properties
AMG043	Generator System - Components/Operating Principles/Characteristics
AMG044	Geometry
AMG045	Ground Operations - Start/Move/Service/Secure Aircraft
AMG046	Helicopter Engine Control System
AMG047	Helicopter Flight Controls
AMG048	Information On An Airworthiness Directive
AMG049	Instrument Panel Mounting
AMG050	Maintenance Error Management
AMG051	Maintenance Publications - Service/Parts/Repair
AMG052	Maintenance Resource Management
AMG053	Mathematics - Percentages/Decimals/Fractions/Ratio/General

SAFETY, GROUND OPERATIONS, AND SERVICING

Shop Safety, Flight Line Safety, Fire Protection, Tiedown Procedures, Land Plane Tiedown, Ground Movement, and Support Equipment

CHAPTER
01

1-1 AMG045
The Material Safety Risk Diamond illustrated in Figure 1-1 below indicates the
- A. material is mildly radioactive.
- B. material flammability risk is high; and reactivity to water is high.
- C. material is biologically hazardous, but not flammable.

1-3 AMG045
What sound level becomes dangerous and requires the use of hearing protection?
- A. 100 db
- B. Varies depending on frequency
- C. Varies depending on duration

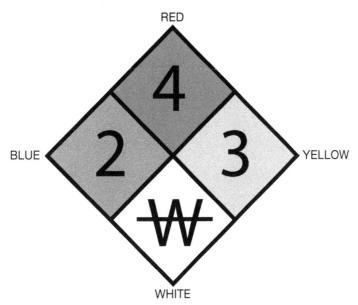

RED

BLUE — 4 2 3 — YELLOW

W

WHITE

Figure 1-1. Risk Diamond.

1-2 AMG045
Which government agency regulates policy regarding workplace safety in aviation facilities?
- A. FAA
- B. EPA
- C. OSHA

1-4 AMG045
A person should approach or leave a helicopter in the pilot's field of vision whenever the engine is running in order to avoid
- A. the tail rotor.
- B. the main rotor.
- C. blowing dust or debris caused by rotor downwash.

SAFETY, GROUND OPERATIONS, AND SERVICING

ANSWERS

1-1 Answer B.
The risk diamond on the Safety Data Sheet (SDS) label provides a quick reference to the risks associated with the product. Its four color segments represent Flammability (Red), Reactivity (Yellow), Health (Blue), and Special Hazards (White). The numbers (0-4) in the blocks represent the various levels for each hazard; the higher the number the higher the risk. There are only two approved symbols for Special Hazards: letter W with a line through it meaning that the material has a high reactivity to water and OX meaning that the material is a strong oxidizer.
[Ref: General Handbook H-8083-30A-ATB, Chapter 01 Page 3]

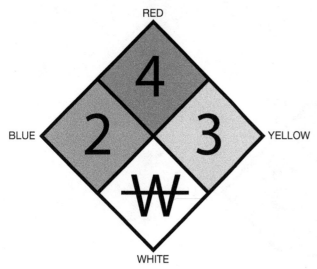

Figure 1-1. Risk Diamond.

1-2 Answer C.
The U.S. Department of Labor's Occupational Safety and Health Administration (OSHA) regulates policy regarding workplace safety. The Federal Aviation Administration deals with aviation safety, among other policies, and the Environmental Protection Agency regulates policy regarding the environment.
[Ref: General Handbook H-8083-30A-ATB, Chapter 01 Page 3]

1-3 Answer C.
Hearing protection is extremely important. Such machines as chainsaws, pneumatic drills, and snowmobiles produce a noise level of 100dB can cause hearing loss. Frequency (vibrations per second) particularly in the high range, such as in musical instruments, can also cause hearing loss. Duration of exposure is extremely critical in determining hearing loss, the longer the duration the greater the potential for loss. In each of the situations, you should wear hearing protection. However, duration plays a significant role when OSHA determines the requirements for mandatory hearing protection, which is what this question implies with the use of the word "requires". The bottom line here is PROTECT your hearing. Always wear hearing protection working with pneumatic drills, rivet guns, or other loud or noisy tools or machinery all producing high dB ranges and high frequency ranges, and even short duration exposure to these sounds can cause a hearing loss. Continued exposure will cause hearing loss. Don't forget to protect your hearing at home and during recreational activities as well. Duration, or how long you are exposed to a noise level, does not stop accumulating when you leave the job site. Listening to loud music on the way home adds to the total duration.
[Ref: General Handbook H-8083-30A-ATB, Chapter 01 Page 4]

1-4 Answer A.
Always approach the helicopter in view of the pilot. Approaching for any other direction is dangerous; the tail rotor is invisible when operating and the pilot will not see you. Additional safety precautions is not to approach the helicopter if the main rotor is turning, unless approved to do so and in the pilot's field of vision. If you should get dust or debris in your eyes while approaching or leaving a helicopter, immediately sit down to avoid further possible injury.
[Ref: General Handbook H-8083-30A-ATB, Chapter 01 Page 5]

1-5 AMG045
Which of the following conditions are required for fire?
  A. Heat, oxygen, fuel
  B. Heat, friction, carbon dioxide
  C. Fuel, combustion, heat

1-8 AMG045
Never use CO2 type fire extinguishers on burning metal because it
  A. can release toxic fumes.
  B. can cause explosive conditions on the metal.
  C. is generally ineffective.

1-6 AMG045
A Class B fire involves
  A. petroleum products or combustible liquids.
  B. energized electrical wiring.
  C. material such as wood, paper, upholstery, etc.

1-9 AMG045
The principle drawback of Halon 104, 1001, and 1202 type fire extinguishers is that they:
  A. Must be stored in high pressure cylinders.
  B. Are extremely toxic.
  C. Are ineffective against electrical fires.

1-7 AMG045
Which of the following is the most satisfactory extinguishing agent for use on a carburetor or intake fire?
  A. Dry chemical
  B. A fine water mist
  C. Carbon dioxide

1-10 AMG045
What class of fire involves the combustion of metallic material such as magnesium?
  A. Class B
  B. Class C
  C. Class D

SAFETY, GROUND OPERATIONS, AND SERVICING

ANSWERS

1-5 Answer A.
Three things are required for a fire:
1. Fuel or a combustible material,
2. Heat to raise the material to its ignition temperature,
3. Oxygen to sustain the combustion.

The chemical reaction caused by the interaction of these three ingredients creates fire. By eliminating even one, a fire cannot occur.
[Ref: General Handbook H-8083-30A-ATB, Chapter 01 Page 5]

1-6 Answer A.
Class B fires are caused by flammable petroleum products of other flammable or combustible liquids, greases, solvents, paints, and so forth.
[Ref: General Handbook H-8083-30A-ATB, Chapter 01 Page 5]

1-7 Answer C.
Because carburetors and intake fires will have grease and fuel associated with them, you can eliminate "a fine water mist" as an answer. Although both dry chemical and carbon dioxide extinguishers can be used on Class B fires, the best answer is carbon dioxide (CO_2), because dry chemical agents can leave chemical residues and dust making cleanup difficult and cause additional damage.
[Ref: General Handbook H-8083-30A-ATB, Chapter 01 Page 6-8]

1-8 Answer B.
Never use CO_2 on Class D fires. As with water extinguishers, the cooling effect of CO_2 on the hot metal can cause explosive expansion of the metal.
[Ref: General Handbook H-8083-30A-ATB, Chapter 01 Page 6]

1-9 Answer B.
Halon 104, 1001, and 1202 all have high Underwriters Laboratory (UL) toxicity ratings and are not recommended for aircraft use.
[Ref: General Handbook H-8083-30A-ATB, Chapter 01 Page 6]

1-10 Answer C.
Class D fire, is defined as fire in flammable metal. Usually Class D fires involve magnesium in the shop or in aircraft wheels and brakes, or are the result of improper or poorly conducted welding operations.
[Ref: General Handbook H-8083-30A-ATB, Chapter 01 Page 6]

1-11 AMG045

A fire extinguisher clearly marked with a white "C" in a blue circle is best suited to which type of fire?

A. Electrical equipment
B. Flammable liquids
C. Ordinary combustibles

1-12 AMG045

Which statement(s) is/are true regarding the tiedown of small aircraft?

1. Manila (hemp) rope has a tendency to stretch when it gets wet.
2. Nylon or Dacron rope is preferred to manila rope.
3. The aircraft should be headed downwind in order to minimize wing lift.
4. Leave the nose wheel or tail wheel unlocked.

A. 1, 2, 3, and 4
B. 1 and 2
C. 2

1-13 AMG045

When tying down an aircraft outside, whenever possible it should be positioned with the

A. nose facing into the wind.
B. tail facing into the wind.
C. anticipated upwind aileron into the wind and positioned downwards.

1-14 AMG094

When tying down a seaplane in strong winds, the practice of flooding the floats

A. is an acceptable method to secure the aircraft.
B. should only be done on the anticipated upwind float.
C. is unacceptable and should never be done.

1-15 AMG094

If a radial engine has been shut down for more than 30 minutes, the propeller should be rotated through at least two revolutions to

A. check for hydraulic lock.
B. check for leaks.
C. prime the engine.

1-16 AMG094

The priming of a fuel injected horizontally opposed engine is accomplished by placing the fuel control lever in the

A. IDLE-CUTOFF position.
B. AUTO RICH position.
C. FULL-RICH position.

SAFETY, GROUND OPERATIONS, AND SERVICING

ANSWERS

1-11 Answer A.
A fire extinguisher with a white "C" in a blue circle is the symbol that indicates it is to be used on Class C fires, which involve energized electrical wiring and equipment.
[Ref: General Handbook H-8083-30A-ATB, Chapter 01 Page 9]

1-12 Answer C.
As noted in the text, Manila rope shrinks when wet so care must be taken to allow for this shrinkage when tying down an aircraft. Nylon and Dacron resist shrinkage, mildew and rot, and have higher tensile strength than Manila rope and therefore preferred. When tying down an airplane it should be headed into the prevailing winds whenever possible and install all control locks.
[Ref: General Handbook H-8083-30A-ATB, Chapter 01 Page 10]

1-13 Answer A.
Positioning the airplane with the nose into prevailing wind whenever possible reduces ground movement from wind striking the empennage and helps prevent ground flutter of the control surfaces.
[Ref: General Handbook H-8083-30A-ATB, Chapter 01 Page 10]

1-14 Answer A.
Seaplanes tied down on land have been saved from high-wind damage by filling the floats with water in addition to tying the aircraft down in the usual manner.
[Ref: General Handbook H-8083-30A-ATB, Chapter 01 Page 11]

1-15 Answer A.
Before starting a radial engine that has been shut down for more than 30 minutes, confirm the ignition switch is OFF then turn the propeller two or three complete revolutions by hand to detect if a hydraulic lock is present.
[Ref: General Handbook H-8083-30A-ATB, Chapter 01 Page 13]

1-16 Answer A.
Generally, the mixture control should be in the "idle cut-off" position for fuel injection and in the "full rich" position for float-type carburetors.
[Ref: General Handbook H-8083-30A-ATB, Chapter 01 Page 13]

1-17 AMG045

When starting and ground operating an aircraft's engine, the aircraft should be positioned to head into the wind primarily

- A. to aid in achieving and maintaining proper air flow into the engine induction system.
- B. to help cancel out engine torque effect.
- C. for engine cooling purposes.

1-18 AMG094

How is a flooded engine, equipped with a float-type carburetor, cleared of excessive fuel?

- A. Crank the engine with the starter or by hand, with the mixture control in cutoff, ignition switch off, and the throttle fully open until the fuel charge has been cleared.
- B. Turn off the fuel and ignition. Discontinue the starting attempt until the excess fuel has been cleared.
- C. Crank the engine with the starter or by hand, with the mixture control in cutoff, ignition switch on, and the throttle fully open until the excess fuel has cleared or until the engine starts.

1-19 AMG094

Generally, when an induction fire occurs during starting of a reciprocating engine, the first course of action should be to

- A. direct carbon dioxide into the air intake of the engine.
- B. continue cranking to start the engine to blow out the fire.
- C. close the throttle.

1-20 AMG045

When approaching the front of an idling jet engine, the hazard area extends forward of the engine approximately

- A. 10 feet.
- B. 15 feet.
- C. 25 feet.

1-21 AMG045

When starting a turbofan engine with the aircraft's onboard APU at what minimum rpm should the APU be turning in order to successfully start the engine?

- A. At least 75% maximum rpm.
- B. 100% of maximum rpm.
- C. Any rpm equal or greater than the engine's self-sustain speed.

1-22 AMG094

During starting of a turbojet powerplant using a compressed air starter, a hot start occurrence was recorded. Select what happened from the following.

- A. The pneumatic starting unit overheated.
- B. The powerplant was preheated before starting.
- C. The fuel/air mixture was excessively rich.

SAFETY, GROUND OPERATIONS, AND SERVICING

ANSWERS

1-17 Answer C.
Position the aircraft to head into the prevailing wind to ensure adequate airflow over the engine for cooling purposes.
[Ref: General Handbook H-8083-30A-ATB, Chapter 01 Page 13]

1-20 Answer C.
This is a general guideline. As shown in Figure 1-17 of the General Handbook H-8083-30A-ATB, the intake hazard area for this aircraft is 25 feet and fan shaped. Always become familiar with specific safety issues of the aircraft with which you work.
[Ref: General Handbook H-8083-30A-ATB, Chapter 01 Page 18]

1-18 Answer A.
If the engine is inadvertently flooded or over-primed, turn the ignition switch OFF and move the throttle to the "full open" position. To rid the engine of the excess fuel, turn it over by hand or by the starter. If excessive force is needed to turn over the engine, stop immediately. Do not force rotation of the engine. If in doubt, remove the lower cylinder spark plugs to remove compression. Immediately after the engine starts, check the oil pressure indicator. If oil pressure does not show within 30 seconds, stop the engine and determine the trouble.
[Ref: General Handbook H-8083-30A-ATB, Chapter 01 Page 14]

1-21 Answer B.
An APU does not have an rpm control. It is either off, or it is operating at 100% of its rated power. As son as the APU reaches this normal operating condition it may be used for various functions.
[Ref: General Handbook H-8083-30A-ATB, Chapter 01 Page 17]

1-19 Answer B.
If an engine fire develops during the starting procedure, continue cranking to start the engine and blow out the fire.
[Ref: General Handbook H-8083-30A-ATB, Chapter 01 Page 15]

1-22 Answer C.
A hot start occurs when the engine starts, but the exhaust gas temperature exceeds specified limits. An excessively rich fuel/air mixture entering the combustion chamber usually causes this. Either too much fuel or not enough airflow can cause this condition.
[Ref: General Handbook H-8083-30A-ATB, Chapter 01 Page 19]

1-23 AMG094

An overly rich mixture of fuel/air when starting a turbine engine will cause a _____.

A. False start
B. Hung start
C. Hot start

1-24 AMG094

Which of the following is a typical cause of a hung start on a turbofan engine?

A. a malfunction of the ignition system
B. the starter cutting off too soon
C. an excessively rich fuel/air mixture

1-25 AMG094

During starting of a turbine engine using a compressed air starter, a hung start occurred. Select the proper procedure.

A. Advance power lever to increase RPM.
B. Re-engage the starter.
C. Shut the engine down.

1-26 AMG094

The most important condition to be monitored during start after fuel flow begins in a turbine engine is the

A. EGT, TIT, or ITT.
B. RPM.
C. oil pressure.

1-27 AMG094

Which is the proper sequence for starting a turboprop engine?

A. Turn on boost pump, turn on starter, turn on ignition, turn fuel on, monitor EGT
B. Turn fuel on, turn on boost pump, turn ignition on, engage the starter, monitor EGT
C. Engage the starter, turn on fuel, turn on boost pump, turn on ignition, monitor EGT.

1-28 AMG045

Which statement(s) below reflect(s) the typical requirement(s) when towing some aircraft?

1. Discharge all hydraulic pressure to prevent accidental operation of the nose wheel steering mechanism.
2. Tail wheel aircraft should be towed backwards.
3. If the aircraft has a steerable nose wheel, the torque-link lock should be set to full swivel.

A. 1 and 2
B. 2
C. 3

SAFETY, GROUND OPERATIONS, AND SERVICING

ANSWERS

1-23 Answer C.
A hot start is caused by an overly rich mixture of fuel and air; either too much fuel or not enough air. This is indicated by an abnormal speed of an increase in EGT temperature as indicated by that gauge. If this occurs the engine should be shut down immediately. A hung start or false start results in by low rpm and typically caused by not enough power to the engine starter.
[Ref: General Handbook H-8083-30A-ATB, Chapter 01 Page 17]

1-24 Answer B.
False or hung starts occur when the engine starts normally, but the rpm remains at some low value rather than increasing to the normal starting rpm. This is often the result of insufficient power to the starter, or the starter cutting off before the engine starts self-accelerating. In this case, the engine should be shut down.
[Ref: General Handbook H-8083-30A-ATB, Chapter 01 Page 17]

1-25 Answer C.
False or hung starts occur when the engine starts normally, but the rpm remains at some low value rather than increasing to the normal starting rpm. This is often the result of insufficient power to the starter, or the starter cutting off before the engine starts self accelerating. In this case, the engine should be shut down. If an air turbine starter is used, the engine should "light off" within a predetermined time after the fuel is turned on. This time interval, if exceeded, indicates a malfunction has occurred and the start should be discontinued.
[Ref: General Handbook H-8083-30A-ATB, Chapter 01 Page 19]

1-26 Answer A.
An important indication of a hot start is the speed at which the needle rises on the EGT (Exhaust Gas Temperature) gauge, other possible indicators include ITT (Interstage Turbine Temperature) or TIT (Turbine Inlet Temperature). If the needle rises abnormally fast, the fuel or power lever should be quickly moved to the fuel cut-off position before the gauge reaches the indicator red line to avoid damage to the engine.
[Ref: General Handbook H-8083-30A-ATB, Chapter 01 Page 19]

1-27 Answer A.
The text provides an example of a typical starting sequence for a turboprop aircraft. Always use the aircraft's checklists to start an engine, never depend on just memory no matter how many times you have done it. However, an understanding of how a turboprop engine operates will provide you with the general knowledge to order a logical sequencing for starting. You will gain this knowledge when you have completed your powerplant course of studies.
[Ref: General Handbook H-8083-30A-ATB, Chapter 01 Page 21]

1-28 Answer C.
Torque links, also called scissors absorb the shock of landing and taxiing the aircraft. The person in charge of the towing operation should verify, on aircraft with a steerable nose wheel, the locking scissors are set to full swivel for towing. The locking device must be reset after the tow bar has been removed from the aircraft. Persons stationed in the aircraft should not attempt to steer or turn the nose wheel when the tow bar is attached to the aircraft.
[Ref: General Handbook H-8083-30A-ATB, Chapter 01 Page 20]

1-29 AMG045

When towing a large aircraft, when crossing of a taxiway or runway is required _____,

A. a person should be in the cockpit to watch for obstructions.
B. persons should be stationed at the nose, each wingtip, and the empennage at all times.
C. a person should be in the cockpit to operate the brakes.

1-30 AMG094

When taxing (or towing) an aircraft, a flashing red light from the control tower means

A. stop and wait for a green light.
B. move clear of the runway/taxiway immediately.
C. return to starting point.

1-31 AMG045

When taxing or towing an aircraft, a flashing white light from the control tower means

A. move clear of the runway/taxiway immediately.
B. OK to proceed but use extreme caution.
C. return to your starting point.

1-32 AMG045

When taxing or towing an aircraft, an alternating red and green light from the control tower means

A. Move clear of the runway/taxiway immediately.
B. OK to proceed but use extreme caution.
C. Return to your starting point

1-33 AMG045

Which marshalling signal, in Figure 1-2, should be given if a taxing aircraft is in imminent danger of striking an object?

A. 1
B. 2
C. 3

Figure 1-2. Marshalling signals.

1-34 AMG045

Referring to Figure 1-3 below, identify the signal to engage the rotor on a rotorcraft.

A. 1
B. 2
C. 3

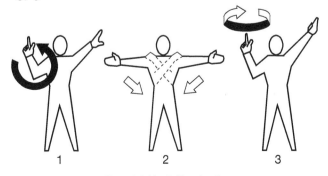

Figure 1-3. Marshalling signals.

SAFETY, GROUND OPERATIONS, AND SERVICING

ANSWERS

1-29 Answer C.
The person in charge should assign team personnel as wing walkers. A wing walker should be stationed at each wingtip in such a position that he or she can ensure adequate clearance of any obstruction in the path of the aircraft. A tail (empennage) walker should be assigned when sharp turns are to be made, or when the aircraft is to be backed into position. A qualified person should occupy the pilot's seat of the towed aircraft to observe and operate the brakes as required. "A" appears to be true, the main task of the person in the pilot seat is to operate the brakes, the wing walkers are the main lookouts for obstructions. Although "B" could easily be considered correct, be cautious of statements that say "all" or "never". There are often times exceptions to almost every rule. In this case, when an aircraft is towed from the gate to a maintenance facility it may well cross active taxi and runways and wing walkers are not allowed on active taxi and runways. Therefore "C" is the most correct answer.
[Ref: General Handbook H-8083-30A-ATB, Chapter 01 Page 21]

1-30 Answer B.
Refer to Figure 1-22 on page 1-21 of the General Handbook H-8083-30A-ATB to learn the light signals used by ATC to communicate with pilots when radio communication is not available. AMTs should know these signals as well in the event of taxiing an aircraft and radio communication with the tower is unavailable. In this question, a flashing red light means that you need to move clear of the runway or taxiway immediately. Light signals should be committed to memory, especially if authorized to taxi aircraft.
[Ref: General Handbook H-8083-30A-ATB, Chapter 01 Page 21]

1-31 Answer C.
Refer to Figure 1-22 on page 1-21 of the General Handbook H-8083-30A-ATB to learn the light signals used by ATC to communicate with pilots when radio communication is not available. AMTs should know these signals as well in the event of taxiing an aircraft and radio communication with the tower is unavailable. In this question, a flashing white light means that you must return to your starting point. Light signals should be committed to memory, especially if authorized to taxi aircraft.
[Ref: General Handbook H-8083-30A-ATB, Chapter 01 Page 21]

1-32 Answer B.
Refer to Figure 1-22 on page 1-21 of the General Handbook H-8083-30A-ATB to learn the light signals used by ATC to communicate with pilots when radio communication is not available. AMTs should know these signals as well in the event of taxiing an aircraft and radio communication with the tower is unavailable. In this question, an alternating red and green light means that you should proceed with extreme caution. Light signals should be committed to memory, especially if authorized to taxi aircraft.
[Ref: General Handbook H-8083-30A-ATB, Chapter 01 Page 21]

1-33 Answer C.
Refer to the Figure below for examples of the various standardized FAA hand taxi signals for aircraft. As with light signals, these should be committed to memory.
[Ref: General Handbook H-8083-30A-ATB, Chapter 01 Page 23]

Answer for Figure 1-2. Marshalling signals.

11-34 Answer C.
Refer to the Figure below for examples of the various standardized FAA hand taxi signals for helicopters. As with light signals, these should be committed to memory.
[Ref: General Handbook H-8083-30A-ATB, Chapter 01 Page 24]

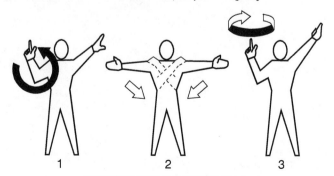
Answer for Figure 1-3. Marshalling signals.

1-35 AMG045
When refilling an aircraft with nitrogen, the system you are typically servicing is
A. landing gear.
B. engine boost pumps.
C. cabin climate control systems.

1-38 AMG040
Federal Specification "BB-0-925A Grade A" refers to the acceptable quality of
A. AVGAS for aircraft reciprocating engines.
B. aviator's breathing oxygen.
C. hydraulic fluid for aircraft flight control systems.

1-36 AMG045
What is a typical use for a ground support Air Cart?
A. Starting engines
B. Pressurizing tires
C. Performing cabin pressure tests

1-39 AMG040
What color fuel would you expect to find in a modern single engine piston powered airplane?
A. Blue
B. Colorless
C. Red

1-37 AMG040
What effect, if any, will aviation gasoline mixed with jet fuel have on a turbine engine?
A. No appreciable effect.
B. The tetraethyl lead in the gasoline forms deposits on the turbine blades.
C. The tetraethyl lead in the gasoline forms deposits on the compressor blades.

1-40 AMG040
Which type of jet fuel is a blend of kerosene and aviation gasoline?
A. JET A
B. JET A-1
C. JET B

SAFETY, GROUND OPERATIONS, AND SERVICING

ANSWERS

1-35 Answer A.
Nitrogen is used in servicing both tires and landing gear struts. While servicing tires or struts with high-pressure nitrogen, the technician must use caution while performing maintenance. Clean areas before connecting filling hose and do not over inflate.
[Ref: General Handbook H-8083-30A-ATB, Chapter 01 Page 25]

1-36 Answer A.
Air carts are used to provide low-pressure (up to 50-psi high volume flow) air, which can be used for starting the engines, and heating and cooling the aircraft on the ground (using the onboard aircraft systems). It generally consists of an APU built into the cart that provides bleed air from the APU's compressor for operating aircraft systems or starting engines. They are NOT used to pressurize tires.
[Ref: General Handbook H-8083-30A-ATB, Chapter 01 Page 26]

1-37 Answer B.
Never mix AVGAS and turbine fuel. Adding jet fuel to AVGAS will cause a decrease in the power developed by the engine and could cause damage to the engine (through detonation) and loss of life. Adding AVGAS to jet fuel, although allowed could cause lead deposits in the turbine engine and lead to reduced service life.
[Ref: General Handbook H-8083-30A-ATB, Chapter 01 Page 26]

1-38 Answer B.
Oxygen is commercially available in three general types: aviator's breathing, industrial, and medical. Only oxygen marked "Aviator's Breathing Oxygen" which meets Federal Specification BB-0-925A, Grade A, or its equivalent should be used in aircraft breathing oxygen systems. Industrial oxygen may contain impurities, which could cause the pilot, crew, and/or passengers to become sick. Medical oxygen, although pure, contains water, which can freeze in the cold temperatures found at the altitudes where oxygen is necessary.
[Ref: General Handbook H-8083-30A-ATB, Chapter 01 Page 27]

1-39 Answer A.
The standard fuel for modern reciprocating engines is 100LL which is dyed blue. Jet fuel is clear or straw colored. Two other rarely used and nearly obsolete grades of AVGAS for piston engines are 80/87 which is dyed red and 100/130 which is dyed green.
[Ref: General Handbook H-8083-30A-ATB, Chapter 01 Page 26]

1-40 Answer C.
JET B is a jet fuel which is a blend of kerosene and aviation gasoline.
[Ref: General Handbook H-8083-30A-ATB, Chapter 01 Page 27]

ORAL EXAM

1-1(O).   For aircraft with a steerable nose gear, what should be done before towing the aircraft?

1-2(O).   Where should team members be stationed when towing an aircraft?

1-3(O).   How fast can an aircraft be towed?

1-4(O).   Describe the brake usage rules when towing aircraft.

1-5(O).   What should be done prior to towing an aircraft on or across an active runway?

1-6(O).   Describe the safety precautions that should be observed while starting and running an engine.

1-7(O).   Describe the safety precautions to be followed when hand cranking an engine.

1-8(O).   Who is authorized to taxi aircraft?

1-9(O).   If radio communication is unavailable, how does the AMT communicate with ATC when taxiing an aircraft?

1-10(O).   Explain the term "hung start".

1-11(O).   Explain the term "hot start".

1-12(O).   Explain why an AMT should be familiar with standard light signals

1-13(O).   Where can you find a listing of standard aircraft taxiing signals?

1-14(O).   Describe the procedures for extinguishing an engine induction fire on a reciprocating engine.

1-15(O).   List at least three possible hazards associated with the ground operations of aircraft.

1-16(O).   Explain the possible results of mixing jet fuel with AVGAS in a reciprocating engine.

ANSWERS

ORAL EXAM

1-1(O).   On aircraft with a steerable nose wheel, the locking scissors are set to full swivel for towing. The locking device must be reset after the tow bar has been removed from the aircraft. Persons stationed in the aircraft should not attempt to steer or turn the nose wheel when the tow bar is attached to the aircraft.
[Ref: General Handbook H-8083-30A-ATB, Chapter 01 Page 21]

1-2(O).   The person in charge should assign team personnel as wing walkers. A wing walker should be stationed at each wingtip in such a position that he or she can ensure adequate clearance of any obstruction in the path of the aircraft. A tail walker should be assigned when sharp turns are to be made, or when the aircraft is to be backed into position. A qualified person should occupy the pilot's seat of the towed aircraft to observe and operate the brakes as required. When necessary, another qualified person is stationed to watch and maintain aircraft hydraulic system pressure.
[Ref: General Handbook H-8083-30A-ATB, Chapter 01 Page 21]

1-3(O).   The towing speed of the aircraft should not exceed that of the walking team members.
[Ref: General Handbook H-8083-30A-ATB, Chapter 01 Page 21]

1-4(O).   Before the aircraft to be towed is moved, a qualified person must be in the cockpit to operate the brakes in case the tow bar should fail or become unhooked. The aircraft can then be stopped, preventing possible damage. When moving aircraft, do not start and stop suddenly. For added safety, aircraft brakes must never be applied during towing except in emergencies, and then only upon command by one of the tow team members.
[Ref: General Handbook H-8083-30A-ATB, Chapter 01 Page 19-21]

1-5(O).   Prior to any movement of aircraft across runways or taxiways, contact the airport control tower on the appropriate frequency for clearance to proceed.
[Ref: General Handbook H-8083-30A-ATB, Chapter 01 Page 21]

1-6(O).   Make sure no property damage or personal injury will occur from the propeller blast or jet exhaust. During any and all starting procedures, a "fireguard" equipped with a suitable fire extinguisher shall be stationed in an appropriate place. If the aircraft is turbine engine powered, the area in front of the jet inlet must be kept clear of personnel, property, and/or debris (FOD). Follow manufacturer's checklists for start procedures and shutdown procedures.
[Ref: General Handbook H-8083-30A-ATB, Chapter 01 Page 13]

1-7(O).   If the aircraft has no self-starter, the engine must be started by turning the propeller by hand (hand propping the propeller). The person who is turning the propeller calls: "Fuel on, switch off, throttle closed, brakes on." The person operating the engine will check these items and repeat the phrase. The switch and throttle must not be touched again until the person swinging the prop calls "contact." The operator will repeat "contact" and then turn on the switch. Never turn on the switch and then call "contact." A few simple precautions will help to avoid accidents when hand propping the engine. While touching a propeller, always assume that the ignition is on. The switches which control the magnetos operate on the principle of short- circuiting the current to turn the ignition off. If the switch is faulty, it can be in the "off" position and still permit current to flow in the magneto primary circuit. This condition could allow the engine to start when the switch is off. Be sure the ground is firm. Slippery grass, mud, grease, or loose gravel can lead to a fall into or under the propeller. Never allow any portion of your body to get in the way of the propeller. This applies even though the engine is not being cranked. Stand close enough to the propeller to be able to step away as it is pulled down. Stepping away after cranking is a safeguard in case the brakes fail. Do not stand in a position that requires leaning toward the propeller to reach it. This throws the body off balance and could cause you to fall into the blades when the engine starts. In swinging the prop, always move the blade downward by pushing with the palms of the hands. Do not grip the blade with the fingers curled over the edge, since "kickback" may break them or draw your body in the blade path.
[Ref: General Handbook H-8083-30A-ATB, Chapter 01 Page 14]

ORAL EXAM

1-17(O).   Can AVGAS be used in a turbine engine and explain why or why not.

1-18(O).   List at least three precautions that should be observed when fueling an aircraft.

1-19(O).   Describe the general safety practices and precautions that should be observed when servicing aircraft oxygen systems.

1-20(O).   What do the numbers represent in AVGAS grade classifications?

1-21(O).   How can the various AVGAS grades be identified?

1-22(O).   What is JET A fuel made of?

1-23(O).   Name three types of contamination that can be found in aviation fuel.

1-24(O).   Describe how each of the three types of contamination can affect the fuel system.

1-25(O).   How can the presence of water be determined in a fuel sample?

1-26(O).   What benefits are achieved when tetraethyl lead (TEL) is added to aviation fuel?

1-27(O).   Is it acceptable to use automotive fuel in aircraft engines?

1-28(O).   Name the four main classifications of fires.

1-29(O).   Give an example of a combustible material associated with each of the four main classifications of fire.

1-30(O).   Describe how to use a fire extinguisher.

1-31(O).   Describe how to identify the correct fire extinguisher for each fire classification.

ORAL EXAM

1-8(O).   As a general rule, only rated pilots and qualified airframe and powerplant technicians are authorized to start, run up, and taxi aircraft.
[Ref: General Handbook H-8083-30A-ATB, Chapter 01 Page 21]

1-9(O).   Using standard taxi light signals.
[Ref: General Handbook H-8083-30A-ATB, Chapter 01 Page 21, Figure 1-22]

1-10(O).   False or hung starts occur when the engine starts normally, but the rpm remains at some low value rather than increasing to the normal starting rpm. This is often the result of insufficient power to the starter, or the starter cutting off before the engine starts self-accelerating. In this case, the engine should be shut down.
[Ref: General Handbook H-8083-30A-ATB, Chapter 01 Page 19]

1-11(O).   A hot start occurs when the engine starts, but the exhaust gas temperature exceeds specified limits. This is usually caused by an excessively rich fuel/air mixture entering the combustion chamber. This condition can be caused by either too much fuel or not enough airflow. The fuel to the engine should be shut off immediately.
[Ref: General Handbook H-8083-30A-ATB, Chapter 01 Page 19]

1-12(O).   Light signals are used if radio communications are unavailable to control and expedite the taxing of aircraft.
[Reference: AC65-9A, Page 520]

1-13(O).   Standard aircraft taxiing signals published in the FAA Aeronautical Information Manual (AIM).
[Ref: General Handbook H-8083-30A-ATB, Chapter 01 Page 22]

1-14(O).   If an engine fire develops during the starting procedure, continue cranking to start the engine and blow out the fire. If the engine does not start and the fire continues to burn, discontinue the start attempt. The fireguard should extinguish the fire using the available equipment. The fireguard must observe all safety practices at all times while standing by during the starting procedure.
[Ref: General Handbook H-8083-30A-ATB, Chapter 01 Page 15]

1-15(O).   Fire, during engine starting. Turning propellers and rotor blades. Jet exhaust or propeller blast. Jet inlets while engines are operating. Foreign object debris. Other aircraft, vehicles, personnel, and other obstacles. Additional hazards include high noise levels, slips, trips, and falls.
[Ref: General Handbook H-8083-30A-ATB, Chapter 01 Page 13]

1-16(O).   Adding jet fuel to AVGAS will cause a decrease in the power developed by the engine and could cause damage to the engine through detonation and engine failure leading to loss of life.
[Ref: General Handbook H-8083-30A-ATB, Chapter 01 Page 21]

1-17(O).   Adding AVGAS to jet fuel, although allowed, can cause lead deposits in the turbine engine and can lead to reduced service life.
[Ref: General Handbook H-8083-30A-ATB, Chapter 01 Page 26]

PRACTICAL EXAM

1-1(P). Given an aircraft or a landing gear mockup, service the tires per the maintenance manual.

1-2(P). Given an aircraft or a landing gear mockup, service the struts per the maintenance manual.

1-3(P). Given an aircraft or simulator, start, run-up, and shut down the aircraft or simulator.
NOTE: Always use the checklist. Aircraft used can be equipped with either a reciprocating or a turbine engine.

1-4(P). Demonstrate the proper hand signals used during aircraft ground operations.
NOTE: This can be accomplished in numerous ways. You may be asked to physically demonstrate various hand signals as called out by the examiner, the examiner may demonstrate them and you must explain what is meant, or you may be provided with pictures of the various hand and light signals and describe their meaning to the examiner.

1-5(P). Given the appropriate documentation, determine the approved engine oil(s) for a specific engine.

1-6(P). Given an aircraft, secure the aircraft for outside storage.
NOTE: Be prepared to tie-down various types of aircraft: tricycle, tail wheel, and/or helicopter.

1-7(P). Given an aircraft, fuel and/or defuel the aircraft, per the maintenance manual.
NOTE: This activity may be simulated.

1-8(P). Given an aircraft, sample the fuel, determining if the proper fuel is used, and whether contaminates have entered the fuel system.

1-9(P). Given an aircraft, set-up and connect an aircraft to a ground power unit.

1-10(P). Given an aircraft, connect a tow bar and prepare the aircraft for towing.

1-11(P). Given the approved hand signals, direct the movement of an aircraft.

1-12(P). Given an aircraft for engine mockup, locate and clear a liquid lock in the aircraft engine.

1-13(P). Given fire extinguishers or pictures of fire extinguishers, identify the types/classes of fires each fire extinguisher can be used for in a shop or on the flight line.

ORAL EXAM

1-18(O).   NOTE: Choose from the any of the following precautions.
Prior to fueling, the person fueling should check the following:

1. Ensure all aircraft electrical systems and electronic devices, including radar, are turned off.
2. Do not carry anything in the shirt pocket. These items could fall into the fuel tanks.
3. Ensure no flame-producing devices are carried by anyone engaged in the fueling operation. A moment of carelessness could cause an accident.
4. Ensure the proper type and grade of fuel is used. Do not mix AVGAS and JET fuel.
5. Ensure all the sumps have been drained.
6. Wear eye protection. Although generally not as critical as eye protection, other forms of protection, such as rubber gloves and aprons, can protect the skin from the effects of spilled or splashed fuel.
7. Do not fuel aircraft if there is danger of other aircraft in the vicinity blowing dirt in the direction of the aircraft being fueled. Blown dirt, dust, or other contaminants can enter an open fuel tank, contaminating the entire contents of the tank.
8. Do not fuel an aircraft when there is lightning within 5 miles.
9. Do not fuel an aircraft within 500 feet of operating ground radar.
10. When using mobile fueling equipment:
    a. Approach the aircraft with caution, positioning the fuel truck so that if it is necessary to depart quickly, no backing will be needed.
    b. Set the hand brake of the fuel truck and chock the wheels to prevent rolling.
    c. Ground the aircraft and then ground the truck. Next, ground or bond them together by running a connecting wire between the aircraft and the fuel truck. This may be done by three separate ground wires or by a "Y" cable from the fuel truck.
    d. Ensure the ground cables are in contact with bare metal or are in the proper grounding points on the aircraft. Do not use the engine exhaust or propeller as grounding points. Damage to the propeller can result, and there is no way of quickly ensuring a positive bond between the engine and the airframe.
    e. Ground the nozzle to the aircraft, then open the fuel tank.
    f. Protect the wing and any other item on the aircraft from damage caused by spilled fuel or careless handling of the nozzle, hose, or grounding wires.
    g. Check the fuel cap for proper installation and security before leaving the aircraft.
    h. Remove the grounding wires in the reverse order. If the aircraft is not going to be flown or moved soon, the aircraft ground wire can be left attached. When fueling from pits or cabinets, follow the same procedures as when using a truck. Pits or cabinets are usually designed with permanent grounding, eliminating the need to ground the equipment. However, the aircraft still must be grounded, and then the equipment must be grounded to the aircraft as it was with mobile equipment.

[Ref: General Handbook H-8083-30A-ATB, Chapter 01 Page 29-30]

1-19(O).   Before servicing any aircraft, consult the specific aircraft maintenance manual to determine the proper type of servicing equipment to be used. Two personnel are required to service an aircraft with gaseous oxygen. One person should be stationed at the control valves of the servicing equipment and one person stationed where he or she can observe the pressure in the aircraft system. Communication between the two people is required in case of an emergency. Aircraft should not be serviced with oxygen during fueling, defueling, or other maintenance work, which could provide a source of ignition. Oxygen servicing of aircraft should be accomplished outside hangars.

[Ref: General Handbook H-8083-30A-ATB, Chapter 01 Page 26-27]

1-20(O).   The two numbers indicate the lean mixture and rich mixture octane rating numbers of the specific fuel. In other words, with 80/87 aviation gasoline, the 80 is the lean mixture rating and 87 is the rich mixture rating number.

[Ref: General Handbook H-8083-30A-ATB, Chapter 01 Page 27]

ORAL EXAM

1-21(O). AVGAS can be identified by its color.
The color of the fuel should match the color band on piping and fueling equipment.
[Ref: General Handbook H-8083-30A-ATB, Chapter 01 Page 27]

1-22(O). Kerosene
[Ref: General Handbook H-8083-30A-ATB, Chapter 01 Page 27]

1-23(O). The types of contamination found in aviation fuel include water, solids, and microbial growths.
[Ref: General Handbook H-8083-30A-ATB, Chapter 01 Page 27]

1-24(O). The dissolved water is not a major problem until, as the temperature lowers, it becomes free water. This then poses a problem if ice crystals form, clogging filters and other small orifices. Solid contaminants are insoluble in fuel. The more common types are rust, dirt, sand, gasket material, lint, and fragments of shop towels. The close tolerances of fuel controls and other fuel-related mechanisms can be damaged or blocked by particles as small as one twentieth the diameter of a human hair. The effects of microorganisms are: 1) Formation of slime or sludge that can foul filters, separators, or fuel controls, 2) Emulsification of the fuel and 3) Corrosive compounds that can attack the fuel tank's structure. In the case of a wet wing tank, the tank is made from the aircraft's structure. They can also have offensive odors.
[Ref: General Handbook H-8083-30A-ATB, Chapter 01 Page 28]

1-25(O). Entrained water is suspended water droplets. These droplets may not be visible to the eye, but will give the fuel a cloudy look. The entrained water will settle out in time.
[Ref: General Handbook H-8083-30A-ATB, Chapter 01 Page 29]

1-26(O). Adding TEL to aviation fuel increases the critical pressure and temperature of a fuel. It also lubricates the engine valves.
[Ref: General Handbook H-8083-30A-ATB, Chapter 01 Page 9]

1-27(O). No. The lower grades of automobile fuel are not held within the tolerances required for aviation gasoline and usually contain a conservable amount of cracked gasoline, which may form excessive gum deposits. For these reasons, automobile fuels should not be used in aircraft engines, especially air-cooled engines operating at cylinder temperatures.
NOTE: Some engines have been issued Supplemental Type Certificates that allow the engine to be modified to use automotive gasoline. This modification will be noted in the aircraft documentation.
[Reference: AC65-9A, Page 74]

ANSWERS

ORAL EXAM

1-28(O). A, B, C, and D
[Ref: General Handbook H-8083-30A-ATB, Chapter 01 Page 5]

1-29(O). Class A fires occur in ordinary combustible materials, such as wood, cloth, paper, upholstery materials, etc.
Class B fires occur in flammable petroleum products of other flammable or combustible liquids, greases, solvents, paints, and so forth.
Class C fires occur involve energized electrical wiring and equipment.
Class D fires involve magnesium.
[Ref: General Handbook H-8083-30A-ATB, Chapter 01 Page 5]

1-30(O). Most extinguishers have a pin to pull that will allow the handle to activate the agent. Stand back 8 feet and aim at the base of the fire or flames. Squeeze the lever and sweep side to side until the fire is extinguished. A great way to remember this is use the acronym PASS – PULL the pin, AIM the hose/nozzle at the base of the fire, SQUEEZE the lever, and SWEEP the hose side to side.
[Ref: General Handbook H-8083-30A-ATB, Chapter 01 Page 9]

1-31(O). Fire extinguishers are marked using the same classification system as fires. Use the corresponding class fire extinguisher with the fire classification. A for A, B for B, C for C, and D for D. There are some fire extinguishers that can be used on multiple fire classifications and these are marked accordingly.
[Ref: General Handbook H-8083-30A-ATB, Chapter 01 Page 8-9, Figure 1-7]

REGULATIONS, MAINTENANCE FORMS, RECORDS, AND PUBLICATIONS

General Requirements, Checklists, Certifications, Civil Air Regulations, Suspected Unapproved Parts, and other FAA Documents

QUESTIONS

2-1 AMG097
What information is generally contained in Aircraft Specifications or Type Certificate Data Sheets?
- A. Empty weight of the aircraft
- B. Useful load of aircraft
- C. Control surface movements

2-2 AMG085
If during a scheduled inspection, a defect is found which makes the aircraft unairworthy; to whom must this defect be reported?
- A. The aircraft owner
- B. The aircraft owner and the FAA
- C. The aircraft owner, the FAA and the aircraft manufacturer.

2-3 AMG085
Upon inspection of an aircraft, it appears to you that the registration number which is visible on the airframe may not be of legal size or placement. Which regulation section would you review to confirm this?
- A. CFR Part 43
- B. CFR Part 45
- C. CFR Part 47

2-4 AMG097
For which of the following are Type Certificate Data Sheets issued for?
1. Engines
2. Propellers
3. Alternators/Generators
4. Avionics Systems
- A. Type Certificate Data sheets are issued for 2 of these 4 products.
- B. Type certificate data Sheets are issued for 3 of these products.
- C. Type Certificate Data Sheets are issued for all 4 of these products.

2-5 AMG066
Which regulation provides the airworthiness standards from an airplane certificated in the normal category?
- A. 14 CFR Part 27
- B. 14 CFR Part 25
- C. 14 CFR Part 23

2-6 AMG077
Which of the following are included in the regulatory definitions of "maintenance"?
- A. Overhaul, repair, parts replacement preservation, and preventive maintenance.
- B. Overhaul, repair, parts replacement, preservation, inspection, and preventive maintenance
- C. Overhaul, repair, parts replacement, preservation, and inspection

ANSWERS

2-1 Answer C.
Control surface movements are listed critical to flight and therefore listed on the TCDS and Aircraft Specifications. The empty weight of the aircraft is not listed as this varies with installed equipment and age. The useful load of the aircraft is also not listed as is dependent on the aircraft's empty weight.
[Ref: General Handbook H-8083-30A-ATB, Chapter 02 Page 33]

2-2 Answer A.
Should the inspector find the aircraft to be unairworthy or it does not meet the applicable type certificate data, airworthiness directives, or other approved data upon which its airworthiness depends, he/she must give the owner or lessee a signed and dated list of those discrepancies.
[Ref: General Handbook H-8083-30A-ATB, Chapter 02 Page 8 and FAR 43.11]

2-3 Answer B.
CFR Part 45 details aircraft identification requirements including the proper size and placement of N numbers. CFR Part 43 details maintenance and preventative maintenance techniques. CFR Part 47 details the processes by which an aircraft is registered.
[Ref: General Handbook H-8083-30A-ATB, Chapter 02 Page 10]

2-4 Answer A.
Type Certificate data sheets are issued for complete aircraft, engines, and propellers. Other items are considered components of the above and may be mentioned in a TCDS, but do not have one of their own.
[Ref: General Handbook H-8083-30A-ATB, Chapter 02 Page 33]

2-5 Answer C.
14 CFR Part 23 provides the airworthiness standards for airplanes certificated in the normal category.
[Ref: General Handbook H-8083-30A-ATB, Chapter 02 Page 5]

2-6 Answer C.
Maintenance is defined as inspection, overhaul, repair, preservation, and the replacement of parts, but excludes preventive maintenance. Preventive maintenance has its own definition and means simple or minor preservation operations and the replacement of small standard parts not involving complex assembly operations.
[Ref: General Handbook H-8083-30A-ATB, Chapter 02 Page 5, and FAR 1.1]

2-7 AMG051
A Technical Standard Order (TSO) is issued by whom?
  A. The aircraft industry
  B. Part manufactures
  C. The FAA administrator

2-10 AMG076
For aircraft operated under part 91, what difference is there, if any, between the record entry requirements for maintenance (e.g. repair or alteration) and the record entry requirements for inspections (beyond the description of the work performed and the type and extent of inspection)?
  A. There is no difference.
  B. Aircraft total time is required to be included only in the maintenance entry.
  C. Aircraft total time is required to be included only in the inspection entry.

2 8 AMG082
Which regulatory document(s) describes the standard for maintaining civilian aircraft in the United States?
  A. FAR Part 21
  B. FAR Part 43
  C. Manufacturer's maintenance manuals along with FAA Airworthiness Directives.

2-11 AMG076
For aircraft operated under Part 91, when is aircraft total time required to be recorded in aircraft maintenance records?
  A. After satisfactorily completing maintenance, preventive maintenance, rebuilding, and alteration (except inspections).
  B. After satisfactorily completing inspections.
  C. After satisfactorily completing maintenance, preventive maintenance, rebuilding, and alteration (including inspections).

2-9 AMG070
Each of the following must be displayed on a fireproof data plate attached to all US aircraft except
  A. manufacturer's name.
  B. aircraft serial number.
  C. owners contact information.

2-12 AMG076
According to regulations, what determines whether an aircraft is considered "large" or "small"?
  A. Maximum certificated takeoff weight is above or below 12,500 pounds.
  B. Maximum certificated capacity is above or below 20 passengers.
  C. Whether or not it is certified for commercial use.

REGULATIONS, MAINTENANCE FORMS, RECORDS, & PUBLICATIONS

ANSWERS

2-7 Answer C.
Technical Standard Orders (TSO) are issued and regulated by the FAA. You will find information regarding TSOs in 14 CFR Part 21.5, Subpart O.
[Ref: General Handbook H-8083-30A-ATB, Chapter 02 Page 5 and CFR 21.5]

2-8 Answer B.
14 CFR Part 43 Maintenance, Preventive Maintenance, Rebuilding, and Alteration provides the standard for maintaining civilian aircraft currently registered in the United States.
[Ref: General Handbook H-8083-30A-ATB, Chapter 02 Page 9]

2-9 Answer C.
Per 14 CFR Part 45 all type-certificated products must have specified information on a fireproof data plate or similar approved fireproof method including both the manufacturer's name and a serial number. The owner's contact information is NOT required.
[Ref: General Handbook H-8083-30A-ATB, Chapter 02 Page 9 and 14 CFR Part 45]

2-10 Answer C.
For inspection entries, the aircraft total time is required to be included. It is not mandatory for a maintenance entry.
[Ref: General Handbook H-8083-30A-ATB, Chapter 02 Page 10 and FAR 43.9, FAR 43.11]

2-11 Answer B.
Aircraft total time is only required when completing maintenance entries after satisfactorily completion of inspections.
[Ref: General Handbook H-8083-30A-ATB, Chapter 02 Page 10 and FAR 43.9, FAR 43.11]

2-12 Answer A.
The maximum certificated takeoff weight, either above or below 12,500 pounds, is used to determine if an aircraft is considered "large" or "small".
[Ref: General Handbook H-8083-30A-ATB, Chapter 02 Page 11 and 14 CFR Part 119]

2-13 AMG062
For how long must a Part 145 repair station keep records of maintenance activity?
- A. Until that aircraft's next scheduled inspection
- B. For a minimum of 2 years
- C. For a minimum of 5 years

2-16 AMG022
In order to reconstruct lost or destroyed aircraft maintenance records, what is it necessary to establish?
- A. Dates of all maintenance, preventive maintenance and alterations.
- B. Dates and/or times of all 100 hour, annual, or progressive inspections.
- C. Total time-in-service of the aircraft.

2-14 AMG064
Which type of FAA designated inspector may conduct maintenance or manufacturing inspections only at the place of their regular employment?
- A. DER
- B. DAR
- C. DMIR

2-17 AMG051
If a required repair to an aircraft does not have previously approved FAA data, how should the repair be approved?
- A. The repair may be approved by an A&P mechanic with Inspection Authorization (IA) approval.
- B. The data may be acquired through an approved document such as AC43.13 1B/2B.
- C. An FAA field approval must be requested.

2-15 AMG082
A certificated mechanic, without an inspection authorization, who signs the appropriate block on FAA Form 337 is doing what?
- A. Certifying that the work was done in accordance with the requirements of 14 CFR part 43.
- B. Approving the work for return to service.
- C. Stating that he/she is the person who has performed the work.

2-18 AMG076
When work is performed on an aircraft that necessitates the use of FAA Form 337, who should prepare the form?
- A. The person who performs or supervises the work.
- B. The person who approves for return to service.
- C. Either the person who approves for return to service, or aircraft owner or operator.

REGULATIONS, MAINTENANCE FORMS, RECORDS, & PUBLICATIONS

ANSWERS

2-13 Answer B.
A Part 145 repair station must keep records of maintenance activity for a minimum of 2 years.
[Ref: General Handbook H-8083-30A-ATB, Chapter 02 Page 14]

2-14 Answer C.
Designated Manufacturing Inspection Representatives (DMIR) make conformity inspections only for their employer. They are similar to "designated repairmen" because they are only authorized to inspect parts at their employers' facility.
[Ref: General Handbook H-8083-30A-ATB, Chapter 02 Page 14]

2-15 Answer C.
He/She is certifying the work was done in accordance with the requirements of 14 CFR Part 43.
[Ref: General Handbook H-8083-30A-ATB, Chapter 02 Page 16 and AC 43.9-1E]

2-16 Answer C.
In order to re-construct lost or destroyed maintenance records, it is necessary to establish the total time-in-service of the airframe. This can be done by reference to other records that reflect the time-in-service; research of records maintained by repair facilities; and reference to records maintained by individual mechanics, etc. Current status of applicable ADs must be established which may require a detailed inspection.
[Ref: Advisory Circular 43.9C]

2-17 Answer C.
If approved data is not available, an FAA field approval may be accomplished by completing FAA form 337 while leaving block 3 empty for later approval. The FAA will then assign specialists to asses the repair prior to giving approval.
[Ref: General Handbook H-8083-30A-ATB, Chapter 02 Page 16]

2-18 Answer A.
FAA Form 337 should be prepared by the person who performs or supervises the work.
[Ref: General Handbook H-8083-30A-ATB, Chapter 02 Page 17 and AC 43.9-1E]

2-19 AMG076
What is/are the appropriate action(s) concerning minor repairs performed on a certified aircraft?
1. FAA Form 337's must be completed.
2. Entries must be made in the aircraft's maintenance record.
3. The owner of the aircraft must submit a record of all minor repairs to the FAA at least annually.
   A. 1 and 2
   B. 2
   C. 2 and 3

2-20 AMG086
After an A&P rated mechanic completes a 100 hour inspection, what is required before the aircraft is returned to service?
   A. A systems check of each observed component.
   B. An operational check of the engine.
   C. A flight test of the aircraft.

2-21 AMG085
When a discrepancy list is provided to an aircraft owner or operator after an inspection is completed, it says in effect that?
   A. The item inspected is unairworthy.
   B. Except for these discrepancies, the item inspected is airworthy.
   C. The item inspected may or may not be airworthy depending on the discrepancies found.

2-22 AMG063
Which of the following are authorized to sign a return to service document following maintenance on an aircraft?
1. A certificated A&P mechanic.
2. A holder of Inspection Authorization (IA) certificate.
3. The aircraft manufacturer.
   A. 1 of these 3 persons may sign a return to service certificate.
   B. 2 of these 3 persons may sign a return to service certificate.
   C. All 3 of these persons may sign a return to service certificate.

2-23 AMG079
Which of the below is an appliance major repair?
   A. Overhaul of a hydraulic pressure pump.
   B. Repairs to a propeller governor or its control.
   C. Troubleshooting and repairing a broken circuit in the landing lights.

2-24 AMG025
When an aircraft is sold domestically, the Airworthiness Certificate
   A. must be surrendered to the local Flight Standards District Office.
   B. becomes invalid until the new owner makes application for a new Airworthiness Certificate.
   C. is transferred with the aircraft at the time of sale.

ANSWERS

2-19 Answer B.
Minor repairs that are completed only need to have the appropriate entries made in the aircraft's maintenance records.
[Ref: General Handbook H-8083-30A-ATB, Chapter 02 Page 17 and FAR 43.11, AC43.9C]

2-22 Answer C.
In addition to those listed in the question, an aircraft return to service document may also be signed by the holder of a repair station certificate, the holder of an air carrier certificate, a certificated private pilot, and in the case of light sport aircraft (LSA) a person with a repairman certificate and LSA maintenance rating.
[Ref: General Handbook H-8083-30A-ATB, Chapter 02 Page 16]

2-20 Answer B.
According to CFR Part 43.15, before authorizing an aircraft's return to service following a 100 inspection, the mechanic must run the aircraft's engine to determine satisfactory performance specifically noting proper power output, magneto operation, fuel and oil pressure, and cylinder and oil temperature. An A&P mechanic is NOT authorized to perform a flight test of the aircraft.
[Ref: General Handbook H-8083-30A-ATB, Chapter 02 Page 18 and FAR 43.11]

2-23 Answer A.
Refer to FAR Part 43 Appendix A for a listing of all major repairs. If the repair is not listed, then it is considered a minor repair. You should study this Appendix and be familiar with some of the more common major repair items.
[Ref: General Handbook H-8083-30A-ATB, Chapter 02 Page 20 and FAR 43 Appendix A]

2-21 Answer B.
When a mechanic has completed an inspection and found discrepancies, he/she is to document the completion of the inspection and note any discrepancies. Once the discrepancies are corrected, the item can be returned to service. No further inspection is required, nor does the original inspector have to be notified.
[Ref: General Handbook H-8083-30A-ATB, Chapter 02 Page 18 and FAR 43.11]

2-24 Answer C.
The Airworthiness Certificate stays with the aircraft and remains valid as long as all required inspections and maintenance items are current and in force.
[Ref: General Handbook H-8083-30A-ATB, Chapter 02 Page 39 and 44]

2-25 AMG079
Which of the following is an example of a major repair performed on an airframe?
- A. The upkeep and preservation of the airframe including the components thereof.
- B. The restoration of the airframe to a condition for safe operation after damage or deterioration.
- C. Simple or minor preservation operations and the replacement of small standard parts not involving complex assembly operations.

2-26 AMG079
The replacement of fabric on fabric-covered parts such as wings, fuselages, stabilizers, or control surfaces is considered to be a
- A. Minor repair unless the new cover is different in any way from the original cover.
- B. Minor repair unless the underlying structure is altered or repaired.
- C. Major repair even though no other alteration or repair is performed.

2-27 AMG079
Which is classified as a major repair?
- A. Splicing of skin sheets.
- B. Installation of new engine mounts obtained from the aircraft manufacturer.
- C. Any repair of damaged stressed metal skin.

2-28 AMG024
Each person performing an annual or 100 hour inspection shall use a checklist that contains at least those items in the appendix of
- A. 14 CFR Part 43.
- B. 14 CFR Part 65.
- C. AC 43.13.

2-29 AMG079
An A&P mechanic services an aircraft by changing its tires, replacing brake pads, and bleeding the brake system. How is this work recorded and the aircraft returned to service.
- A. An entry is made in the aircraft's maintenance log.
- B. A form 337 is submitted to FAA.
- C. A form 337 is placed in the aircraft's maintenance record but not submitted to FAA.

2-30 AMG076
After making a repair to an aircraft engine that is to be returned to service, an FAA Form 337 is prepared. How many copies are required and what is the disposition of the completed forms?
- A. Two; one copy for the owner and one copy for the FAA.
- B. Two; one copy for the FAA and one copy for the permanent records of the repairing agency or individual.
- C. Three; one copy for the aircraft owner, one copy for the FAA, and one copy for the permanent records of the repairing agency or individual.

REGULATIONS, MAINTENANCE FORMS, RECORDS, & PUBLICATIONS

ANSWERS

2-25 Answer B.
Refer to FAR Part 43 Appendix A for a listing of all major repairs. If the repair is not listed, then it is considered a minor repair. You should study this Appendix and be familiar with some of the more common major repair items.
[Ref: General Handbook H-8083-30A-ATB, Chapter 02 Page 20 and FAR Part 43 Appendix A]

2-26 Answer C.
Refer to FAR Part 43 Appendix A for a listing of all major repairs. If the repair is not listed, then it is considered a minor repair. You should study this Appendix and be familiar with some of the more common major repair items.
[Ref: General Handbook H-8083-30A-ATB, Chapter 02 Page 20 and FAR Part 43 Appendix A]

2-27 Answer A.
Refer to FAR Part 43 Appendix A for a listing of all major repairs. If the repair is not listed, then it is considered a minor repair. You should study this Appendix and be familiar with some of the more common major repair items.
[Ref: General Handbook H-8083-30A-ATB, Chapter 02 Page 20 and FAR Part 43 Appendix A]

2-28 Answer A.
A sample checklist for the completion of an annual or 100 hour inspection is contained in 14 CFR Part 43. Other checklists may be used, but at a minimum must include all those items listed in this sample checklist.
[Ref: General Handbook H-8083-30A-ATB, Chapter 02 Page 22, Chapter 12 Page 20 and FAR Part 43.15]

2-29 Answer A.
This work is considered a minor repair as it does effect weight & balance, strength, performance, or flight characteristics. As a minor repair, a form 337 is not required and a simple log book entry will suffice.
[Ref: General Handbook H-8083-30A-ATB, Chapter 02 Page 16, 20]

2-30 Answer A.
FAA Form 337 must be in duplicate, at a minimum. Although keeping a copy of the work you have performed, either as an individual or for your repair agency, is not uncommon.
[Ref: General Handbook H-8083-30A-ATB, Chapter 02 Page 21 and FAR Part 43.9 Appendix B]

2-31 AMG076

Which minimum license is required to perform a 100 hour inspection and authorize that aircraft for return to service?

A. An Airframe and Powerplant (A&P) license.

B. An A&P license with Inspection Authorization (IA).

C. A repairman's certificate.

2-32 AMG076

A regular 100 hour inspection is performed on an aircraft which is partially used for hire and on which the hobbs meter (time in use) reads 1,407 hours. When is the next 100 hour inspection due?

A. 1,507 hours.

B. 1,500 hours.

C. At the next 100 hours of commercial use.

2-33 AMG076

What is the regulatory definition of "preventive maintenance"?

A. Simple or minor preservation operations and the replacement of small standard parts not involving complex assembly operations.

B. All preservation operations and the replacement of standard parts, including any required assembly operations.

C. All preservation operations and the replacement of standard parts not involving complex assembly operations.

2-34 AMG068

How often must an altimeter static system or altitude encoding transponder be inspected by a properly rated inspector?

1. Every 24 months.

2. Anytime the static system is opened and closed.

3. As part of every annual, or 100 hour inspection.

A. All of the above

B. 1 & 2 above

C. 2 & 3 above

2-35 AMG076

For aircraft operated under Part 91, which of the following records must be retained and transferred with the aircraft when it is sold?

A. Records of maintenance, alterations, preventive maintenance, 100 hour, annual, and progressive inspections.

B. Records of inspections performed in accordance with 14 CFR part 43, Appendix D.

C. Records of the current status of applicable ADs, and date and time when recurring ADs are next due.

2-36 AMG062

How long are AD compliance records to be kept?

A. Until the work is repeated or superseded by other work.

B. For one year after the work is performed, or until the work is superseded.

C. They shall be retained and transferred with the aircraft when it is sold.

REGULATIONS, MAINTENANCE FORMS, RECORDS, & PUBLICATIONS

ANSWERS

2-31 Answer A.
The difference between 100 hour and annual inspections is that an annual inspection must be performed by a person with an Inspection Authorization while a 100 hour inspection requires only an A&P license.
[Ref: General Handbook H-8083-30A-ATB, Chapter 02 Page 21, and 14 CFR Section 65.95]

2-32 Answer B.
An aircraft subject to 100 hour inspections may exceed the 100 hour increments by up to 10 hours, but only for the purpose of ferrying that aircraft to the location where the inspection will be performed. But in either case, the time of that excess use will be subtracted from the time allowed before the next inspection.
[Ref: General Handbook H-8083-30A-ATB, Chapter 02 Page 22]

2-33 Answer A.
Preventative maintenance is defined as the "simple or minor preservation operations and the replacement of small standard parts not involving complex assembly operations."
[Ref: General Handbook H-8083-30A-ATB, Chapter 02 Page 22, and FAR Part 1]

2-34 Answer B.
Per the FAR, the altimeter system and altitude recording equipment must be tested every 24 months and, except for the use of system drain and alternate static pressure valves, following any opening and closing of the static pressure system. The system should be tested and inspected and found to comply with paragraph (a), appendix E, of part 43 of this chapter.
[Ref: General Handbook H-8083-30A-ATB, Chapter 02 Page 23, and FAR Part 91.411]

2-35 Answer C.
Although A and B seem logical as correct answers, only C is correct as specified in FAR 91.419. Additional records are also required to be transferred but not as stated in the other answers.
[Ref: General Handbook H-8083-30A-ATB, Chapter 02 Page 24, and FAR Part 91.419]

2-36 Answer C.
The registered owner shall maintain the current status of applicable airworthiness directives (AD) and safety directives including the method of compliance, the AD or safety directive number and revision date. If the AD or safety directive involves recurring action, the time and date when the next action is required, and shall be retained and transferred with the aircraft at the time the aircraft is sold.
[Ref: General Handbook H-8083-30A-ATB, Chapter 02 Page 24, and FAR Part 91.417]

2-37 AMG075
When inspecting an aircraft you suspect an unapproved part has been installed at a prior time, you should
  A. Remove the part and report to FAA Surveillance and Analysis division.
  B. Contact your supervisor.
  C. Note your finding in the aircraft maintenance log. If it appears faulty, replace it.

2-40 AMG062
If an airworthiness directive is issued without an NPRM, typically when is compliance required?
  A. At the time of the next scheduled inspection.
  B. Within 30 days of its issuance.
  C. Prior to the next flight.

2-38 AMG062
Civil Aviation Regulations (CARs) are referred to when?
  A. Inspecting or repairing aerobatic aircraft.
  B. Inspecting or repairing aircraft certified outside the US.
  C. Inspecting or repairing aircraft which entered service prior to the 1960s.

2-41 AMG062
Airworthiness Directives are issued primarily to?
  A. Provide information about malfunction or defect trends.
  B. Present recommended maintenance procedures for correcting potentially hazardous defects.
  C. Correct an unsafe condition

2-39 AMG051
Which of these publications contains standards for protrusion of bolts, studs, and screws through self-locking nuts?
  A. AC 43.13-2B
  B. Aircraft Specifications or Type Certificate Data Sheets
  C. AC 43.13-1B

2-42 AMG062
When is a mechanic responsible for checking AD compliance?
  A. Never; the owner or operator is solely responsible.
  B. When performing an inspection required under part 91, 125, or 135.
  C. Anytime an aircraft or a critical part is returned to service.

ANSWERS

2-37 Answer B.
If either the physical part or the paperwork associated with the part is questionable, it is best to contact the shop foreman, shift supervisor, or the assigned quality individual to discuss your concerns. Suspected unapproved parts (SUPs) should be segregated and quarantined until proper disposition can be determined. Contacting the manufacturer of the product is a good way to start gathering the facts concerning the product in question.
[Ref: General Handbook H-8083-30A-ATB, Chapter 02 Page 27]

2-38 Answer C.
The CARs were a part of the original certification basis through the 1960s and are still used as a reference regarding aircraft which were first certified before those dates. Later aircraft are certified under regulation 14 CFR Part 25.
[Ref: General Handbook H-8083-30A-ATB, Chapter 02 Page 27, and AC 43.9-1E]

2-39 Answer C.
Advisory Circular 43.13-1B contains this information. AC 43.13-2B contains information on aircraft alterations.
[Ref: General Handbook H-8083-30A-ATB, Chapter 02 Page 27, and AC 43.13-1B]

2-40 Answer C.
Typically an NPRM (Notice of Proposed Rule Making) is issued 60 days prior to the actual issuance of the AD. However in the case of a critical safety issue, an emergency AD may be issued without the prior NPRM. In this case, all corrective actions required by the AD are critical and typically must be performed immediately.
[Ref: General Handbook H-8083-30A-ATB, Chapter 02 Page 27]

2-41 Answer C.
Airworthiness Directives (ADs) are issued to provide guidance on correcting unsafe conditions.
[Ref: General Handbook H-8083-30A-ATB, Chapter 02 Page 30]

2-42 Answer B.
Whenever performing an inspection required under part 91, 125, or 135, the mechanic must perform a check for compliance with all applicable ADs.
[Ref: General Handbook H-8083-30A-ATB, Chapter 02 Page 30, and AC39-7C]

2-43 AMG051
In order to replace a critical component of an older aircraft with a modern component of superior quality, which is the minimum required?
   A. Documentation of the superior quality.
   B. A supplemental type certificate.
   C. Approval of an A&P with Inspection Authorization.

2-44 AMG062
An aircraft has a total time in service of 468 hours. An airworthiness directive requiring 200 hour recurring inspections was initially complied with at 454 hours in service. How many additional hours in service may be accumulated before the airworthiness directive must again be complied with?
   A. 46
   B. 132
   C. 186

2-45 AMG051
Regarding the statements below:
   1. Manufacturer's data and FAA publications such as Airworthiness Directives, Type Certificate Data Sheets, and Advisory Circulars are all approved data.
   2. FAA publications such as Technical Standard Orders, Airworthiness Directives, Type Certificate Data Sheets, Aircraft Specifications and Supplemental Type Certificates are all approved data.
   A. Both 1 and 2 are true
   B. Only 1 is true
   C. Only 2 is true

2-46 AMG089
What FAA-approved document gives the leveling means to be used when weighing an aircraft?
   A. Type Certificate Data Sheet
   B. AC43.13-1B
   C. Manufacturer's maintenance manual

2-47 AMG097
Regarding the statements below,
   1. A Supplemental Type Certificate may be issued to more than one applicant for the same design change, providing each applicant shows compliance with the applicable airworthiness requirement.
   2. An installation of an item manufactured in accordance with the Technical Standard Order system requires no further approval for installation in a particular aircraft.
   A. Both 1 and 2 are true
   B. Neither 1 nor 2 is true
   C. Only 1 is true

2-48 AMG051
Aviation Maintenance Alerts (formerly General Aviation Airworthiness Alerts) do what?
   A. Provide mandatory procedures to prevent or correct serious aircraft problems.
   B. Provide information about aircraft problems and suggested corrective actions.
   C. Provide temporary emergency procedures until Airworthiness Directives can be issued.

ANSWERS

2-43 Answer B.
A Supplemental Type Certificate (STC) is issued by the FAA to approve a product modification of the airframe, engine, or propeller and serves as an acceptable change to the aircraft's original type certificate.
[Ref: General Handbook H-8083-30A-ATB, Chapter 02 Page 30]

2-46 Answer A.
The Type Certificate Data Sheet provides information on the leveling means to be used when weighting an aircraft.
[Ref: General Handbook H-8083-30A-ATB, Chapter 02 Page 30, and Chapter 12 Page 31-35]

2-44 Answer C.
The AD was complied with at 454 hours total time. It has accumulated 14 hours since the last inspection. Subtract 14 from the 200 hour inspection interval, which leaves an additional 186 hours before the next inspection is due.
[Ref: General Handbook H-8083-30A-ATB, Chapter 02 Page 30]

2-47 Answer C.
Number 1 is true. Number 2 is not true, as the installation of a TSO item requires approval.
[Ref: General Handbook H-8083-30A-ATB, Chapter 02 Page 30, and Chapter 12 Page 31, and FAR 21.115]

2-45 Answer C.
Although ADs provide guidance for the correction of unsafe conditions, they are not considered approved data to actually comply with the maintenance. They usually refer you to other approved data sources for the actual completion of the maintenance.
[Ref: General Handbook H-8083-30A-ATB, Chapter 02 Page 8]

2-48 Answer B.
These alerts provide information about aircraft problems and suggested corrective actions.
[Ref: General Handbook H-8083-30A-ATB, Chapter 02 Page 31, and AC 43.16]

2-49 AMG097
A Type Certificate Data Sheet (TCDS) specifies?
  A. The make and model engine allowed.
  B. The minimum and maximum horsepower and weight of an allowed engine.
  C. Airworthiness directives effecting the engine.

2-50 AMG075
Where would you find information regarding the overhaul schedule for a propeller?
  A. Type certificate data sheet.
  B. Manufacturer's service bulletin.
  C. Manufacturer's maintenance manual.

2-51 AMG072
Placards required on an aircraft are specified in
  A. AC 43.13-1B.
  B. FAR's under which the aircraft was type certificated.
  C. Aircraft Specifications or Type Certificate Data Sheets.

2-52 AMG063
Regarding the statements below:
  1. The FARs require approval after compliance with the data of a Supplemental Type Certificate.
  2. An installation of an item manufactured in accordance with the Technical Standard Order system requires no further approval for installation in a particular aircraft.
  A. Only 2 is true
  B. Neither 1 nor 2 are true
  C. Only 1 is true

2-53 AMG026
The Air Transport Association of America (ATA) Specification No. 100 does what?
  1. Establishes a standard for the presentation of technical data in maintenance manuals.
  2. Divides the aircraft into numbered systems and subsystems in order to simplify locating maintenance instructions.

Regarding the above statements;
  A. Both 1 and 2 are true.
  B. Neither 1 nor 2 are true.
  C. Only 1 is true.

2-54 AMG025
In which of the following cases would a Special Airworthiness certificate be issued, rather than a Standard Certificate?
  A. For transport category aircraft.
  B. For acrobatic aircraft.
  C. For Light Sport Aircraft (LSA) category airplanes.

ANSWERS

2-49 Answer A.
The type certificate data sheet describes the specifications of the aircraft as it was designed and constructed by its manufacturer for which a type certificate is given. As a particular engine is specified by the manufacturer, details of an alternative engine is not relevant. As airworthiness directives would be created after the manufacture of the aircraft, they would be found as issued in the Federal Register, or a regulatory guidance library.
[Ref: General Handbook H-8083-30A-ATB, Chapter 02 Page 27-33]

2-50 Answer C.
Inspections and maintenance schedules, as well as the required techniques are published in the manufacturer's maintenance manual. The TCDS will only identify the component required, Service bulletins will advise on newly recommended procedures to perform the specific task.
[Ref: General Handbook H-8083-30A-ATB, Chapter 02 Page 33]

2-51 Answer C.
This question is referring to a specific aircraft and its required placard information will be found in the Aircraft Specifications or Type Certificate Data Sheets.

Note: These requirements are derived from the FAR that the aircraft was type certificated under.
[Ref: General Handbook H-8083-30A-ATB, Chapter 02 Page 5, Chapter 12 Page 33]

2-52 Answer C.
Only 1 is true.
The installation of a TSO item requires approval.
[Ref: General Handbook H-8083-30A-ATB, Chapter 02 Page 31, and FAR Part 21 Subpart E]

2-53 Answer A.
Both 1 and 2 are true. You will want to note ATA Specification 100 has been superseded by ATA iSpec 2200 and is now a global aviation industry standard for the content, structure, and electronic exchange of aircraft engineering, maintenance, and flight operations information.
[Ref: General Handbook H-8083-30A-ATB, Chapter 02 Page 36]

2-54 Answer C.
Standard Airworthiness Certificates are available in the following categories: Normal, Utility, Acrobatic, Commuter, Transport, and Manned Balloon. In all other cases (notably here LSA aircraft) a Special certificate is authorized.
[Ref: General Handbook H-8083-30A-ATB, Chapter 02 Page 39]

2-55 AMG076

Which statement is true regarding the use of FAA Form 337?

A. FAA Form 337 is authorized for use with both U.S. and foreign registered aircraft.
B. FAA Form 337 is authorized for use with U.S. registered aircraft, and foreign registered aircraft when located in the United States.
C. FAA Form 337 is not authorized for use with other than U.S. registered aircraft.

2-56 AMG076

Where should you find this entry?

"Removed right wing from aircraft and removed skin from outer 6 feet. Repaired buckled spar 49 inches from tip in accordance with Figure 8 in the manufacturer's structural repair manual No. 28-1."

A. Engine Maintenance Record
B. Aircraft Minor Repair and Alteration Record
C. FAA Form 337

2-57 AMG076

If more space is needed for a work description entered on FAA Form 337, what information should be included on the attached sheet(s), in addition to the rest of the work description?

A. Make, model, and serial number of the aircraft,
B. Aircraft nationality and registration mark, and the date the work was accomplished.
C. Name, date, and office designator of the FAA inspector from the supervising district office.

2-58 AMG059

Where do you record the compliance of an Airworthiness Directives or manufacturers' service bulletin?

A. FAA Form 337
B. Aircraft Maintenance Records
C. Flight Manual

2-59 AMG059

Which statement is true regarding the requirements for maintenance record format?

A. Any format that provides record continuity and includes the required information may be used.
B. The format provided by the manufacturer of the aircraft must be retained.
C. Any desired change from the manufacturer provided format requires approval from the Federal Aviation Administration.

2-60 AMG076

For how long must records of required scheduled inspections performed on an aircraft be kept?

A. For 1 year.
B. For 5 years.
C. Permanently.

REGULATIONS, MAINTENANCE FORMS, RECORDS, & PUBLICATIONS

ANSWERS

2-55 Answer C.
FAA Form 337 is not authorized for use with aircraft not registered in the United States.
[Ref: General Handbook H-8083-30A-ATB, Chapter 02 Page 40, and FAR Part 43.9 and AC 43.9-1F]

2-56 Answer C.
This is an example of a maintenance record entry. However, you would not put it in the engine maintenance record (log), and there is no such document "aircraft minor repair and alteration record", therefore FAA Form 337 is the most correct answer.
[Ref: General Handbook H-8083-30A-ATB, Chapter 02 Page 40-41, and FAR 43 Appendix A&B]

2-57 Answer B.
Attach sheets showing the aircraft nationality, registration mark, and the date the work was completed. All attachments to item 8 must be submitted on 8 1/2- by 11-inch paper to allow for proper processing into the aircraft historical record at the aircraft registry.
[Ref: General Handbook H-8083-30A-ATB, Chapter 02 Page 40-41, and AC 43.9-1F]

2-58 Answer B.
Record the compliance to an AD and service bulletins in the aircraft maintenance records.
[Ref: General Handbook H-8083-30A-ATB, Chapter 02 Page 43]

2-59 Answer A.
Maintenance records can be of any format that provides for record continuity and includes the required information.
[Ref: General Handbook H-8083-30A-ATB, Chapter 02 Page 43, FAR 43.9, and AC 61-23C]

2-60 Answer B.
Records of regularly scheduled inspection such as 100 hour or annual inspections must be kept until the next scheduled inspection is performed. As all aircraft must undergo at least an annual inspection, those records must be kept for a minimum of 1 year.
[Ref: General Handbook H-8083-30A-ATB, Chapter 02 Page 44]

2-61 AMG086
Where would one find information related to the current status of life limited parts on an aircraft?
A. The aircraft's temporary records.
B. The aircraft's permanent record.
C. The form 337 submitted when that part was installed.

2-62 AMG062
In which manner must permanent records of an aircraft be kept?
A. Permanent records must be preserved in writing as a physical document.
B. Permanent records may be preserved in either electronic or physical format.
C. Permanent records must be preserved as stated by the local FSDO office.

2-63 AMG076
In order to conduct line maintenance on a Light Sport Aircraft (LSA) such as replacing a fuel pump, the technician must hold the minimum rating of _____.
A. A&P.
B. LSA repairman –maintenance.
C. LSA repairman – inspection.

2-64 AMG079
What constitutes a major repair on a Light Sport Aircraft (LSA)?
A. Any procedure which alters the weight and balance or operational characteristics of the aircraft, powerplant or propeller.
B. Any procedure involving structural aspects of the aircraft.
C. Any procedure for which instructions are not included in the maintenance manual.

ANSWERS

2-61 Answer B.
Per CFR 43.9, permanent records of an aircraft includes total time in service, time since last overhaul, current inspection status, status of applicable ADs, and the status of life limited parts, and major alteration forms.
[Ref: General Handbook H-8083-30A-ATB, Chapter 02 Page 44]

2-63 Answer C.
An A&P certificate is not required to work on a light sport aircraft. Instead, the ratings for LSA are repairman-inspection and repairman-maintenance. The repairman-inspection rating allows the holder to perform any procedure consider a minor repair, whereas the instructions to perform that procedure are given in the aircraft maintenance manual.
[Ref: General Handbook H-8083-30A-ATB, Chapter 02 Page 45]

2-62 Answer B.
Permanent records may be kept in the manner chosen, typically by the Part 145 maintenance organization, so long as they remain in fact permanent and accessible on demand. These choices include on paper, electronically within the repair station's own servers, or through a number of commercial agencies who provide this service.
[Ref: General Handbook H-8083-30A-ATB, Chapter 02 Page 44]

2-64 Answer C.
For Light Sport Aircraft, a minor repair or alterations are considered any procedure in which the instructions to carry out the work are included in the aircraft maintenance manual. Any other maintenance or alteration in which the process must be determined by other sources or by the technician's personal knowledge is considered a major repairs.
[Ref: General Handbook H-8083-30A-ATB, Chapter 02 Page 45]

ORAL EXAM

2-1(O).   How is a major structural repair documented?

2-2(O).   Where can a mechanic find a listing of items considered to be a major airframe repair?

2-3(O).   What information is required to be entered into the maintenance record upon completion of maintenance or alteration and approving for return to service?

2-4(O).   Upon completion of a 100 hour inspection, what is required of the mechanic holding an airframe and powerplant rating?

2-5(O).   Who is responsible for making the entry in the maintenance records after an annual, 100 hour, or progressive inspection?

2-6(O).   If defects are found during an annual inspection, what is required of the inspector?

2-7(O).   Can an owner fly an aircraft that was not approved for return to service after an annual inspection to another maintenance base for the completion of the repairs? Explain your answer.

2-8(O).   Can an aircraft fly with inoperative instruments or equipment?

2-9(O).   Define "overhaul" as it relates to aviation maintenance.

2-10(O).   Define "rebuilt" as it relates to aviation maintenance.

2-11(O).   Explain the phrase "time in service" as it relates to aviation maintenance.

2-12(O).   Define "maintenance" as it relates to aviation.

2-13(O).   Define "preventive maintenance".

2-14(O).   Define a major alteration

2-15(O).   Define a major repair.

2-16(O).   Provide at least three examples of what information can be found in a Type Certificate Data Sheet?

2-17(O).   Where would a mechanic find information on how to level an aircraft?

2-18(O).   Who is responsible for determining materials used in aircraft maintenance and repair are of the proper type and conform to the appropriate standards?

2-19(O).   Where can you find a checklist to complete a 100 hour or annual inspection?

2-20(O).   What is required of the person performing work to comply with an Airworthiness Directive?

REGULATIONS, MAINTENANCE FORMS, RECORDS, & PUBLICATIONS

ANSWERS

ORAL EXAM

2-1(O). Major repairs are documented on FAA Form 337. Upon completion of the repair and Form 337, an entry is made in the maintenance records referencing the Form 337 by its date.
[Reference: FAR 43.9, AC 43.9-1F]

2-2(O). FAR 43 Appendix A provides a list of items that are considered major repairs.
[Ref: General Handbook H-8083-30A-ATB, Chapter 02 Page 20, and FAR 43 Appendix A]

2-3(O). A maintenance record must include the following information: a description (or reference to acceptable data) of work performed, date of completion, the name of the person performing the work (if someone else), signature, certificate number, and kind of certificate held.
[Ref: General Handbook H-8083-30A-ATB, Chapter 02 Page 43, and FAR 43.9]

2-4(O). Make the proper entries in the aircraft's maintenance record.
[Ref: General Handbook H-8083-30A-ATB, Chapter 02 Page 18, and FAR 43.11]

2-5(O). The person approving or disapproving the item for return to service must document the completion of the inspection and note any discrepancies in the maintenance record.
[Ref: General Handbook H-8083-30A-ATB, Chapter 02 Page 43, Chapter 13 Page 4, and FAR 43.11]

2-6(O). The inspector must make a maintenance entry for the completion of the inspection, noting the discrepancies and give the owner or lessee a signed and dated list of those discrepancies.
[Ref: General Handbook H-8083-30A-ATB, Chapter 02 Page 14, and FAR 43.11]

2-7(O). Yes, however the owner must obtain a special flight permit from the FAA to be authorized to ferry the aircraft to another maintenance base.
[Ref: General Handbook H-8083-30A-ATB, Chapter 02 Page 18, and FAR 21.197]

2-8(O). Yes, under FAR 91.213 an aircraft can fly with inoperative instruments or equipment if it meets this regulation in regards to a minimum equipment list and has the approved documentation/authorization.
[Ref: General Handbook H-8083-30A-ATB, Chapter 02 Page 10, and FAR 91.213]

2-9(O). An article is considered overhauled when it has been disassembled, cleaned, inspected, repaired as necessary, reassembled, and tested per approved standards and technical data.
[Reference: FAR 43.2]

2-10(O). An article is considered rebuilt when it has been disassembled, cleaned, inspected, repaired as necessary, reassembled, and tested to the same tolerances and limits as a new item and conforms to the new part tolerances and limits or to approved oversized or undersized dimensions.
[Reference: FAR 43.2]

2-11(O). Time in service, with respect to maintenance time records, means the time from the moment an aircraft leaves the surface of the earth until it touches it at the next point of landing.
[Reference: FAR 1.1]

2-12(O). Inspection, overhaul, repair, preservation, and the replacement of parts, but excludes preventive maintenance.
[Reference: FAR 1.1]

ORAL EXAM

2-21(O).   What is the purpose of Airworthiness Directives?

2-22(O).   When is a mechanic responsible for checking AD compliance?

2-23(O).   Name the three categories of airworthiness directives and explain each category.

2-24(O).   In what formats can individuals receive Airworthiness Directives?

2-25(O).   How are Airworthiness Directives identified?

2-26(O).   Aviation Maintenance Alerts (formerly General Aviation Airworthiness Alerts) provide what types of information?

2-27(O).   The Air Transport Association of America (ATA) Specification No. 100 was established for what reason?

PRACTICAL EXAM

2-1(P).   Given the required information and a sample maintenance logbook, record the maintenance entry for the completion of a minor repair.

2-2(P).   Given the required information and a sample maintenance logbook, record the maintenance entry for the completion of a minor alteration.

2-3(P).   Given the required information and a sample maintenance logbook, record the maintenance entry for the completion of a preventative maintenance task.

2-4(P).   Given the required information and a sample maintenance logbook, record the maintenance entry for the completion of a maintenance task for compliance with an Airworthiness Directive.

2-5(P).   Given the required information and a sample maintenance logbook, record the maintenance entry for the completion of a 100 hour inspection with disapproval for return to service due to needed maintenance or noncompliance with applicable specifications or airworthiness directive(s).

2-6(P).   Given the required information and a sample maintenance logbook, record the maintenance entry for the completion of a 100 hour inspection with approval for return to service. Include a list of two allowable inoperative instruments and/or equipment in accordance with the provision of 14 CFR part 91.

2-7(P).   Given the required information, a sample maintenance logbook, and FAA Form 337, Major Repair and Major Alteration, document the performance of a major repair and make the appropriate corresponding aircraft maintenance record entry. (Level 3)

2-8(P).   Given the required information, a sample maintenance logbook, and FAA Form 337, Major Repair and Major Alteration, document the installation of additional equipment and make the appropriate maintenance record entry.

ANSWERS

ORAL EXAM

2-13(O).   Preventative maintenance is defined as the "simple or minor preservation operations and the replacement of small standard parts not involving complex assembly operations."
[Ref: General Handbook H-8083-30A-ATB, Chapter 02 Page 22, and FAR 1.1]

2-14(O).   A major alteration is an alteration not listed in the aircraft, aircraft engine, or propeller specifications and might appreciably affect weight, balance, structural strength, performance, powerplant operation, flight characteristics, or other qualities affecting airworthiness, is not done according to accepted practices or cannot be done by elementary operations.
[Reference: FAR 1.1]

2-15(O).   A major repair is defined as a repair that, if improperly done, might appreciably affect weight, balance, structural strength, performance, powerplant operation, flight characteristics, or other qualities affecting airworthiness, or if not done according to accepted practices or cannot be done by elementary operations.
[Reference: FAR 1.1]

2-16(O).   Model designation of all approved engine types; minimum fuel grade; maximum continuous and takeoff ratings; name of manufacturer and model of approved propellers and their limits and operating restrictions; airspeed limits; center of gravity range; empty weight center of gravity; location of the datum; means for leveling the aircraft; pertinent maximum weights; number of seats and moment arms; oil and fuel capacity; control surface movements; required equipment; additional or special equipment; and required placard information.
[Ref: General Handbook H-8083-30A-ATB, Chapter 02 Page 5]

2-17(O).   In the Type Certificate Data Sheet.
[Ref: General Handbook H-8083-30A-ATB, Chapter 02 Page 5]

2-18(O).   It is the responsibility of the installing person or agency.
[Ref: General Handbook H-8083-30A-ATB, Chapter 02 Page 18, and FAR 43.13]

2-19(O).   Appendix D of FAR 43.
[Ref: General Handbook H-8083-30A-ATB, Chapter 02 Page 18, and FAR 43.15]

2-20(O).   Make an entry in the maintenance record of that equipment.
[Ref: General Handbook H-8083-30A-ATB, Chapter 02 Page 43]

2-21(O).   Airworthiness Directives are FAA publications that notify aircraft owners and other interested persons of unsafe conditions and prescribes the condition under which the product may continue to be operated.
[Ref: General Handbook H-8083-30A-ATB, Chapter 02 Page 30]

2-22(O).   When performing an inspection required under part 91, 125, or 135.
[Ref: General Handbook H-8083-30A-ATB, Chapter 02 Page 30, and AC 39-7D]

2-23(O).   Airworthiness directives can be issued in three ways: Notice of Proposed Rulemaking (NPRM) followed by a final rule, Final Rule Request for Comment or Immediately Adopted Rule, and Emergency ADs. NPRMs allow for a comment period by the public prior to being adopted as a final rule. Immediately Adopted ADs are of a higher priority and are adopted immediately, but do allow for comments by the public. Emergency ADs are those situations where safety is critical and are issued to aircraft owners/operators without first being published in the Federal Register. Emergency ADs are published in the next update up the Federal Register.
[Reference: AC 39-7D]

PRACTICAL EXAM

2-9(P).   Given the required information, a sample maintenance logbook, and FAA Form 337, Major Repair and Major Alteration, document an alteration in accordance with a supplemental type certificate (STC) and make the appropriate maintenance record entry.

2-10(P).   Given the required information, complete FAA Form 8010-4, Malfunction or Defect Report.

2-11(P).   Given a manufacturer's maintenance manual, answer specific questions as determined by the examiner.*

2-12(P).   Given a manufacturer's illustrated parts manual, answer specific questions as determined by the examiner.*

2-13(P).   Given a specific make, model, and serial number of an aircraft, locate and list all applicable ADs.

2-14(P).   Given a specific make, model, and serial number of an engine, locate and list all applicable ADs.

2-15(P).   Given a specific make, model, and serial number of a propeller, locate and list all applicable ADs.

2-16(P).   Given a specific make, model, and serial number of an appliance, locate and list all applicable ADs.

2-17(P).   Given a specific make, model, and serial number of an aircraft, determine if a specified AD is required for the aircraft. Be prepared to answer questions about the AD and explain your answers/decisions.

2-18(P).   Given a service bulletin, answer specific questions as determined by the examiner.*

2-19(P).   Given an overhaul manual, answer specific questions as determined by the examiner.*

2-20(P).   Given a structural repair manual, answer specific questions as determined by the examiner.*

2-21(P).   Given the instructions for continued airworthiness, answer specific questions as determined by the examiner.*

2-22(P).   Given access to 14 CFR, locate and interpret specific regulations by applying the information to an assigned task or answer specific questions as determined by the examiner.*

2-23(P).   Given the Aircraft Specifications or TCDS for a specific aircraft, apply the information provided to a maintenance task and/or answer specific questions as determined by the examiner.*

Note: These questions may be written or verbal. Also, these skills are required for all maintenance tasks you are asked to complete during your exam and therefore can be tested as part of another practical application project.

ANSWERS

ORAL EXAM

2-24(O).   ADs can be retrieved from the government website: FAA.gov. Emergency ADs are mailed and/or faxed to owners/operators.
[Reference: AC39-7D]

2-25(O).   ADs have a three-part number designator. The first part is the calendar year of issuance; the second part is the biweekly period of the year when the number is assigned; and the third part is the sequential release number within each biweekly period.
[Ref: General Handbook H-8083-30A-ATB, Chapter 02 Page 30]

2-26(O).   These alerts provide information about aircraft problems and suggested corrective actions.
[Ref: General Handbook H-8083-30A-ATB, Chapter 02 Page 31, and AC43.16]

2-27(O).   ATA Spec 100, also referred to as ATA codes, provides a standard for the presentation of technical data in maintenance manuals by dividing aircraft systems in to various chapters.
[Ref: General Handbook H-8083-30A-ATB, Chapter 02 Page 36]

MATHEMATICS IN AVIATION MAINTENANCE

Fractions, Mixed Numbers, the Decimal System, Proportion, Ratio, Percentage, Powers, Scientific Notation, Algebra, Volume and Area

CHAPTER 03

3-1 AMG053
When working with fractions, the common denominator can be found by multiplying all of the denominators together.
A. True
B. False
C. Cannot be determined

3-2 AMG053
When dividing fractions, it is best to invert the second fraction and multiply the resulting numbers.
A. True
B. False
C. Cannot be determined

3-3 AMG053
Which decimal is most nearly equal to a bend radius of 31/64?
A. 0.2065B
B. 0.3164
C. 0.4844

3-4 AMG053
An aircraft bolt has an overall length of 1-1/2 inches, a shank length of 1-3/16 inches, and a threaded portion length of 5/8 inch. What is the grip length?
A. 0.3125 inch
B. 0.5625 inch
C. 0.8750 inch

3-5 AMG053
Select the fractional equivalent for a 0.0625 inch thick sheet of aluminum.
A. 1/16
B. 11/32
C. 3/64

3-6 AMG053
A blueprint shows a hole of 0.17187 to be drilled. Which fraction size drill bit is most nearly equal?
A. 9/32
B. 11/32
C. 11/64

MATHEMATICS IN AVIATION MAINTENANCE

ANSWERS

3-1 Answer A.
Mathematical principle states that when adding and subtracting fractions the fractions must have a common denominator. A simple way to find the common denominator is to multiply all the denominators together. Note, however, that this number will not always be the Least Common Denominator (LCD) but can be used to continue the calculations. When the final fraction is determined, it may have to be reduced to its lowest terms and/or corrected so it is not an improper fraction.
[Ref: General Handbook H-8083-30A-ATB, Chapter 03 Page 3]

3-2 Answer A.
Mathematical principle states that to divide fractions, invert the second fraction and then multiply the first fraction by the new inverted second fraction.
[Ref: General Handbook H-8083-30A-ATB, Chapter 03 Page 4]

3-3 Answer C.
This question is asking you to convert a fraction to a decimal. To convert fractions to a decimal divide the numerator by the denominator. The context in which the work is being done will determine how accurate (how many decimal places) the answer will need to be. Usually this will be to the ten thousandths (four decimal places) and round up if the fifth decimal place is a five or higher, unless otherwise noted.
[Ref: General Handbook H-8083-30A-ATB, Chapter 03 Page 8]

3-4 Answer B.
This question provides you more information than needed. The overall length of the bolt is not important to determine the grip length. To find the grip length subtract the length of the threaded portion from the length of the shank.
Grip length = shank - threaded portion
Shank = 1-3/16 = 19/16 or 1.1875
Threaded portion = 5/8 = 10/16 or .625
Grip length = 1.1875 − .625
Grip length = .5625
[Ref: General Handbook H-8083-30A-ATB, Chapter 03 Page 4-8]

3-5 Answer A.
To convert a decimal number to a fraction "read" the fraction, this is six hundred twenty-five ten thousandths. As a fraction, it is written as 625/10,000. Find the lowest common denominator, which happens to be 625, reducing the fraction to 1/16.
[Ref: General Handbook H-8083-30A-ATB, Chapter 03 Page 7]

3-6 Answer C.
To convert a decimal number to a fraction "read" the fraction, this is seventeen thousand one hundred eighty-seven hundred thousandths. As a fraction, this is written as 17,187/100,000. However, this fraction cannot be reduced any lower. How do we determine which drill bit to use, since this obviously is not an option? In this question, divide each answer to turn the fractions into decimals: 9/32 = 0.28125, 11/32 = 0.34375 and 11/64 = 0.171875; 11/64th is the closest drill bit size without over-sizing the hole.
[Ref: General Handbook H-8083-30A-ATB, Chapter 03 Page 6-7]

3-7 AMG053
An airplane flying a distance of 750 miles used 60 gallons of gasoline. How many gallons will it need to travel 2,500 miles?
- A. 200
- B. 325
- C. 180

3-8 AMG053
What is the ratio of a gasoline fuel load of 200 gallons to one of 1,680 pounds?
- A. 2:3
- B. 5:7
- C. 5:42

3-9 AMG053
What is the speed of a spur gear with 42 teeth driven by a pinion gear with 14 teeth turning 420 RPM?
- A. 588 RPM
- B. 160 RPM
- C. 140 RPM

3-10 AMG053
What is the speed ratio of an input gear with 36 teeth meshed to a gear with 20 teeth?
- A. 9:5
- B. 1:0.56
- C. 1:1.8

3-11 AMG053
A pinion gear with 14 teeth is driving a spur gear with 42 teeth at 140 RPM. Determine the speed of the pinion gear.
- A. 10 RPM
- B. 420 RPM
- C. 47 RPM

3-12 AMG053
What is the definition of proportion?
- A. A statement of equality between two or more ratios.
- B. A statement of inequity between two or more ratios.
- C. All ratios are proportionate.

MATHEMATICS IN AVIATION MAINTENANCE

ANSWERS

3-7 Answer A.
This is a proportion question. A proportion is a statement of equality between two or more rations. Here the ratio is miles/gallon. Based on the questions a distance of 750 miles can be flown using 60 gallons. What the pilot needs to know is how many gallons will need to fly 2,500 miles. Put the quantities into the appropriate ratio (miles/gallon), then cross multiply, then divide and solve for the unknown.

   750 miles × 2,500 miles
   60 gallons: # of gallons
   60 × 2,500 = 150,000
   150,000 / 750 = 200

[Ref: General Handbook H-8083-30A-ATB, Chapter 03 Page 10]

3-8 Answer B.
A ratio is a comparison of two numbers or quantities. First, you must use the same measurement to compare the two, either gallons or pounds. The standard weight for aviation gasoline is 6.0 lb./gal. 200 gallons weighs 1,200 pounds. Now you can write this as a ratio of 1,200/1,680. Like fractions, ratios need to be expressed in the lowest terms. There are two ways to get to the answer. The mathematical way is to reduce the ratio to its lowest terms.
1200/1680 / 10/10 = 120/168 / 6/6 = 20/28 / 4/4 = 5/7

Or the test taking way, turn everything into a decimal and compare the values:
   1200/1680 = .7142
   2/3 = .6667
   5/7 = .7142
   5/42 = .1190

NOTE: Remember, when working in the real world you are not going to be given options for your answers so you must know how to calculate them the mathematical way, but understanding how numbers work can give you the advantage during testing.

[Ref: General Handbook H-8083-30A-ATB, Chapter 03 Page 8]

3-9 Answer C.
The ratio of the two gears is 42:14 or simplified to 3:1. Since the driving gear (pinion gear) is smaller than the gear it is turning (spur gear), the speed of the spur gear must also be less. Thus to find the speed of the spur gear, divide the pinion gear speed by 3.420 divided by 3 = 140

[Ref: General Handbook H-8083-30A-ATB, Chapter 03 Page 10]

3-10 Answer C.
The ratio of the input (driving) gear to the driven gear is 36:20 or simplified to 9:5. The speed ratio is the inverse of this; 9 divided by 5 = 1.8.

[Ref: General Handbook H-8083-30A-ATB, Chapter 03 Page 10]

3-11 Answer B.
The ratio of the two gears is 14:42, which can be simplified to 1:3, the spur gear turns 3 times for every time the driven gear turns once. "140 RPM of the spur gear then results in 420 RPM for the pinion gear (140 × 3 = 420)".

[Ref: General Handbook H-8083-30A-ATB, Chapter 03 Page 10]

3-12 Answer A.
A proportion is a statement of equality between two or more ratios. For example, A is to B as C is to D can be represented as A:B = C:D or A/B = C/D.

[Ref: General Handbook H-8083-30A-ATB, Chapter 03 Page 10]

3-13 AMG053
A pilot flies .81 of the way to her destination before she stops and refuels. How much is left of her trip?
- A. Cannot be determined
- B. 19 miles
- C. 19%

3-16 AMG053
An engine of 98 horsepower maximum is running at 75 percent power. What is the horsepower being developed?
- A. 87.00
- B. 33.30
- C. 73.50

3-14 AMG053
An airplane is flying at 22,000 feet above sea level. The current temperature at sea level is -4° and the temperature at 22,000 feet above sea level is 25° cooler. If the ratio of temperature change remains constant as altitude is increased, what is the temperature at 30,000 feet?
- A. -21°
- B. -29°
- C. -38°

3-17 AMG053
If an engine is turning 1,965 RPM at 65 percent power, what is its maximum RPM?
- A. 2,653
- B. 3,023
- C. 3,242

3-15 AMG053
The battery of an unmanned aircraft is 21% discharged. The capacity of the battery is 2,400 amps. How many amps remain in the battery?
- A. 1,896 amps
- B. 189.6 amps
- C. 504 amps

3-18 AMG053
Maximum life for a certain part is 1,100 hours. Recently, 15 of these parts were removed from different aircraft with an average life of 835.3 hours. What percent of the maximum part life has been achieved?
- A. 75.9 percent
- B. 76.9 percent
- C. 75.0 percent

MATHEMATICS IN AVIATION MAINTENANCE

ANSWERS

3-13 Answer C.
This is a percentage question. 0.81 is equivalent to 81%. Subtracting 81% from 100% equals 19%. Read the whole question and all the answers. Although percentages are defined as "parts of one-hundred", 19% of 1,200-mile trip is 228 miles.
[Ref: General Handbook H-8083-30A-ATB, Chapter 03 Page 11]

3-14 Answer C.
Take the 25° C difference in temperature and divide it by 22,000 (25/22000= .0011364), which gives us the degree change per foot. Now we know we are increasing by 8,000 ft. .0011364 × 8000 = 9.09°. The best answer is C -38°. If the temperature change between 0 and 22,000 feet is 25°, dividing 25,000 by 22,000 tells you that for each 1,000 feet of altitude gained, the temperature decreases 1.136°. 1.136 × 30 (30,000 feet) = 34.08°, meaning that the temperature at 30,000 feet is approximately 34 degrees less than at sea level. -4 minus 34 = -38° at 30,000 feet.
[Ref: General Handbook H-8083-30A-ATB, Chapter 03 Page 10]

3-15 Answer A.
If we take 2,400 amps and multiply it by 21%, we get 504 amps. This is the amount of amps discharged. To determine the number of amps remaining subtract 504 from 2,400, which leaves 1,896 amps remaining.
[Ref: General Handbook H-8083-30A-ATB, Chapter 03 Page 10]

3-16 Answer C.
Multiply the maximum horsepower by 75% to get horsepower being developed (98 × .75 = 73.5).
[Ref: General Handbook H-8083-30A-ATB, Chapter 03 Page 11]

3-17 Answer B.
In this equation, we need to calculate the maximum RPM. Use the following equation to calculate maximum RPM:
Max RPM × .65 = 1965
Max RPM = 1965/.65 = 3023
[Ref: General Handbook H-8083-30A-ATB, Chapter 03 Page 11]

3-18 Answer A.
To determine maximum life achieved divide 835.3 by 1100 (835.3/1100 = .759), move the decimal two places to the right to get a percentage, which is the equivalent of multiplying the answer by 100, either method getting you the percentage.
[Ref: General Handbook H-8083-30A-ATB, Chapter 03 Page 11]

3-19 AMG053
Express 7/8 as a percent.
 A. 8.75 percent
 B. .875 percent
 C. 87.5 percent

3-20 AMG053
Solve the equation below.

$$\sqrt{(-4)^\circ + 6 + (\sqrt[4]{1296})\,(\sqrt{3})^2} =$$

 A. 115
 B. 4.472
 C. 5

3-21 AMG053
Square root of 36 + square root of 49/17 squared.
 A. 3757
 B. 22.23
 C. .045

3-22 AMG053
Solve the equation below.

$$\frac{(-35 + 25)\,(-7) + (\pi)\,(16\text{-}2)}{\sqrt{25}} =$$

 A. 174.85
 B. 81.49
 C. 14.02

3-23 AMG044
Which form of mathematics can be used to determine the relationship between the radius of a circle to its area?
 A. trigonometry
 B. algebra
 C. calculus

3-24 AMG053
Which of the following is the correct formula to determine the area of a circle?
 A. Area = $\pi \times r^2$
 B. Area = $\pi \times d$
 C. Area = $\pi^2 \times r$

MATHEMATICS IN AVIATION MAINTENANCE

ANSWERS

3-19 Answer C.
Dividing 7 by 8 you get .875 then multiply by 100 to get the percentage equivalent.
[Ref: General Handbook H-8083-30A-ATB, Chapter 03 Page 11]

3-20 Answer C.
Use the following steps to calculate this equation (do not round up):

Complete all the operations within parentheses first, then do any multiplication, followed by addition and then determine the square root of the final number.

Any number raised to the zero power equals one. The fourth root of 1,296 is equivalent to raising 1,296 to the 1/4 power or $1{,}296^{0.25}$ and equals 6.

The squared square root of 3 equals 3 (when rounded up).
Multiply 6 and 3 to equal 18.
Add the remaining numbers: 1 + 6 + 18 to equal 25. The square root of 5 equals 5.
[Ref: General Handbook H-8083-30A-ATB, Chapter 03 Page 13-17]

3-21 Answer C.
Use the following steps to calculate this equation (do not round up)
The square root of 36 is 6
The square root of 49 is 7
The square of 17 is 289
6 + 7 = 13. 13 / 289 = .045
[Ref: General Handbook H-8083-30A-ATB, Chapter 03 Page 17]

3-22 Answer C.
Use the following steps to calculate this equation (do not round up):
Complete all the operations within parentheses first, then do any multiplication, followed by addition and then divide.
(-35 + 25) = -10
16^{-2} this is equivalent $1/16^2$ or 1/256, which equals 0.039
-10 × -7 = 70
π = 3.1516 × .039 = .1229
70 + .1229 = 70.1229
Square root of 25 = 5
70.1229/5 = 14.02
[Ref: General Handbook H-8083-30A-ATB, Chapter 03 Page 17-18]

3-23 Answer B.
Algebra is defined as a branch of mathematics dealing with general statements of relations, utilizing letters and other symbols representing specific sets of numbers, values, etc.
[Ref: General Handbook H-8083-30A-ATB, Chapter 03 Page 17]

3-24 Answer A.
The formula for the area of a circle is $\pi \times r^2$ (squared). Where as π = 3.14 and r = the radius of the circle, or 1/2 the diameter. The formula for the circumference of a circle is $\pi \times$ diameter. The formula in answer C is made up.
[Ref: General Handbook H-8083-30A-ATB, Chapter 03 Page 21]

3-25 AMG053
Which is the correct order of operations when solving an algebraic equation?
  A. exponents – parentheses – multiplication – division – addition – subtraction
  B. parentheses – exponents – multiplication – division – addition – subtraction
  C. exponents – parentheses – division – multiplication – addition – subtraction

3-26 AMG053
Solve the equation below:

[(4 x -3) + (-9 x 2)] ÷ 2 =

  A. 29
  B. -15
  C. -5

3-27 AMG053
What power of 10 is equal to 1,000,000?
  A. 10 to the fourth power
  B. 10 to the fifth power
  C. 10 to the sixth power

3-28 AMG053
Find the value of 10 raised to the negative sixth power.
  A. 0.000010
  B. 0.000001
  C. 0.0001

3-29 AMG053
The number 3.47 × 10 to the negative fourth power is equal to:
  A. .00347
  B. 34,700.0
  C. .000347

3-30 AMG053
Which alternative answer is equal to 16,300?
  A. 1.63 × 10 to the fourth power
  B. 1.63 × 10 to the negative third power
  C. 163 × 10 to the negative second power

MATHEMATICS IN AVIATION MAINTENANCE

ANSWERS

3-25 Answer B.
Remember the acronym PEMDAS to determine which
sections of an algebraic equation to solve first. PEMDAS =
parentheses/exponents/multiplication/division/addition/
subtraction.
[Ref: General Handbook H-8083-30A-ATB, Chapter 03 Page 23]

3-28 Answer B.
Remember that negative powers mean that you divide the
number by itself the same amount of times as is equal to the
power, which would be $10 \div 10 \div 10 \div 10 \div 10 \div 10$. Another
way to calculate this would be to use its reciprocal or $1/10^6$,
which is 1 divided by 1,000,000 or 0.000001.
[Ref: General Handbook H-8083-30A-ATB, Chapter 03 Page 12]

3-26 Answer B.
$[(4 \times -3) + (-9 \times 2)] \div 2 =$
$[(-12) + (-18)] \div 2 =$
$[(-30)] \div 2 =$
-15
[Ref: General Handbook H-8083-30A-ATB, Chapter 03 Page 17]

3-29 Answer C.
Use the reciprocal operation. $1/3.47 \times 10^4$, which is 1/34,700
or 0.000347.
[Ref: General Handbook H-8083-30A-ATB, Chapter 03 Page 12]

3-27 Answer C.
The power (or exponent) of a number is a shorthand method
of indicating how many times a number, called the base, is
multiplied by itself. Ten to the sixth power or 10^6 equals $10 \times
10 \times 10 \times 10 \times 10 \times 10$ equally 1,000,000. For a base number
of 10 simply add zeros to equal the power, e.g.
$10^2 = 100$, $10^4 = 10,000$ etc.
[Ref: General Handbook H-8083-30A-ATB, Chapter 03 Page 12]

3-30 Answer A.
1.63×10^4 is equivalent to 16,300. 1.63×10^{-3} is equivalent to
.00163 and 163×10^{-2} is equivalent to 1.63.
[Ref: General Handbook H-8083-30A-ATB, Chapter 03 Page 12]

3-31 AMG053

Find the square root of 124.9924.

   A. 111.8 × 10 to the third power

   B. .1118 × 10 to the negative second power

   C. 1,118 × 10 to the negative second power

3-32 AMG053

The result of 7 raised to the third power plus the square root of 39 is equal to?

   A. 349.24

   B. .34924

   C. 343.24

3-33 AMG053

Find the square root of 1,824.

   A. 42.708 × 10 to the negative second power

   B. .42708

   C. .42708 × 10 to the second power

3-34 AMG053

Which of the following is equal to the square root of (-1776) ÷ (-2) - 632?

   A. 128

   B. 256

   C. 16

3-35 AMG053

What is the cube root of 216?

   A. 10,077,696

   B. 72

   C. 6

3-36 AMG053

Which of the equations is using scientific notation?

#1 $3.47 \times 10^4 = 34,700$

#2 $2(4^{10}) = 2,097,152$

   A. 1

   B. 2

   C. Both 1 and 2

MATHEMATICS IN AVIATION MAINTENANCE

ANSWERS

3-31 Answer C.
The square root of 124.9924 is 11.18, which is equivalent to $1,118 \times 10^{-2}$.
[Ref: General Handbook H-8083-30A-ATB, Chapter 03 Page 12-13]

3-34 Answer C.
The order of operation for algebraic equations are: Parenthesis, Exponents, Multiplication and Division (from left to right), Addition and subtraction (from left to right).
$\sqrt{[(-1,776) / (-2) - 632]} =$
$\sqrt{(888 - 632)} =$
$\sqrt{256} =$
16
[Ref: General Handbook H-8083-30A-ATB, Chapter 03 Page 18]

3-32 Answer A.
$73 = 7 \times 7 \times 7 = 343$
Square root of 39 is 6.24
$343 + 6.24 = 349.24$
[Ref: General Handbook H-8083-30A-ATB, Chapter 03 Page 12-13]

3-35 Answer C.
When 6 is multiplied by itself 3 times it equals 216 ($6 \times 6 \times 6$). The other two answers are incorrect. $72 = 216/3$ and 10,077,696 is actually 216^3 or $216 \times 216 \times 216$.
[Ref: General Handbook H-8083-30A-ATB, Chapter 03 Page 13]

3-33 Answer C.
The square root of 1,824 is 42.708, which can also be expressed as $.42708 \times 10^2$.
[Ref: General Handbook H-8083-30A-ATB, Chapter 03 Page 13]

3-36 Answer A.
The equation marked 1 is an example of scientific notation.

#1 | $3.47 \times 10^4 = 34,700$ |

[Ref: General Handbook H-8083-30A-ATB, Chapter 03 Page 18]

3-37 AMG044
A triangle includes one 90° angle. It stands 9 inches tall and has a base of 8 inches. What is its area?
   A. 72 square inches.
   B. 36 square inches.
   C. 144 square inches.

3-38 AMG044
Compute the area of the trapezoid.

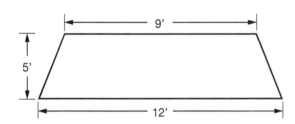

   A. 52.5 square feet
   B. 60 square feet
   C. 76.5 square feet

3-39 AMG044
What is the opening area of an aircraft's engine cylinder if the inside diameter or bore is 6 inches?
   A. 113.098 square inches
   B. 18.850 square inches
   C. 28.274 square inches

3-40 AMG044
What is the piston displacement of a master cylinder with a 1.5-inch diameter bore and a piston stroke of 4 inches?
   A. 9.4248 cubic inches
   B. 7.0686 cubic inches
   C. 6.1541 cubic inches

3-41 AMG044
A four-cylinder aircraft engine has a cylinder bore of 3.78 inches and is 8.5 inches deep. With the piston on bottom center, the top of the piston measures 4.0 inches from the bottom of the cylinder. What is the approximate piston displacement of this engine?
   A. 200 cubic inches
   B. 360 cubic inches
   C. 235 cubic inches

3-42 AMG044
32,000 feet = _____ kilometers.
   A. 198.4
   B. 3.76
   C. 9.77

MATHEMATICS IN AVIATION MAINTENANCE

ANSWERS

3-37 Answer B
The area of any triangle can be considered half of a square. Thus the formula for the area of a triangle is: A = ½ (base × height). In this case the base is 8" and the height is 9". 8 × 9 = 72. Half of that is 36.
[Ref: General Handbook H-8083-30A-ATB, Chapter 03 Page 20]

3-40 Answer B.
πr^2 × H. The bore is 1.5 inches diameter which equals a radius of .75".
.75 squared (.75 × .75) = .5625.
So 3.1416 × .752 × 4 inch stroke distance = 9.4248
[Ref: General Handbook H-8083-30A-ATB, Chapter 03 Page 24]

3-38 Answer A.
The area of a trapezoid can be found by multiplying the altitude by the average length of the bases.
The altitude in this figure is 5 feet. The average of the bases is 10.5 ((9+12)/2).
[Ref: General Handbook H-8083-30A-ATB, Chapter 03 Page 20]

3-41 Answer A.
Piston Displacement is πr^2 × H × number of cylinders. So, 3.1416 × (3.78/2)^2 × 4.5 × 4 cylinders = 201.99
The question is asking for the approximate piston displacement and 200 is the closest answer. To solve this problem you must determine the correct stroke length. This will discussed in more detail when you study aircraft engines. For now, the stroke is 4.5 inches. It is calculated as the depth of the cylinder minus the distance from the top of the piston at bottom dead center (BDC) to the bottom of the cylinder.
[Ref: General Handbook H-8083-30A-ATB, Chapter 03 Page 24]

3-39 Answer C.
The area of circle is πr^2. The area is calculated as 3.1415 × (6/2)^2 = 3.1415 × 9 = 28.274.
[Ref: General Handbook H-8083-30A-ATB, Chapter 03 Page 21]

3-42 Answer C.
5,280 feet = 1 mile. .62 miles = 1 kilometer. Thus 32,000 feet = 6.06 miles and 6.06 miles = 9.77 kilometers.
[Ref: General Handbook H-8083-30A-ATB, Chapter 03 Page 22]

3-43 AMG044
A rectangular-shaped fuel tank measures 60 inches in length, 30 inches in width, and 12 inches in depth. How many cubic feet are within the tank?
   A. 12.5
   B. 15.0
   C. 21.0

3-44 AMG044
Select the container size that is equal in volume to 60 gallons of fuel.
   A. 7.5 cubic feet
   B. 8.0 cubic feet
   C. 8.5 cubic feet

3-45 AMG044
How many gallons of fuel will be contained in a rectangular shaped tank, which measures 2 feet in width, 3 feet in length, and 1 foot 8 inches in depth? (7.5 gal = 1 cu. ft.)
   A. 66.6
   B. 75
   C. 45

3-46 AMG044
What is the entire surface area of a cube when each side edge measures 7.25 inches?
   A. 381.078 cu. in.
   B. 315.375 sq. in.
   C. 52.5625 sq. in.

3-47 AMG044
What is the volume of a sphere with a radius of 4.5 inches?

$V = 1/6 \, \pi \, D^3$

   A. 47.71 cubic inches
   B. 381.7 square inches
   C. 381.7 cubic inches

3-48 AMG044
If the circumference of a circle is 24 inches, what is the approximate diameter?
   A. 7.64 inches
   B. 3.82 inches
   C. 2.43 inches

MATHEMATICS IN AVIATION MAINTENANCE

ANSWERS

3-43 Answer A.
Volume = Length × Width × Height
However, note the question gives you the measurements in inches and the answer is to calculated in feet. Divide each measurement by 12.
(12 inches in a foot).
60 ÷ 12 × 30 ÷ 12 × 12 ÷ 12 = 5 × 2.5 × 1 = 12.5
[Ref: General Handbook H-8083-30A-ATB, Chapter 03 Page 23]

3-44 Answer B.
Divide 60 by 7.5 = 8, since 7.5 gallons equals 1 cubic foot of space, 60 gallons of fuel will need to have a container that can hold 8 cubic feet of volume.
[Ref: General Handbook H-8083-30A-ATB, Chapter 03 Page 22-23]

3-45 Answer B.
Volume = Length × Width × Height
3 × 2 × (20/12) = 10 cubic feet × 7.5 gallons = 75 gallons.
Note: Make sure all measurements are in the same units.
[Ref: General Handbook H-8083-30A-ATB, Chapter 03 Page 23]

3-46 Answer B.
Area = length × width = 7.25 × 7.25 = 52.5625 × 6 (sides of a cube) = 315.375 sq. in.
[Ref: General Handbook H-8083-30A-ATB, Chapter 03 Page 24]

3-47 Answer C.
The equation for the volume of a sphere is:
$V = 4/3 \times \pi \times r^3$
$V = 1.3333333 \times 3.1415 \times (4.5)^3 = 1.333 \times 3.1415 \times 91.125 = 381.7$ cubic inches.
Note: Confirm units before choosing an answer.
[Ref: General Handbook H-8083-30A-ATB, Chapter 03 Page 24]

3-48 Answer A.
The key to solving this is remembering the value of ∏ (pi) which is approximately 3.14. As the formula for circumference is diameter × ∏; dividing the circumference by ∏ (3.14) gives you the diameter.
[Ref: General Handbook H-8083-30A-ATB, Chapter 03 Page 21]

3-49 AMG044

When solving a complex mathematical equation, which is the proper order of which function to determine first?

A. Multiplications, then additions, then exponents.

B. Parentheses, then multiplications, then exponents.

C. Exponents, then divisions, then subtractions.

3-52 AMG044

Determine the area of the triangle formed by points A, B, and C. A-B = 7.5 inches. A-C = 16.8 inches.

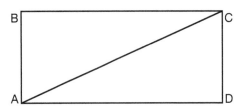

A. 42 square inches

B. 63 square inches

C. 126 square inches

3-50 AMG044

A special delivery needs to be made for a large painting. The painting measures 9 feet tall by 9 feet wide. It is being delivered by a cargo plane that has a door opening of 6 1/2 feet tall and 8 1/2 feet wide.

Can the painting fit through the opening?

A. Yes, the diagonal measurement is 10.7 feet.

B. No, the diagonal measurement is 7.5 feet.

C. Yes, the diagonal measurement is 15 feet.

3-53 AMG044

Which of the following problems can be solved by using the Pythagorean theorem?

A. How many gallons of fuel will fit in a cylindrical tank?

B. What is the displacement of a piston in an engine?

C. What is the height from the ground of an aircraft's vertical stabilizer?

3-51 AMG044

Find the area of the triangle shown.

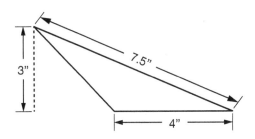

A. 12 square inches

B. 6 square inches

C. 15 square inches

3-54 AMG053

Examples of units used in the conventional (U.S. or English) measurement include _____.

A. inch, meter, gram

B. inch, kilo, liter

C. inch, ounce, pounds

MATHEMATICS IN AVIATION MAINTENANCE

ANSWERS

3-49 Answer C.
Use the acronym PEMDAS to remember the order in which to solve an algebraic equation. Parentheses, exponents, multiplication, division, addition, subtraction.
[Ref: General Handbook H-8083-30A-ATB, Chapter 03 Page 23]

3-50 Answer A.
The answers give you the clues to what formula to use, the Pythagorean Theorem ($a^2 + b^2 = c^2$).

Diagonal measurement of the cargo door:
$c^2 = (6.5)^2 + (8.5)^2 = 42.25 + 72.25 = 114.5$
$c = \sqrt{114.5} = 10.7$.
[Ref: General Handbook H-8083-30A-ATB, Chapter 03 Page 23]

3-51 Answer B.
Area of a triangle =
$1/2 \times$ Base $\times$ Height = $.5 \times 3 \times 4 = 6$ square inches.
[Ref: General Handbook H-8083-30A-ATB, Chapter 03 Page 19]

3-52 Answer B.
Area of a triangle =
$1/2 \times$ Base $\times$ Height = $.5 \times 7.5 \times 16.8 = 63$ square inches.
[Ref: General Handbook H-8083-30A-ATB, Chapter 03 Page 19]

3-53 Answer C.
The Pythagorean Theorem is used to measure the angles and length of the sides of a right triangle. As a perceived triangle can be formed based on your distance from an aircraft (base of the triangle) and the angle from your position to the top of the stabilizer (hypotenuse), the height of the triangle (height of the stabilizer) can also be determined.
[Ref: General Handbook H-8083-30A-ATB, Chapter 03 Page 26]

3-54 Answer C.
Meters, kilos, and grams are metric measurements.
[Ref: General Handbook H-8083-30A-ATB, Chapter 03 Page 27]

3-55 AMG053

How many miles are in a distance of 10 kilometers?

A. 2.2
B. 6.2
C. 12.2

3-56 AMG053

One millionth of a meter is known as a?

A. millimeter
B. nanometer
C. micrometer

3-57 AMG100

Which of the following is the correct sequence of number prefixes, from the smallest to the largest?

A. nano; hecto; tera
B. deca; deci; peta
C. kilo; giga; pico

3-58 AMG100

The binary number system is most useful in aircraft electronics because those systems are either

A. ON/OFF.
B. ON/OFF/ON.
C. FALSE/TRUE/FALSE.

3-59 AMG044

Which of the following is a purpose of the binary number system?

A. To determine whether a switch is ON or OFF.
B. To compare the relative value of two functions.
C. To simplify a complex equation into its basic parts.

3-60 AMG100

Convert the binary number 11011001 to a decimal number. Refer to Figure 3-1.

A. 38
B. 217
C. 233

BINARY PLACE VALUE TABLE

2^7 = 128	2^6 = 64	2^5 = 32	2^4 = 16	2^3 = 8	2^2 = 4	2^1 = 2	2^0 = 1

Figure 3-1. Binary Place Value Table.

3-61 AMG100

Convert the decimal number 147 to a binary number. Refer to Figure 3-1.

A. 10001001
B. 10100001
C. 10010011

BINARY PLACE VALUE TABLE

2^7 = 128	2^6 = 64	2^5 = 32	2^4 = 16	2^3 = 8	2^2 = 4	2^1 = 2	2^0 = 1

Figure 3-1. Binary Place Value Table.

MATHEMATICS IN AVIATION MAINTENANCE

ANSWERS

3-55 Answer B.
Note: 1 Kilometer (Km) is equivalent to 0.6214 miles.
$10 \times .6214 = 6.214$ miles.
[Ref: General Handbook H-8083-30A-ATB, Chapter 03 Page 22]

3-56 Answer C.
Micro is the prefix equivalent to 10^{-6} power or
.000001, therefore one millionth of a meter is one micrometer.
[Ref: General Handbook H-8083-30A-ATB, Chapter 03 Page 28]

3-57 Answer A.
The full sequence of number prefixes from the smallest (one quintillionth 10^{-18} to exa (quintillion 10^{18}) is atto, femto, pico, nano, micro, milli, centi, deci, unit (one), deca, hector, kilo, mega, giga, tera, peta, exa.
[Ref: General Handbook H-8083-30A-ATB, Chapter 03 Page 27]

3-58 Answer A.
Using the binary numbering system digital electronics send a signal to indicate whether an electrical pulse has been received. "1" indicates an electrical pulse has been received or on and a "0" indicates no pulse or off. There are only two options, not three as shown in B and C.

Special Note: In a digital electronic logic circuit, the "1" indicates true and a "0" indicates false.
[Ref: General Handbook H-8083-30A-ATB, Chapter 03 Page 28]

3-59 Answer A.
a simple electric or other switch has two possible conditions; ON or OFF. Thus its condition can be represented using either a "1" or a "0" in binary code.
[Ref: General Handbook H-8083-30A-ATB, Chapter 03 Page 28]

3-60 Answer B.
$128 + 64 + 0 + 16 + 8 + 0 + 0 + 1 = 217$

2^7 = 128	2^6 = 64	2^5 = 32	2^4 = 16	2^3 = 8	2^2 = 4	2^1 = 2	2^0 = 1
1	1	0	1	1	0	0	1

3-61 Answer C.
$147 - 128 = 19$
$19 - 16 = 3$
$3 - 2 = 1$
$1 - 1 = 0$

2^7 = 128	2^6 = 64	2^5 = 32	2^4 = 16	2^3 = 8	2^2 = 4	2^1 = 2	2^0 = 1
1	0	0	1	0	0	1	1

ORAL EXAM

3-1(O).   State the formula to calculate the area of a circle.

3-2(O).   State the formula to calculate the area of a rectangle.

3-3(O).   State the formula to calculate the area of a triangle.

3-4(O).   State the formula to calculate the volume of a cylinder.

3-5(O).   State the formula to calculate the volume of a rectangle.

3-6(O).   What is the numerical value for the mathematical constant ⊓?

3-7(O).   Define a negative number and how it is expressed.

3-8(O).   Define ratio and describe how it is expressed.

3-9(O).   Define a proportion.

3-10(O).   Define percentage.

MATHEMATICS IN AVIATION MAINTENANCE

ORAL EXAM

3-1(O).   Area = $\pi \times radius^2$ or A = $\pi \times r^2$
           [Ref: General Handbook H-8083-30A-ATB, Chapter 03 Page 21]

3-2(O).   Area = Length × Width or A=L × W
           [Ref: General Handbook H-8083-30A-ATB, Chapter 03 Page 19]

3-3(O).   Area = 1/2 × (Base × Height) or A = 1/2 × (B × H)
           [Ref: General Handbook H-8083-30A-ATB, Chapter 03 Page 19]

3-4(O).   Volume = $\pi \times radius^2 \times$ Height of the cylinder or V = $\pi \times r^2 \times H$
           [Ref: General Handbook H-8083-30A-ATB, Chapter 03 Page 24]

3-5(O).   Volume = Length × Width × Height or V = L × W × H
           [Ref: General Handbook H-8083-30A-ATB, Chapter 03 Page 23]

3-6(O).   Pi (π) = 3.1416
           [Ref: General Handbook H-8083-30A-ATB, Chapter 03 Page 21]

3-7(O).   A negative number is a number less than zero, and is expressed by placing a negative sign in front of the number.
           [Ref: General Handbook H-8083-30A-ATB, Chapter 03 Page 12]

3-8(O).   A ratio is the comparison of two numbers or quantities. It can be expressed in three ways: as a fraction, with a colon, or with the word "to".
           [Ref: General Handbook H-8083-30A-ATB, Chapter 03 Page 8]

3-9(O).   A proportion is a statement of equality between two or more rations.
           [Ref: General Handbook H-8083-30A-ATB, Chapter 03 Page 10]

3-10(O).   Percentage means "parts out of one hundred."
           [Ref: General Handbook H-8083-30A-ATB, Chapter 03 Page 10]

PRACTICAL EXAM

NOTE: The practical portion of the Mathematics subject area may be tested simultaneously when performing calculation(s) in subject areas of Basic Electricity and/or Weight and Balance.

3-1(P).   Given specific measurements, calculate the area of a circle, a rectangle, and a triangle.

3-2(P).   Given specific measurements, calculate the volume of a sphere, a cube, and a cylinder.

3-3(P).   Be able to locate the mathematical formulas needed to complete maintenance, preventative maintenance, or alteration of the an aircraft, e.g. piston displacement of a cylinder, compression ratio of a cylinder, area of a wing, volume of a fuel tank, find the rotational speed of a shaft.

3-4(P).   Convert a list of fractions convert them to their decimal equivalent and vice versa.

3-5(P).   Calculate the square root of a given number.

3-6(P).   Calculate the square and cube of a given number.

3-7(P).   Add, subtract, multiply, and divide both positive and negative numbers.

3-8(P).   Convert common fractions into percentages.

PAGE LEFT BLANK INTENTIONALLY

AIRCRAFT DRAWINGS

Computer Graphics, Types of Drawings, Universal Numbering System, Title Blocks, Methods of Illustration, Symbols, Graphs and Charts

CHAPTER
04

QUESTIONS

4-1 AMG013
In a sectional view drawing, what sections illustrate particular parts of an object?
  A. Removed.
  B. Revolved.
  C. Half.

4-3 AMG013
The -100 in the title block (Area 1) is applicable to which doubler part number(s) diagram in the Figure 4-1 below?
  A. -101
  B. -102
  C. Both

4-2 AMG014
Which of the following best describes what is shown by a sectional drawing?
  A. An interior details of the object from the plane in which it was intersected.
  B. A detailed view of a particular section or component of an object.
  C. The details of how certain sections of a component are assembled into a single unit.

4-4 AMG014
Where are title blocks normally located on an aircraft drawing?
  A. upper left-hand corner
  B. lower left-hand corner
  C. lower right-hand corner

							REV.	B
4	4	MS20470AD-4-4	Rivet					
8	8	NAS1097-3-4	Rivet					
4	4	NAS1473-3A	Domed Nutplate					
5	5	NAS1097-4-5	Rivet					
37	37	NAS1097-4-4	Rivet					
2	2	-103	Clip	.040 sheet	2024-T3 CLAD AL.			
1		-102	Doubler	.040 sheet	7075-0 AL.			
	1	-101	Doubler	.040 sheet	2024-T3 CLAD AL.			
		Part number	NAME	stock size	MAT'L DESCR	MAT'L SPEC.	Zone	

Area 1

			-200	-100	DASH NUMBERS SHOWN	DASH NUMBERS OPPOSITE	UNIT WT.	DWG. AREA
					All	N/A	FIRST	RELEASE
					Unless otherwise noted	For continuation see zone		
REQ'd. PER ASSEM.								
							PROJECT T. Smith	J. Smith
							DESIGN R. Eamer	R. Eamer
						1 -200 36TCP 001-All	Engineer FAA D.E.R G. Winn	G. Winn
						1 -200 36P 088-All		
B	ADD-200					1 -200 36P 001-087	DWG. Checker I. Wright	D Wright
A	MAT'L THKNESS				Break all sharp edges	No. req. per Airplane Type A/C EFF		
LET.	CHANGE	BY	Date	Appr.	Scale full	992-148-XXX	DFTSMIN. S. Linz	S. Linz

1 The use of this document shall be restricted to conveyance of information to customers of vendors only. Neither classified nor unclassified documents may be reproduced without the written consent of THE SPEEDWIND AIRCRAFT CORP.

Speedwind aircraft engineering section last chance airport anytown OK 73125-1234

TAH

Figure 4-1. Maintenance Data.

AIRCRAFT DRAWINGS

ANSWERS

4-1 Answer A.

The removed section illustrates the parts of an object. The revolved section shows the shape of the cross section of an object. The Half section splits the object to show both the exterior and interior shapes.

[Ref: General Handbook H-8083-30A-ATB, Chapter 04 Page 3]

4-2 Answer A.

A sectional drawing depicts an object by cutting away part of the object to show the shape and construction at the cutting plane, they can be full, half, revolved and removed section drawings depending on the objective of the drawing.

[Ref: General Handbook H-8083-30A-ATB, Chapter 04 Page 3]

4-3 Answer A.

Locate the specific information in the title block pertaining to -100 (see Figure 4-1). Locate the doubler. There are two doublers required; reading to the left will tell you which part number is applicable to -100 part assemblies.

[Ref: General Handbook H-8083-30A-ATB, Chapter 04 Page 3]

4-4 Answer C.

Title blocks are normally located in the lower right hand corner, but may also extend along the entire distance across the bottom of a drawing.

[Ref: General Handbook H-8083-30A-ATB, Chapter 04 Page 7]

	4	4	MS20470AD-4-4	Rivet						REV.	B
	8	8	NAS1097-3-4	Rivet							
	4	4	NAS1473-3A	Domed Nutplate							
	5	5	NAS1097-4-5	Rivet							
Area 1	37	37	NAS1097-4-4	Rivet							
	2	2	-103	Clip	.040 sheet	2024-T3 CLAD AL.					
	1		-102	Doubler	.040 sheet	7075-0 AL.					
		1	-101	Doubler	.040 sheet	2024-T3 CLAD AL.					
			Part number	NAME	stock size	MAT'L DESCR	MAT'L SPEC.			Zone	

		-200	-100	DASH NUMBERS SHOWN	DASH NUMBERS OPPOSITE		UNIT WT.	DWG. AREA			
				All	N/A		FIRST	RELEASE			
				Unless otherwise noted	For continuation see zone						
REQ'd. PER ASSEM.											
								PROJECT	T. Smith	*J. Smith*	
								DESIGN	R. Eamer	*R. Eamer*	
					1	-200	36TCP	001-All	Engineer FAA D.E.R	G. Winn	*G. Winn*
					1	-200	36P	088-All			
					1	-200	36P	001-087	DWG. Checker	I. Wright	*D Wright*
B	ADD-200			Break all sharp edges	No. req. per Airplane	Type A/C	EFF				
A	MAT'L THKNESS			Scale full				DFTSMIN.	S. Linz	*S. Linz*
LET.	CHANGE	BY	Date	Appr.	992-148-XXX						

1 The use of this document shall be restricted to conveyance of information to customers of vendors only. Neither classified nor unclassified documents may be reproduced without the written consent of THE SPEEDWIND AIRCRAFT CORP.

Speedwind aircraft engineering section last chance airport anytown OK 73125-1234

TAH

Answer for Figure 4-1. Maintenance Data.

4-5 AMG014

Zone numbers on aircraft blueprints are used to
  A. locate parts, sections, and views on large drawings.
  B. indicate different sections of the aircraft fuselage.
  C. locate parts in the aircraft relative to the mean aerodynamic chord.

4-7 AMG014

A dimension on a drawing is given as 4.387" +005, -002. What is the maximum tolerance?
  A. .005
  B. .003
  C. .007

4-6 AMG013

The diameter of the holes in the finished object in the diagram (Figure 4-2) are
  A. 3/4 inch.
  B. 31/64 inch.
  C. 1/2 inch.

4-8 AMG014

What is the allowable manufacturing tolerance for a bushing where the outside dimensions shown on the blueprint are: 1.0625 +.0025 -.0003?
  A. .0028
  B. 1.0650
  C. 1.0647

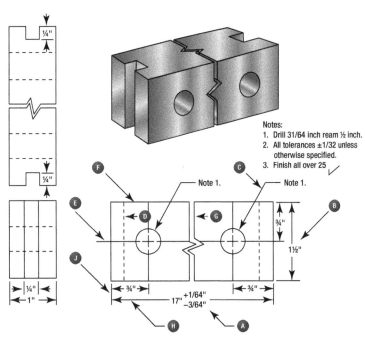

Figure 4-2. Aircraft Drawing.

AIRCRAFT DRAWINGS

ANSWERS

4-5 Answer A.
Zone numbers on drawings are there to help you locate a specific area on the drawing. To locate the referenced area on a drawing, locate the letter and number and then mentally draw horizontal and vertical lines from the letter and number to where they intersect on the drawing. This is the location where you will find the referenced point.
[Ref: General Handbook H-8083-30A-ATB, Chapter 04 Page 9]

4-7 Answer C.
Tolerance is defined as the combined total of the maximum and minimum allowances. Thus +.005 and -.002 = .007
[Ref: General Handbook H-8083-30A-ATB, Chapter 04 Page 9]

4-6 Answer C.
Refer to the notes in the Figure 4-2.
Answer: They state the holes are to be drilled to diameter of 31/64 and then reamed to 1/2 inch.
[Ref: General Handbook H-8083-30A-ATB, Chapter 04 Page 9]

4-8 Answer A.
Tolerance is the sum of the plus and minus allowable deviation of the dimensions. Therefore, in this example you would add the maximum allowable deviation of .0025 and the minimum allowable deviation of .0003 (ignoring the negative sign) for a tolerance of .0028.
[Ref: General Handbook H-8083-30A-ATB, Chapter 04 Page 9]

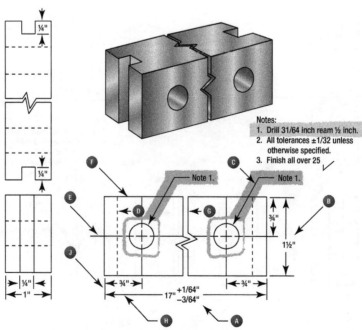

Answer for Figure 4-2. Aircraft Drawing.

4-9 AMG014

What are the maximum number of views possible on an orthographic projection?

   A. 3
   B. 8
   C. 6

4-10 AMG014

1. A measurement should not be scaled from an aircraft print because the paper shrinks or stretches when the print is made.
2. When a detail drawing is made, it is carefully and accurately drawn to scale, and is dimensional.

Regarding the above statements:

   A. Only #2 is true.
   B. Both #1 and #2 are true.
   C. Neither #1 or #2 is true.

4-11 AMG014

Which of these numbers indicates the horizontal distance from the manufacturer's datum to the location of a component on an aircraft?

   A. Zone number.
   B. Station number.
   C. Moment number.

4-12 AMG014

When reading aircraft blueprints, the term "tolerance" used in association with aircraft parts or components

   A. is the tightest permissible fit for proper construction and operation of mated parts.
   B. is the difference between extreme permissible dimensions that a part may have and still be acceptable.
   C. represents the limits of galvanic compatibility between different adjoining material types in aircraft parts.

4-13 AMG014

Figure 4-3 depicts the front view of an object along with three possible bottom views of that same object. Which is the correct depiction of the bottom view?

   A. 1
   B. 2
   C. 3

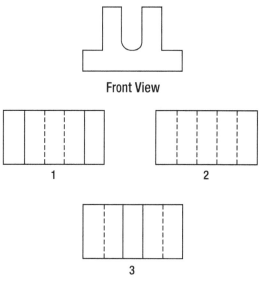

Figure 4-3. Object views.

AIRCRAFT DRAWINGS

ANSWERS

4-9 Answer C.
An orthographic projection shows an object from its 6 possible sides; front, back, left side, right side, top, and bottom.
[Ref: General Handbook H-8083-30A-ATB, Chapter 04 Page 11]

4-10 Answer B.
Scaled drawings are representations drawn in the same proportions as the original. They can be the same (1:1), smaller (1/4 inch), or larger (2:1). Never re-measure the paper drawing to determine a measurement, even if noted as scaled 1:1. The paper can shrink or stretch and with today's technology, copies are easily reduced or enlarged yet will still note a scale of 1:1.
ALWAYS use the dimensions on the drawing.
[Ref: General Handbook H-8083-30A-ATB, Chapter 04 Page 11]

4-11 Answer B.
A station number is a reference measure from a reference point. For aircraft, these reference points are the datum for fuselage measurement, the buttock line for measurements left and right of the aircraft's longitudinal axis, and the waterline for measurements below and above a reference line running from the nose of the aircraft to the tail.
[Ref: General Handbook H-8083-30A-ATB, Chapter 04 Page 9]

4-12 Answer B.
Tolerance is defined as the difference between extreme permissible dimensions that a part may have and still be acceptable. This definition is equivalent to "the sum of the plus and minus allowance figures" used in the text. In the text definition, you ignored the signs and added the numbers. For this definition, you keep the signs. Difference in this context means subtraction; remember that subtracting a negative is the same as adding a positive.
[Ref: General Handbook H-8083-30A-ATB, Chapter 04 Page 9]

4-13 Answer B.
View 2 in Figure 4-3 is the correct orthographic view for this part. The bottom of the object is solid, remembering that dashed vertical lines represent features of the part that are hidden from the view being represented, here the bottom.
[Ref: General Handbook H-8083-30A-ATB, Chapter 04 Page 11]

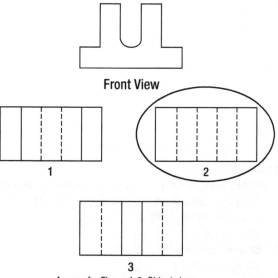

Answer for Figure 4-3. Object views.

4-14 AMG014

According to Figure 4-4, the vertical distance between the top of the plate and the bottom of the lowest 15/64 inch hole is?

    A. 2.250

    B. 2.242

    C. 2.367

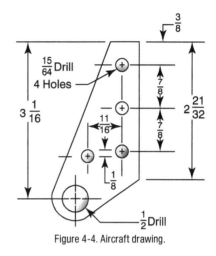

Figure 4-4. Aircraft drawing.

4-15 AMG014

Refer to Figure 4-5; identify the left side of the object shown.

    A. 1

    B. 2

    C. 3

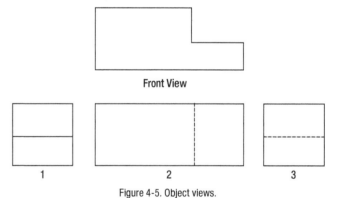

Figure 4-5. Object views.

4-16 AMG004

Refer to Figure 4-6. Identify the bottom view of the object shown.

    A. 1

    B. 2

    C. 3

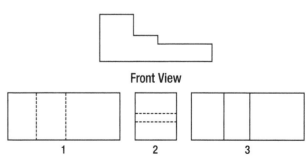

Figure 4-6. Object views.

AIRCRAFT DRAWINGS

ANSWERS

4-14 Answer C.
Add the following dimensions from Figure 4-4:
Distance from the top of the plate to center of the top hole is
3/8" or 0.375"
Distance from the center of first hole to the center of the
center of second hole is 7/8" or 0.875" Distance from the
center of the second hole to the center of the third hole is
7/8" or 0.875"
Distance from the center of the third hole to the center of the
fourth hole is 1/8" or 0.125" Distance from the center of the
fourth hole to the bottom edge is 15/128" or 0.117" 0.375 +
0.875 + 0.875 + 0.125 + 0.117 = 2.367"
[Ref: General Handbook H-8083-30A-ATB, Chapter 04 Page 3]

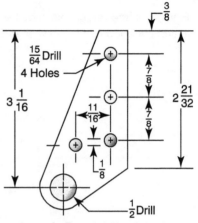

Answer for Figure 4-4. Aircraft drawing.

4-15 Answer C.
View 3 in Figure 4-5 on previous page is the correct view of
the left side of the object.
[Ref: General Handbook H-8083-30A-ATB, Chapter 04 Page 12]

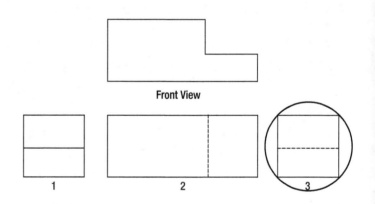

4-16 Answer A.
View 1 in Figure 4-6 is the correct orthographic view for this
part. The bottom of the object is solid, remembering that
dashed vertical lines represent features of the part that are
hidden from the view being represented.
[Ref: General Handbook H-8083-30A-ATB, Chapter 04 Page 12]

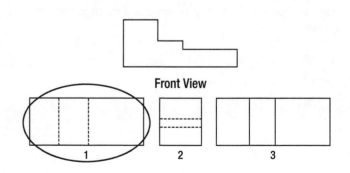

4-17 AMG013
What is the class of working drawing that is the description/depiction of a single part?
  A. Installation drawing
  B. Assembly drawing
  C. Detail drawing

4-20 AMG014
A drawing in which the sub-assemblies or parts are shown as brought together on the aircraft is called
  A. an assembly drawing.
  B. an installation drawing.
  C. a detail drawing.

4-18 AMG014
The drawings often used in illustrated parts catalogs/manuals are
  A. exploded view.
  B. block view.
  C. detail view.

4-21 AMG014
In what type of electrical diagram are images of components used instead of conventional electrical symbols?
  A. a pictorial diagram.
  B. a schematic diagram.
  C. a block diagram.

4-19 AMG013
Refer to Figure 4-7. In the isometric view of a typical aileron balance weight, identify the view indicated by the arrow.
  A. 1
  B. 3
  C. 2

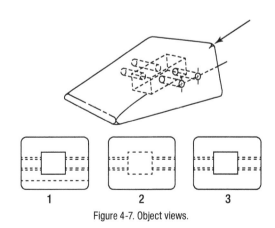

Figure 4-7. Object views.

AIRCRAFT DRAWINGS

ANSWERS

4-17 Answer C.
Detail drawings depict single parts, providing information for construction of the part including specifications on size, shape, material, and method of construction.
[Ref: General Handbook H-8083-30A-ATB, Chapter 04 Page 11]

4-18 Answer A.
An exploded view is a pictorial drawing of two or more parts that fit together as an assembly. The view shows the individual parts and their relative position to other parts before assembled.
[Ref: General Handbook H-8083-30A-ATB, Chapter 04 Page 13]

4-19 Answer B.
An isometric view uses a combination of the views from an orthographic projection and tilts the object forward so that portions of three views are seen at once.
[Ref: General Handbook H-8083-30A-ATB, Chapter 04 Page 12]

4-20 Answer B.
Installation drawings are used extensively in aircraft maintenance and repair manuals. They provide the AMT a visual representation of how the various parts and/or subassemblies are assembled.
[Ref: General Handbook H-8083-30A-ATB, Chapter 04 Page 15]

4-21 Answer A.
This is not specifically addressed within the text. However, based on your knowledge of the three answers determine the one that best fits the question. Block diagrams used blocks to simplify the relationship between components of a more complex system and do not use electrical systems. Schematic diagrams show the location of components with respect to each other within a system and do not use electrical systems. Pictorial drawings are similar to photographs. The question refers to images of the components, therefore this would be the most correct answer.
[Ref: General Handbook H-8083-30A-ATB, Chapter 04 Page 11]

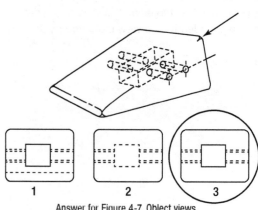

Answer for Figure 4-7. Object views.

4-22 AMG014
One purpose for schematic drawings is to show the
 A. functional location of components within a system.
 B. physical location of components within a system.
 C. size and shape of components within a system.

4-23 AMG014
Review the two statements below. Which are correct?
1. Schematic diagrams indicate the location of individual components in the aircraft.
2. Schematic diagrams indicate the location of components with respect to each other within the system.

Regarding the above statements:
 A. Only #1 is true.
 B. Both #1 and #2 are true.
 C. Only # 2 is true.

4-24 AMG014
A schematic diagram of a hydraulic system would indicate the
 A. specific location of individual components within the aircraft.
 B. direction of fluid flow through the system.
 C. type and quantity of the hydraulic fluid.

4-25 AMG014
What type of diagram is used to explain a principle of operation, rather than show the parts as they actually appear?
 A. A pictorial diagram.
 B. A schematic diagram.
 C. An assembly drawing.

4-26 AMG014
What do flowcharts illustrate?
 A. The flow of hydraulic and fuel lines.
 B. The flow of air over an airfoil.
 C. The flow of events or a particular sequence.

4-27 AMG014
The measurements showing the ideal or "perfect" sizes of parts on drawings are called
 A. tolerances.
 B. allowances.
 C. dimensions.

AIRCRAFT DRAWINGS

ANSWERS

4-22 Answer A.
Schematic diagrams show the location of components with respect to each other within a system. In other words, their functional location not necessarily their actual location within the system.
[Ref: General Handbook H-8083-30A-ATB, Chapter 04 Page 16]

4-23 Answer C.
Schematic diagrams show the location of components with respect to each other within a system, not their actual location in the aircraft.
[Ref: General Handbook H-8083-30A-ATB, Chapter 04 Page 16]

4-24 Answer B.
Schematic diagrams show the location of components with respect to each other within a system. In other words, their functional location. In this question, the direction of fluid flow within the system would be depicted as part of its functionality. Actual location, type, and quantity of hydraulic fluid would not be found in a schematic diagram.
[Ref: General Handbook H-8083-30A-ATB, Chapter 04 Page 16]

4-25 Answer B.
Schematic diagrams show functional location of components within a system, and by studying the various components and how they are related within the system the AMT can learn how the system operates. Schematic diagrams of this type are often used in troubleshooting.
[Ref: General Handbook H-8083-30A-ATB, Chapter 04 Page 16]

4-26 Answer C.
Flowcharts illustrate a particular sequence or flow of events. There are troubleshooting flowcharts used to aid you in detecting a faulty component. You will find these in the Fault Isolation Manuals. Another flowchart you will use in your career is the logic flowchart that uses standardized symbols to indicate specific types of logic gates and their relationship to other digital devices in a system. This type of flowchart is also used for troubleshooting by illustrating decisions and reactions. By using standardized symbols, decisions and actions can be indicated.
[Ref: General Handbook H-8083-30A-ATB, Chapter 04 Page 17]

4-27 Answer C.
Although not specifically defined, dimensions are the preferred (ideal/perfect) measurements for a part. Allowances and tolerances define deviations from these preferred measurements, if acceptable.
[Ref: General Handbook H-8083-30A-ATB, Chapter 04 Page 18]

4-28 AMG014

What would be the minimum diameter of 4130 round stock required for the construction of the clevis that would produce a machined surface? Refer to Figure 4-8 below.

    A. 55/64 inch

    B. 1 inch

    C. 7/8 inch

4-30 AMG014

In an aircraft drawing, what type of line would be drawn if it was composed of one long and two short evenly spaced dashes indicating the alternate position of parts of an object or relative position of a missing part

    A. a sectioning line.

    B. a break line.

    C. a phantom line.

4 29 AMG014

What is the maximum diameter of the hole for the clevis pin? Refer to Figure 4-8 below.

    A. 0.3175

    B. 0.3130

    C. 0.31255

4-31 AMG014

Using the information, what size drill would be required to drill the clevis bolt hole? Refer to Figure 4-8 below.

    A. 5/16 inch

    B. 21/64 inch

    C. 1/2 inch

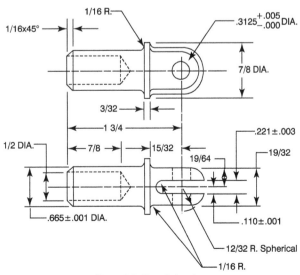

Figure 4-8. Aircraft drawing.

AIRCRAFT DRAWINGS

ANSWERS

4-28 Answer B.
The question is stating that all the surfaces of the clevis are machined. Therefore the part needs to be larger than its largest finished dimension which is 7/8 inch. 55/64 is equivalent to 0.859375 which is too small, and 7/8 is also too small if it must be machined. Therefore the minimum diameter of 4130 round stock must be 1 inch.
[Ref: General Handbook H-8083-30A-ATB, Chapter 04 Page 3 & 18]

4-30 Answer C.
Phantom lines composed of one long and two short evenly spaced dashes indicate the alternate position of parts of the object or the relative position of a missing part.
[Ref: General Handbook H-8083-30A-ATB, Chapter 04 Page 19]

4-29 Answer A.
The diameter of the clevis hole is 0.3125 with an allowance of +0.005 and -0.000, which means the maximum size the hole can be 0.3175.
[Ref: General Handbook H-8083-30A-ATB, Chapter 04 Page 3 & 18]

4-31 Answer A.
The drawing below notes that the clevis bolt hole should have a diameter of .3125.
The drill bit size decimal equivalents are:
5/16 = .3125, 21/64 = .3281, and 1/2 = .5, therefore the 5/16th would be the correct drill bit to use.
[Ref: General Handbook H-8083-30A-ATB, Chapter 04 Page 19]

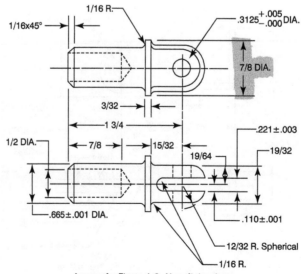

Answer for Figure 4-8. Aircraft drawing.

4-32 AMG014
Identify the extension line in Figure 4-9 below.
- A. 3
- B. 1
- C. 2

4-34 AMG014
Which statement is applicable when using a sketch for
making a part?
- A. The sketch may be used only if supplemented with a
     3-view orthographic projection drawing.
- B. The sketch must show all information to manufacture
     the part.
- C. The sketch need not show all necessary construction
     details.

4-33 AMG014
What does the type of line below on an aircraft technical
drawing represent?

———— —— ———— —— ———— —— ———— —— ———— —

- A. edges of an object which are invisible from the
     drawn perspective.
- B. the center line of an object or portion of an object.
- C. the alternating position of a hinged portion of an object.

4-35 AMG001
What are the proper procedural steps for sketching repairs
and alterations? Refer to Figure 4-10 below.
- A. 3, 1, 4, and 2
- B. 4, 2, 3, and 1
- C. 1, 3, 4, and 2

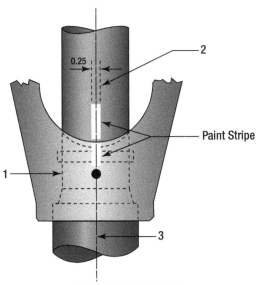

Figure 4-9. Aircraft drawing.

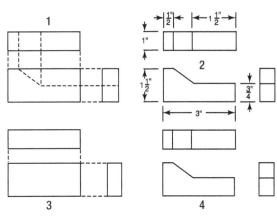

Figure 4-10. Sketches.

AIRCRAFT DRAWINGS

ANSWERS

4-32 Answer A.
Extensions are used to extend the line showing the side or edge of a figure for placing a dimension to that side or edge. They are very narrow and have a short break where they extend from the object and extend a short distance past the arrow of the dimensioning line. Item #3 in Figure 4-9 from the previous page represents extension lines.
[Ref: General Handbook H-8083-30A-ATB, Chapter 04 Page 19]

4-33 Answer B.
Alternating long and short lines are center lines. Invisible edges of an object are known as hidden lines and drawn as a long dashed, evenly spaced segmented line.

— — — — — — — — — — — — — — — — — — —

The depiction of an alternate position of a hinged component is done with phantom lines and shaped as so:

——— —— —— ——— —— —— ——— —— —— ———

[Ref: General Handbook H-8083-30A-ATB, Chapter 04 Page 18-21]

4-34 Answer B.
The degree to which a sketch is complete will depend on its intended use. However, it must show all information necessary for its intended use. In the example, for making a part, it must have all the information to manufacture the part.
[Ref: General Handbook H-8083-30A-ATB, Chapter 04 Page 23]

4-35 Answer A.
To make a sketch, first determine what views are necessary to portray the object, then block in the views, using light construction lines. Next, complete the details, darken the object outline, and sketch extension and dimension lines. Complete the drawing by adding notes, dimensions, title, date, and when necessary, the sketcher's name.
[Ref: General Handbook H-8083-30A-ATB, Chapter 04 Page 23]

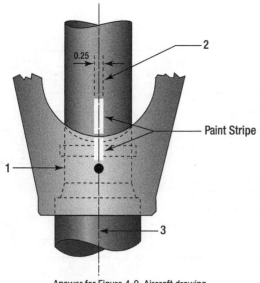

Answer for Figure 4-9. Aircraft drawing.

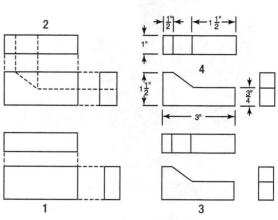

Answer for Figure 4-10. Sketches.

4-36 AMG001
Refer to Figure 4-11 below. What is the next step required for a working sketch of the illustration?
   A. Darken the object outlines.
   B. Sketch extension and dimension lines.
   C. Add notes, dimensions, title, and date.

4-38 AMG001
What should be the first step of the procedure in sketching an aircraft wing repair?
   A. Draw heavy guidelines.
   B. Lay out the repair.
   C. Block in the views.

4-37 AMG014
Refer to Figure 4-12 below. Which material section-line symbol indicates cast iron?
   A. 1
   B. 2
   C. 3

4-39 AMG001
1. According to FAR Part 91, repairs to an aircraft skin should have a detailed dimensional sketch included in the permanent record.
2. On occasion, a mechanic may need to make a simple sketch of a proposed repair to an aircraft, a new design, or a modification.

For the above statements,
   A. Only #1 is true
   B. Only #2 is true
   C. Both #1 and #2 are true

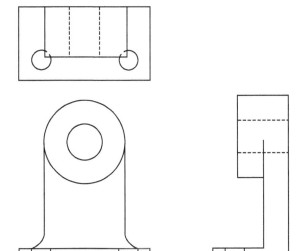

Figure 4-11. Sketches.

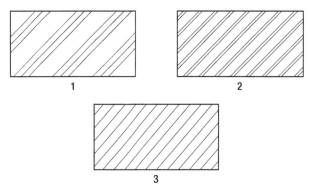

Figure 4-12. Material symbols.

AIRCRAFT DRAWINGS

ANSWERS

4-36 Answer B.
To make a sketch, first determine what views are necessary to portray the object; then block in the views, using light construction lines. Next, complete the details, darken the object outline, and sketch extension and dimension lines. Complete the drawing by adding notes, dimensions, title, date, and when necessary, the sketcher's name.
[Ref: General Handbook H-8083-30A-ATB, Chapter 04 Page 23]

4-38 Answer C.
Blocking in the views is the first step for this type of sketching. The second step is to complete the drawing details, the third step is to sketch extension and dimension lines and the fourth step is to add notes and dimensions.
[Ref: General Handbook H-8083-30A-ATB, Chapter 04 Page 23]

4-37 Answer C.
Item #3 in Figure 4-12 on the previous page represents cast iron, #2 is steel, and #1 represents rubber, plastic, or electrical insulation.
[Ref: General Handbook H-8083-30A-ATB, Chapter 04 Page 22]

4-39 Answer B.
To determine this answer you have to know the FARs. Although statement 1 appears logical, not all repairs need to have detailed dimensional sketches included.
[Ref: General Handbook H-8083-30A-ATB, Chapter 04 Page 23]

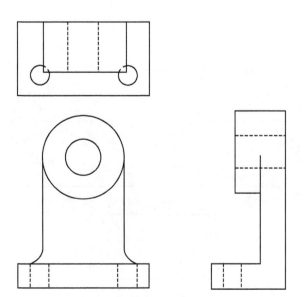

Answer for Figure 4-11. Sketches.

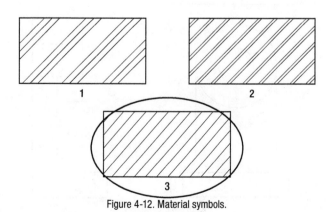

Figure 4-12. Material symbols.

4-40 AMG001
For sketching purposes, almost all objects are composed
of one or more combinations of six basic shapes. These
include:
  A. angle, arc, line, plane, square, and circle.
  B. triangle, circle, cube, cylinder, cone, and sphere.
  C. triangle, plane, circle, line, and square.

4-41 AMG014
An aircraft reciprocating engine has a 1,830 cubic inch
displacement and develops 1,250 brake horsepower at 2500
RPM. What is the brake mean effective pressure? Refer to
Figure 4-13 below.
  A. 217
  B. 205
  C. 225

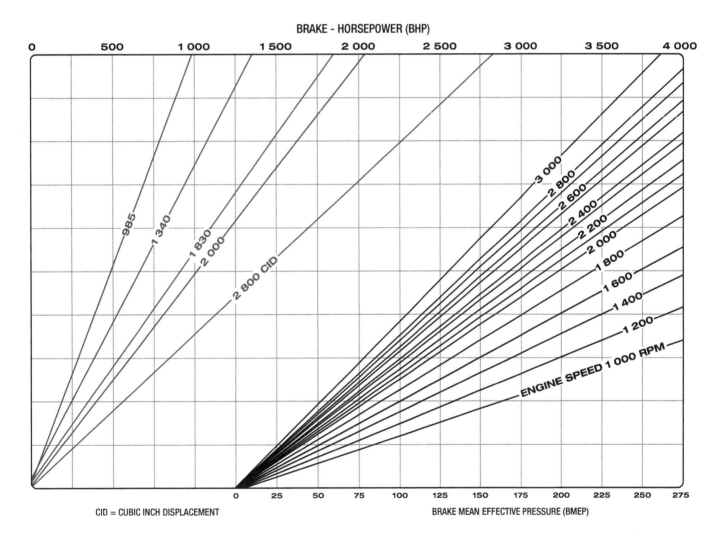

Figure 4-13. BHP performance chart.

AIRCRAFT DRAWINGS

ANSWERS

4-40 Answer B.

The six basic shapes used in sketching include the triangle, circle, cube, cylinder, cone, and sphere.

[Ref: General Handbook H-8083-30A-ATB, Chapter 04 Page 23]

4-41 Answer A.

Start at the 1,250 brake-horsepower vertical line, follow it to where it intersects with the diagonal line representing the 1830 cubic inch displacement engine. Then, follow the vertical line from this intersection to the diagonal line for 2,500 RPM, at this intersection follow the vertical line to the bottom to read the brake mean effective pressure. The graph is hard to read but the closest answer is 217 BMEP.

[Ref: General Handbook H-8083-30A-ATB, Chapter 04 Page 25]

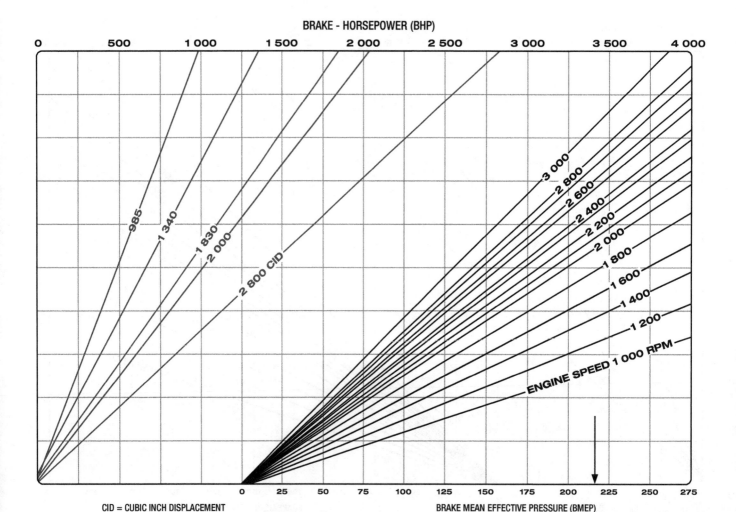

Answer for Figure 4-13. BHP performance chart.

4-42 AMG013

An aircraft reciprocating engine has a 2,800 cubic inch displacement and develops 2,000 brake horsepower, and indicates 270 brake mean effective pressure. What is the engine speed RPM? Refer to Figure 4-13 on the previous page.

   A. 2,200
   B. 2,100
   C. 2,300

4-43 AMG014

Determine the maximum length of No. 16 cable to be installed from a bus to the equipment in a 28-volt system with a 25-ampere intermittent load and a 1-volt drop. Refer to Figure 4-14 below.

   A. 8 feet
   B. 10 feet
   C. 12 feet

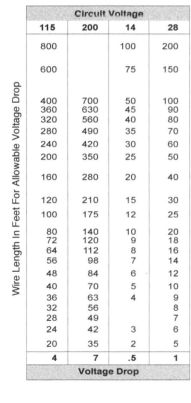

Circuit Voltage			
115	200	14	28
800		100	200
600		75	150
400	700	50	100
360	630	45	90
320	560	40	80
280	490	35	70
240	420	30	60
200	350	25	50
160	280	20	40
120	210	15	30
100	175	12	25
80	140	10	20
72	120	9	18
64	112	8	16
56	98	7	14
48	84	6	12
40	70	5	10
36	63	4	9
32	56		8
28	49		7
24	42	3	6
20	35	2	5
4	7	.5	1
Voltage Drop			

(Left axis: Wire Length In Feet For Allowable Voltage Drop)

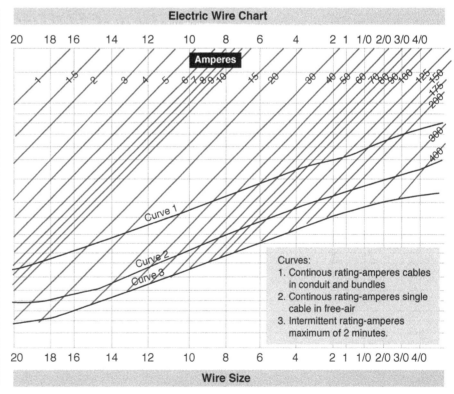

Electric Wire Chart

Curves:
1. Continous rating-amperes cables in conduit and bundles
2. Continous rating-amperes single cable in free-air
3. Intermittent rating-amperes maximum of 2 minutes.

Figure 4-14. Electric wire chart.

AIRCRAFT DRAWINGS

ANSWERS

4-42 Answer B.
Utilizing Figure 4-13 on the previous page, start at the 2,000 brake-horsepower vertical line, follow it to where it intersects with the diagonal line representing the 2,800 cubic inch displacement engine. Draw a horizontal line from this intersection to the right of the chart. Locate the 270 brake mean effective pressure on the bottom scale, draw a vertical line up until it intersects with the horizontal line you drew previously; from here, you can determine that the RPM for this engine will be 2100.
[Ref: General Handbook H-8083-30A-ATB, Chapter 04 Page 25]

4-43 Answer A.
Utilizing Figure 4-14 on the previous page, first draw a line mid-way between the 20 and 30 amperes lines to use as a guide to represent the 25 amperes in this question. Find the 16-gage wire size we will be using, follow this line until it intersects with the 25-ampere line drawn, draw a line from this intersection to the left column for a 28-volt circuit with a 1-volt drop and the answer is 8 feet.
[Ref: General Handbook H-8083-30A-ATB, Chapter 04 Page 25]

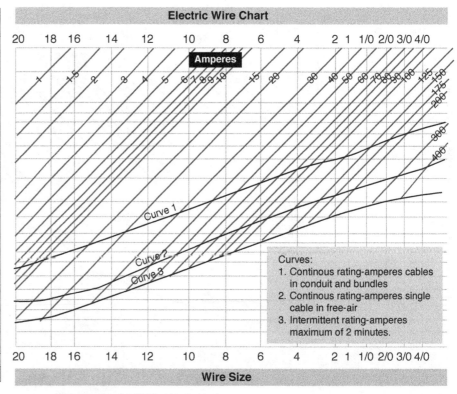

Answer for Figure 4-14. Electric wire chart.

4-44 AMG014
Determine the proper tension for a 3/16 inch cable (7 × 19 extra flex) if the temperature is 87°F.
Refer to Figure 4-15 below.

   A. 135 pounds
   B. 125 pounds
   C. 140 pounds

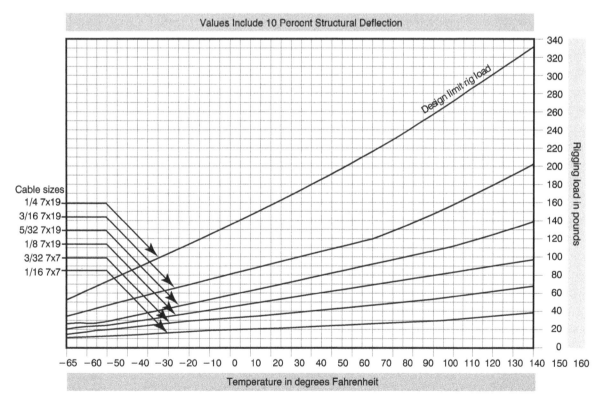

Figure 4-15. Cable tension chart.

AIRCRAFT DRAWINGS

ANSWERS

4-44 Answer B.
Utilizing Figure 4-15 below, from the 87° mark on the bottom of the graph, draw a vertical line up until it intersects with the 3/16 7 × 19 cable curve. From this intersection draw a horizontal line to the right scale on the graph to read the proper rigging load in pounds, 125 is the closest answer.
[Ref: General Handbook H-8083-30A-ATB, Chapter 04 Page 25]

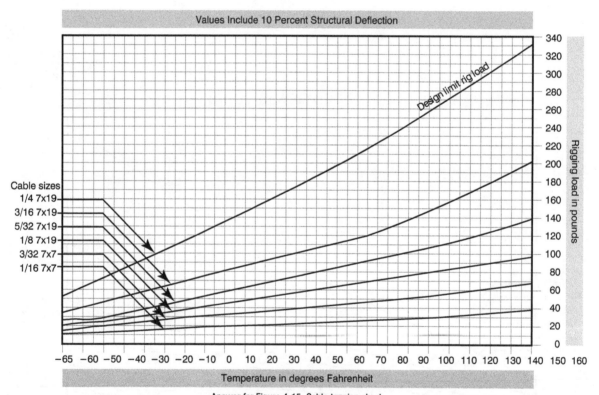

Answer for Figure 4-15. Cable tension chart.

ORAL EXAM

4-1(O).   Define tolerance as it relates to aircraft drawings.

4-2(O).   Define clearance as it relates to aircraft drawings.

4-3(O).   What information can you find on the title block of an aircraft drawing?

4-4(O).   Explain a dimension line and what is it used for.

ANSWERS

ORAL EXAM

4-1(O).   Tolerance is the allowable variation, the plus (+) figure indicates the maximum, and the minus (–) figure indicates the minimum allowable variation. The sum of the plus and minus allowance figures is called tolerance.
[Ref: General Handbook H-8083-30A-ATB, Chapter 04 Page 9]

4-2(O).   The dimensions given for tolerances signify the amount of clearance allowable between moving parts. A positive allowance is indicated for a part that is to slide or revolve upon another part. A negative allowance is one given for a force fit.
[Ref: General Handbook H-8083-30A-ATB, Chapter 04 Page 9]

4-3(O).   The information found in a title block is as follows: A drawing number to identify the print for filing purposes and to prevent confusing it with any other print.
     1. The name of the part or assembly.
     2. The scale to which it is drawn.
     3. The date.
     4. The name of the firm.
     5. The name of the draftsmen, the checker, and the person approving the drawing.
[Ref: General Handbook H-8083-30A-ATB, Chapter 04 Page 3]

4-4(O).   A dimension line is a light solid line, broken at the midpoint for insertion of measurement indications, and having opposite pointing arrowheads at each end to show origin and termination of a measurement. They are generally parallel to the line for which the dimension is given, and are usually placed outside the outline of the object and between views if more than one view is shown.
[Ref: General Handbook H-8083-30A-ATB, Chapter 04 Page 18]

PRACTICAL EXAM

NOTE: The practical portion of the Mathematics subject area may be tested simultaneously when performing calculation(s) in subject areas of Basic Electricity and/or Weight and Balance.

4-1(P).   Given an aircraft drawing, blueprint, and/or system schematic identify the lines and symbols as requested.

4-2(P).   Given a system schematic, answer questions regarding the system and explain how it can be used to assist in troubleshooting a discrepancy with the system.

4-3(P).   Given a performance chart, a specific RPM, and BMEP, determine the brake horsepower.

4-4(P).   Given a control cable tension chart, find the proper tension for a specified cable at a given temperature.

4-5(P).   Using a servicing chart or graph, determine if a component is within limits.

4-6(P).   Given specific details, draw a sketch of an alteration or repair.

4-7(P).   Given an electrical wiring diagram, explain the various symbols and explain how it can be used to assist in troubleshooting the system.

PAGE LEFT BLANK INTENTIONALLY

PHYSICS FOR AVIATION

Matter, Energy, Force, Work, Power, Torque, Simple Machines, Pulleys, Gears, Inclined Planes, Stresses, Motion, Heat, Pressure, Gas, and Sound

CHAPTER 05

QUESTIONS

5-1 AMG027
Which of the following is not a characteristic of matter?
  A. Porosity.
  B. Impenetrability.
  C. Energy.

5-2 AMG027
A fully charged aircraft battery is an example of?
  A. Potential Energy.
  B. Kinetic Energy.
  C. Power.

5-3 AMG055
What force is exerted on the piston in a hydraulic cylinder if the area of the piston is 1.2 square inches and the fluid pressure is 850 PSI?
  A. 1,020 pounds
  B. 960 pounds
  C. 850 pounds

5-4 AMG099
An engine that weighs 350 pounds is removed from an aircraft by means of a mobile hoist. The engine is raised 3 feet above its attachment mount, and the entire assembly is then moved forward 12 feet. A constant force of 70 pounds in required to move the loaded hoist. What is the total work input required to move the hoist?
  A. 840 foot-pounds
  B. 1,890 foot-pounds
  C. 1,050 foot-pounds

5-5 AMG099
How much work input is required to lower (not drop) a 120-pound weight from the top of a 3-foot table to the floor?
  A. 120 pounds of force
  B. 360 foot-pounds
  C. 40 foot-pounds

5-6 AMG099
Which of the following is not a kind of friction?
  A. Rolling friction.
  B. Static friction.
  C. Resisting friction.

PHYSICS FOR AVIATION

ANSWERS

5-1 Answer C.
The characteristics of matter are: mass and weight, attraction, porosity, impenetrability, density, and specific gravity.
[Ref: General Handbook H-8083-30A-ATB, Chapter 05 Page 2]

5-2 Answer A.
Energy in storage is potential energy. Once a circuit is closed and the energy stored in the battery is actually performing work, such as starting an engine or powering a light, it is considered kinetic energy. Power is the actual force being applied over distance and time.
[Ref: General Handbook H-8083-30A-ATB, Chapter 05 Page 4]

5-3 Answer A.
Work = Force (F) × distance (d). F = W/d.
F = 850 PSI times 1.2 square inches = 1,020
[Ref: General Handbook H-8083-30A-ATB, Chapter 05 Page 5]

5-4 Answer A.
Work = Force (F) × distance (d)
[Ref: General Handbook H-8083-30A-ATB, Chapter 05 Page 5]

5-5 Answer B.
Work = Force (F) × distance (d)
[Ref: General Handbook H-8083-30A-ATB, Chapter 05 Page 5]

5-6 Answer C.
Thus, the three kinds of friction may be classified as:
1. starting (static) friction,
2. sliding friction, and,
3. rolling friction.
[Ref: General Handbook H-8083-30A-ATB, Chapter 05 Page 6]

5-7 AMG099

In physics, which of the following factors are necessary to determine power?

1. Force exerted
2. Distance moved
3. Time required
   A. 1 and 2
   B. 2 and 3
   C. 1, 2, and 3

5-8 AMG099

The simplest machine and probably the most familiar is

A. the gear.
B. the lever.
C. the inclined plane.

5-9 AMG099

If you tried to lift a 200lb aircraft part, which type of pulley design would make for the least effort needed?

A. Single movable pulley.
B. Block and tackle.
C. Single fixed pulley.

5-10 AMG099

The amount of force applied to rope A in Figure 5-1 (below) to lift the weight is?

A. 12 pounds.
B. 15 pounds.
C. 20 pounds.

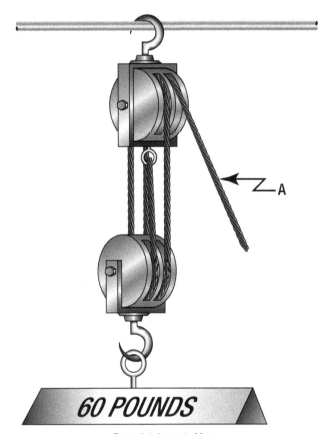

Figure 5-1. Amount of force.

PHYSICS FOR AVIATION

ANSWERS

5-7 Answer C.
Power = Force × distance × time
[Ref: General Handbook H-8083-30A-ATB, Chapter 05 Page 7]

5-10 Answer B.
The block and tackle shown in the figure has four ropes supporting the weight and therefore provides a mechanical advantage of four. To determine the force to be exerted divide the weight to be moved by the mechanical advantage (60/4 = 15). It will take 15 pounds of force to lift the weight. Note that the rope must be pulled four times the distance the weight is to be lifted, e.g. if the weight must be lifted 10 feet, you will have to pull the rope 40 feet.
[Ref: General Handbook H-8083-30A-ATB, Chapter 05 Page 11]

5-8 Answer B.
The simplest machine, and perhaps the most familiar one, is the lever.
[Ref: General Handbook H-8083-30A-ATB, Chapter 05 Page 9]

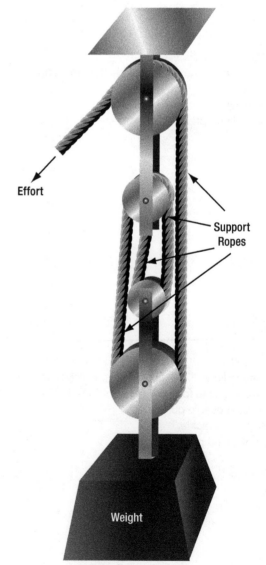

5-9 Answer B.
A block and tackle is made up of multiple pulleys, some of them fixed and some movable. In Figure 5-2 (right), the block and tackle is made up of four pulleys, the top two being fixed and the bottom two being movable. Viewing the figure from right to left, notice there are four ropes supporting the weight and a fifth rope where the effort is applied. The number of weight supporting ropes determines the mechanical advantage of a block and tackle, in this case the mechanical advantage is four. If the weight was 200 lb., it would require a 50 lb. effort to lift it.
[Ref: General Handbook H-8083-30A-ATB, Chapter 05 Page 11]

Figure 5-2. Block and tackle.

5-11 AMG099
The type of stress that can cause an object to become distorted or change its shape is
A. torsion.
B. strain.
C. bending.

5-12 AMG099
_____ is the type of stress that tries to pull the object apart.
A. Compression
B. Shear
C. Tension

5-13 AMG099
We need to calculate the acceleration of an airplane traveling at 300 mph. The pilot pushes the throttle to a speed of 600 mph in 30 seconds. What is the airplane's average acceleration in mph/s?
A. 20 mph/s
B. 300 mph/s
C. 10 mph/s

5-14 AMG099
Which of the following is Newton's First Law of Motion, generally termed the Law of Inertia?
A. Every action has an equal and opposite reaction.
B. Force is proportional to the product of mass and acceleration.
C. Objects at rest tend to remain at rest and objects in motion tend to remain in motion at the same speed and direction, unless acted on by an external force.

5-15 AMG099
Based on Newton's second law of motion, the formula to calculate thrust is?

A. $F = \dfrac{W\,(Vf\text{-}Vi)}{Gt}$

B. $F = MA$

C. $F = \dfrac{W\,(Vf\text{-}Vi)}{Gt}$

5-16 AMG099
Newton's Third Law of motion is often called?
A. Momentum.
B. The law of potential energy.
C. The law of action and reaction.

PHYSICS FOR AVIATION

ANSWERS

5-11 Answer B.
If the stress acting on an object is great enough, it can cause the object to change its shape or to become distorted.
[Ref: General Handbook H-8083-30A-ATB, Chapter 05 Page 14-15]

5-12 Answer C.
Tension is a force that tries to pull an object apart. For example, if a rope was suspending a heavy object, it is the weight of the object which causes tension to be applied to the rope.
[Ref: General Handbook H-8083-30A-ATB, Chapter 05 Page 14]

5-13 Answer C.
Acceleration is the rate of change of speed of an object. For example, if an object increases its speed by 10 mph over a 5 second period of time, the rate of change of speed is 2 miles per hour per second. Acceleration (A) = Velocity Final (Vf) - Velocity Initial (Vi) / Time (t)
[Ref: General Handbook H-8083-30A-ATB, Chapter 05 Page 16]

5-14 Answer C.
By Newton's first law of motion, stating that objects at rest tend to remain at rest and objects in motion tend to remain in motion at the same speed and in the same direction, unless acted on by an external force.
[Ref: General Handbook H-8083-30A-ATB, Chapter 05 Page 17]

5-15 Answer A.
A body that has great momentum has a strong tendency to remain in motion and is therefore hard to stop. Force = Weight (Velocity final - Velocity initial); Gravity (Time)

$$Force = \frac{W\ (Vf-Vi)}{Gt}$$

[Ref: General Handbook H-8083-30A-ATB, Chapter 05 Page 17]

5-16 Answer C.
Newton's third law of motion is often called the law of action and reaction.
[Ref: General Handbook H-8083-30A-ATB, Chapter 05 Page 18]

5-17 AMG099
Which of the following scenarios is an example of centripetal force?
   A. The G forces felt by the flight crew during a steep turn.
   B. The forces on spinning propeller blade at it works to pull itself from the hub.
   C. The forces on turbine engine shaft as it works to hold onto each attached compressor blade.

5-20 AMG027
The heat transfer process of convection occurs in
_____.
   A. Solids and liquids.
   B. Liquids and gasses.
   C. Solids only.

5-18 AMG027
Which of the following is not used to express quantities of heat energy?
   A. Calorie
   B. Degree
   C. BTU

5-21 AMG027
Which statement concerning heat and/or temperature is true?
   A. There is an inverse relationship between temperature and heat.
   B. Temperature is a measure of the kinetic energy of the molecules of any substance.
   C. Temperature is a measure of the potential energy of the molecules of any substance.

5-19 AMG027
An airplane engine is burning enough fuel to produce 680 horsepower but it is only creating 285. What is the thermal efficiency of this airplane's engine?
   A. 238.59%
   B. 41.91%
   C. 58.08%

5-22 AMG099
Thermal expansion is very slight in
   A. gases.
   B. liquids.
   C. solids.

PHYSICS FOR AVIATION

ANSWERS

5-17 Answer C.
Centripetal force is the force that acts on a body moving in a circular path and is directed toward the center around which the body is moving. An example is a ball attached to a string when it is swung in a circular motion. Another example is the force on a shaft such as in a turbine engine which is exerted by the mass of the fan blades as they rotate with the shaft.
[Ref: General Handbook H-8083-30A-ATB, Chapter 05 Page 18]

5-18 Answer B.
Two different units are used to express quantities of heat energy. They are the calorie and the BTU.
[Ref: General Handbook H-8083-30A-ATB, Chapter 05 Page 19]

5-19 Answer B.
Thermal Efficiency = Horsepower Produced ÷ Horsepower in Fuel
[Ref: General Handbook H-8083-30A-ATB, Chapter 05 Page 19-20]

5-20 Answer B.
Convection is the process of transferring heat by the movement of fluids. Liquids and gasses are considered fluids. Convection is often used for removing heat or cooling an object. In the convective process, the faster the movement of those fluids, the more heat will be transferred.
[Ref: General Handbook H-8083-30A-ATB, Chapter 05 Page 21]

5-21 Answer B.
Temperature and heat have a direct relationship, as heat increases temperature increases. Potential energy is stored energy. Kinetic energy is the energy possessed by an object in motion.
[Ref: General Handbook H-8083-30A-ATB, Chapter 05 Page 22]

5-22 Answer C.
Because the molecules of solids are much closer together and are more strongly attracted to each other, the expansion of solids when heated is very slight in comparison to the expansion in liquids and gases.
[Ref: General Handbook H-8083-30A-ATB, Chapter 05 Page 23]

5-23 AMG099
Which pressure includes atmospheric pressure in its reading?
  A. Gauge pressure
  B. Absolute pressure
  C. Differential pressure

5-26 AMG055
What force is exerted on the piston in a hydraulic cylinder if the area of the piston is 1.2 square inches and the fluid pressure is 850 PSI?
  A. 1,020 pounds
  B. 960 pounds
  C. 850 pounds

5-24 AMG027
If the volume of a confined gas is double (without the addition of more gas), assuming the temperature remains constant, the pressure will
  A. increase in direct proportion to the volume increase.
  B. remain the same.
  C. be reduced to one-half of its original value.

5-27 AMG055
If a double-acting actuating cylinder in a 3,000 PSI system has a piston with a surface area of three square inches on the extension side, and a rod with a cross-section area of one square inch attached to the piston on the other side, approximately how much force will the actuator be able to produce when retracting?
  A. 9,000 pounds
  B. 6,000 pounds
  C. 3,000 pounds

5-25 AMG027
Which gas law states that all gases expand and contract in direct proportion to the change in the absolute temperature provided the pressure is held constant?
  A. Dalton's Law
  B. General Gas Law
  C. Charles' Law

5-28 AMG027
Which statement concerning Bernoulli's principle is true?
  A. The pressure of a fluid increases at points where the velocity of the fluid increases.
  B. The pressure of a fluid decreases at points where the velocity of the fluid increases.
  C. It applies only to gases and the expansion or contraction when exposed to heat.

PHYSICS FOR AVIATION

ANSWERS

5-23 Answer B.
A gauge that includes atmospheric pressure in its reading
is measuring what is known as absolute pressure, or
PSIA. Absolute pressure is equal to gauge pressure plus
atmospheric pressure.
[Ref: General Handbook H-8083-30A-ATB, Chapter 05 Page 24]

5-24 Answer C.
Boyle's law is normally stated as: "The volume of an
enclosed dry gas varies inversely with its absolute pressure,
provided the temperature remains constant."
[Ref: General Handbook H-8083-30A-ATB, Chapter 05 Page 25]

5-25 Answer C.
Charles found that all gases expand and contract in direct
proportion to the change in the absolute temperature,
provided the pressure is held constant.
[Ref: General Handbook H-8083-30A-ATB, Chapter 05 Page 26]

5-26 Answer A.
Pascal's law states that a force applied to a confined liquid is
transmitted equally in all directions.
Force = Pressure × Area.
Thus 850 pounds/sq. in. × 1.2 = 1020 pounds
[Ref: General Handbook H-8083-30A-ATB, Chapter 05 Page 28]

5-27 Answer B.
Force = Pressure × Area. In a double-acting actuating
cylinder, the rod on the retraction side reduces the overall
surface area of the piston equal to the surface area of the
cross-section of the retraction side. In this example, the 3
sq. in. piston area is reduced by 1 sq. in. of the retraction
piston area.
[Ref: General Handbook H-8083-30A-ATB, Chapter 05 Page 29]

5-28 Answer B.
The static pressure of a fluid (liquid or gas) decreases at
points where the velocity of the fluid increases, provided no
energy is added to nor taken away from the fluid.
[Ref: General Handbook H-8083-30A-ATB, Chapter 05 Page 30-31]

5-29 AMG099

What does the following describe? *"When two adjacent objects have the same natural frequency and one starts to vibrate; that wave energy can be transferred to the other object causing it to vibrate as well."*

A. Resonance.
B. Doppler Effect.
C. Propagation.

5-32 AMG008

Which mixture of a cubic foot of air will be the most dense?

A. Air containing 2% water vapor.
B. Air containing 65% water vapor.
C. Air which is completely saturated with water vapor.

5-30 AMG099

Decibels are a measure of a sound's?

A. Wave length.
B. Amplitude.
C. Frequency.

5-33 AMG008

Which condition is the actual amount of water vapor in a mixture of air and water?

A. Relative Humidity
B. Dew point
C. Absolute Humidity

5-31 AMG008

Which atmospheric conditions will cause the true landing speed of an aircraft to be the greatest?

A. Low temperature with low humidity
B. High temperature with low humidity
C. High temperature with high humidity

5-34 AMG008

Which is the ratio of the water vapor actually present in the atmosphere to the amount that would be present if the air were saturated at the prevailing temperature and pressure?

A. Absolute Humidity
B. Relative Humidity
C. Dew point

PHYSICS FOR AVIATION

ANSWERS

5-29 Answer A.
The statement describes the phenomena of resonance. Doppler effect refers to the changing of perceived frequency of sound related to its motion to or from the observer. Propagation refers to the movement of a vibration from its source.
[Ref: General Handbook H-8083-30A-ATB, Chapter 05 Page 33]

5-30 Answer B.
Sound intensity (or its amplitude) is measured in decibels, with a decibel being the ratio of one sound to another. One decibel (dB) is the smallest change in sound the human ear can detect. Wave length and frequency are perceived as a measure of a sounds pitch or tone.
[Ref: General Handbook H-8083-30A-ATB, Chapter 05 Page 33]

5-31 Answer C.
The density of air determines the true landing speed for an aircraft. Both its temperature and its humidity determine air density, with density decreasing as temperature and humidity increase. Air density is one factor in determining aerodynamic lift, in addition to the shape of the airfoil and the speed of the airfoil through the air. Thus, the lower the air density the faster the aircraft will have to travel to maintain the required lift.
[Ref: General Handbook H-8083-30A-ATB, Chapter 05 Page 35]

5-32 Answer A.
Water vapor weighs less than dry air, therefore the weight of an air water vapor mixture decreases as the amount of water vapor increases.
[Ref: General Handbook H-8083-30A-ATB, Chapter 05 Page 35-37]

5-33 Answer C.
Absolute humidity is the actual amount of the water vapor in a mixture of air and water. Dew point is the temperature that air must be cooled to reach saturation. Relative humidity is the ratio of vapor present if the air was saturated.
[Ref: General Handbook H-8083-30A-ATB, Chapter 05 Page 36]

5-34 Answer B.
Relative humidity is the ratio of the amount of water vapor actually present in the atmosphere to the amount that would be present if the air were saturated at the prevailing temperature and pressure.
[Ref: General Handbook H-8083-30A-ATB, Chapter 05 Page 36]

5-35 AMG099
Which of the following is not a true statement about the Four Forces of Flight?
- A. When an airplane is at a constant altitude, lift and weight are equal.
- B. When an airplane is decelerating, it has less thrust than drag.
- C. When an airplane is climbing, it has more weight than lift.

5-36 AMG099
Which term below is best described "as the velocity of a fluid increases, the static pressure of that fluid will decrease, provided there is no energy added or energy taken away"?
- A. Bernoulli's Principle
- B. Newton's Third Law
- C. Pascal's Law

5-37 AMG007
An increase in the speed at which an airfoil passes through the air increases lift because
- A. the increased speed of the airflow creates a greater pressure differential between the upper and lower surfaces.
- B. the increased speed of the airflow creates a lesser pressure differential between the upper and lower surfaces.
- C. the increased velocity of the relative wind increases the angle of attack.

5-38 AMG007
Aspect ratio of a wing is defined as the ratio of the
- A. wingspan to the wing root.
- B. square of the chord to the wingspan.
- C. wingspan to the mean chord.

5-39 AMG099
Which one of the below is not a method of controlling boundary layer air?
- A. Air suction through small holes on the wing's upper surface.
- B. Wing leading edge slots.
- C. Wingtip electrical generators.

5-40 AMG099
The term that best describes the approach of the boundary layer to the center of the wing that begins to lose speed due to skin friction and becomes thicker and turbulent is?
- A. Transition point.
- B. Turbulent layer.
- C. Laminar layer.

ANSWERS

5-35 Answer C.

During flight, there are four forces acting on an airplane. These forces are lift, weight, thrust, and drag. All four of these forces are measured in pounds. Any time the forces are not in balance, something about the airplane's condition is changing. The possibilities are as follows:

1. When an airplane is accelerating, it has more thrust than drag.
2. When an airplane is decelerating, it has less thrust than drag.
3. When an airplane is at a constant velocity, thrust and drag are equal.
4. When an airplane is climbing, it has more lift than weight.
5. When an airplane is descending, it has more weight than lift.
6. When an airplane is at a constant altitude, lift and weight are equal.

[Ref: General Handbook H-8083-30A-ATB, Chapter 05 Page 37]

5-36 Answer A.

Bernoulli's principle, as we refer to it today, states "as the velocity of a fluid increases, the static pressure of that fluid will decrease, provided there is no energy added or energy taken away."

[Ref: General Handbook H-8083-30A-ATB, Chapter 05 Page 37-39]

5-37 Answer A.

The increased speed of the airflow creates a greater pressure differential between the upper and lower surfaces. The lift on the wing as described by Bernoulli's principle, and lift on the wing as described by Newton's third law, are not separate or independent of each other. They are just two different ways to describe the same thing, namely the lift on a wing. The wing of an airplane moves through the air because the airplane is in motion, and generates lift by the process previously described.

[Ref: General Handbook H-8083-30A-ATB, Chapter 05 Page 37-39]

5-38 Answer C.

The aspect ratio of a wing is the relationship between its span (wingtip to wingtip measurement) and the chord of the wing.

[Ref: General Handbook H-8083-30A-ATB, Chapter 05 Page 40]

5-39 Answer C.

One way of keeping the boundary layer air under control, or lessening its negative effect, is to make the wing's surface as smooth as possible and to keep it free of dirt and debris. Other methods of controlling boundary layer air include wing leading edge slots, air suction through small holes on the wing's upper surface, and the use of devices called vortex generators.

[Ref: General Handbook H-8083-30A-ATB, Chapter 05 Page 40]

5-40 Answer B.

As the boundary layer approaches the center of the wing, it begins to lose speed due to skin friction and it becomes thicker and turbulent. Here it is called the turbulent layer.

[Ref: General Handbook H-8083-30A-ATB, Chapter 05 Page 40]

5-41 AMG007
The purpose of an aircraft wing dihedral is to
A. increase lateral stability.
B. increase longitudinal stability
C. increase lift coefficient of the wing.

5-44 AMG039
The ailerons or the spoilers on a jet transport are types of flight controls or lateral control for the
A. vertical axis.
B. lateral axis.
C. longitudinal axis.

5-42 AMG007
What type of stability for an airplane involves the tendency for the nose to pitch up or pitch down, rotating around the lateral axis?
A. Lateral stability
B. Directional stability
C. Longitudinal stability

5-45 AMG039
The rudder is a type of flight control or directional control for the
A. vertical axis.
B. lateral axis.
C. longitudinal axis.

5-43 AMG007
Which stability term represents a small amount of oscillation around both the longitudinal and vertical axes?
A. Static stability
B. Dutch Roll
C. Dynamic stability

5-46 AMG038
The elevator attached to the horizontal stabilizer is a type of flight control or directional control for the
A. vertical axis.
B. lateral axis.
C. longitudinal axis.

PHYSICS FOR AVIATION

ANSWERS

5-41 Answer A.
One design characteristic that tends to give an airplane good lateral stability is called dihedral. Dihedral is an upward angle for the wings with respect to the horizontal, and it is usually just a few degrees.
[Ref: General Handbook H-8083-30A-ATB, Chapter 05 Page 43]

5-42 Answer C.
Longitudinal stability for an airplane involves the tendency for the nose to pitch up or pitch down, rotating around the lateral axis (wingtip to wingtip).
[Ref: General Handbook H-8083-30A-ATB, Chapter 05 Page 42]

5-43 Answer B.
The aircraft tendency to move in the opposite direction of how it is slipping, and the lift of the vertical fin will try to yaw the airplane in the direction of the slip. If the wing dihedral has the greatest effect, the airplane will have a tendency to experience a Dutch roll. A Dutch roll is the oscillation around both the longitudinal and vertical axes.
[Ref: General Handbook H-8083-30A-ATB, Chapter 05 Page 43]

5-44 Answer C.
The middle of the airplane, from nose to tail, passing through the center of gravity. Movement around this axis is known as roll, and control around this axis is called lateral control. Movement around this axis is controlled by the ailerons, and on some airplanes, it is aided by surfaces on the wing known as spoilers.
[Ref: General Handbook H-8083-30A-ATB, Chapter 05 Page 43]

5-45 Answer A.
The vertical axis of an airplane runs from top to bottom through the middle of the airplane, passing through the center of gravity. Movement around this axis is known as yaw, and control around this axis is called directional control. Movement around this axis is controlled by the rudder.
[Ref: General Handbook H-8083-30A-ATB, Chapter 05 Page 43]

5-46 Answer B.
The lateral axis of an airplane is a line that runs below the wing, from wingtip to wingtip, passing through the airplane's center of gravity. Movement around this axis is called pitch, and control around this axis is called longitudinal control.
[Ref: General Handbook H-8083-30A-ATB, Chapter 05 Page 43]

5-47 AMG038
Which type of flight control tabs move in the opposite direction of the control surface on which it is attached?
- A. trim tabs
- B. anti-servo tabs
- C. balance tabs

5-48 AMG038
How many of the following devices are primarily used to modify the amount of lift produced by a wing?
- • Flaps   • Slats   • Tabs
- • Slots   • Spoilers
- A. 2 of the 5 listed devices are primarily used to modify lift.
- B. 3 of the 5 listed devices are primarily used to modify lift.
- C. 4 of the 5 listed devices are primarily used to modify lift.

5-49 AMG007
The speed of sound in the atmosphere is affected by variations in which of the following?
- A. Sound frequency (cps)
- B. Ambient temperature
- C. Barometric pressure

5-50 AMG007
At which speed does the airplane experience stability problems?
- A. Subsonic
- B. Transonic
- C. Supersonic

5-51 AMG007
Which type of wave is not a shock wave?
- A. Expansion
- B. Oblique
- C. Normal

5-52 AMG091
Name four of the seven main components of a helicopter.
- A. Landing gear, transmission, tail rotor, main rotor
- B. Cabin, tail boom, transmission, powerplant
- C. Blades, tail rotor, landing gear, tail boom

PHYSICS FOR AVIATION

ANSWERS

5-47 Answer C.
Just the opposite of anti-servo tabs, balance tabs move in the opposite direction of the flight control's trailing edge, providing a force that helps the flight control move. The servo tab is acting like a balance tab, but rather than assisting the normal force that moves the elevator, it becomes the sole force that makes the elevator move. Like the balance tab, the servo tab moves in the opposite direction of the flight control's trailing edge.
[Ref: General Handbook H-8083-30A-ATB, Chapter 05 Page 45-46]

5-48 Answer C.
Flaps, slots, slats, and spoilers effect the airflow, velocities, and pressures over and under a wing. Tabs are used primarily to adjust control pressures required by various larger flight controls.
[Ref: General Handbook H-8083-30A-ATB, Chapter 05 Page 46-47]

5-49 Answer B.
The speed of sound in air changes with temperature, increasing as temperature increases.
[Ref: General Handbook H-8083-30A-ATB, Chapter 05 Page 48]

5-50 Answer B.
Stability problems can be encountered during transonic flight, because the shock wave can cause the airflow to separate from the wing.
[Ref: General Handbook H-8083-30A-ATB, Chapter 05 Page 48]

5-51 Answer A.
An expansion wave occurs when supersonic air turns away from the direction of flow as determined by the airfoil shape and follows a new direction. Expansion waves are not shock waves. Shock waves are formed when pressure waves (sound energy) compresses in front of, and cannot get away from the airplane.
[Ref: General Handbook H-8083-30A-ATB, Chapter 05 Page 49]

5-52 Answer B.
The main parts that make up a helicopter are the cabin, landing gear, tail boom, powerplant, transmission, main rotor, and tail rotor.
[Ref: General Handbook H-8083-30A-ATB, Chapter 05 Page 51]

5-53 AMG091
The rotor system on a helicopter that has blades which are rigidly attached to the hub with the blades and a hub able to teeter like a seesaw is the
A. rigid rotor system.
B. fully articulated rotor system.
C. semi-rigid rotor system.

5-54 AMG091
Identify which anti-torque system of a helicopter presents the least amount of risk to personnel on the ground and creates less drag in flight?
A. NOTAR
B. Fenestron
C. Tail rotor

PHYSICS FOR AVIATION

ANSWERS

5-53 Answer C.
The semi-rigid rotor system is used with a two blade main rotor. The blades are rigidly attached to the hub, with the hub and blades able to teeter like a seesaw.
[Ref: General Handbook H-8083-30A-ATB, Chapter 05 Page 51-52]

5-54 Answer B.
An alternative to the tail rotor seen in Figure 5-86, General Handbook H-8083-30A-ATB, is a type of anti-torque rotor known as a fenestron, or "fan-in-tail" design as seen in Figure 5-87, General Handbook H-8083-30A-ATB. Because the rotating blades in this design are enclosed in a shroud, they present less of a hazard to personnel on the ground and they create less drag in flight.
[Ref: General Handbook H-8083-30A-ATB, Chapter 05 Page 53]

ORAL EXAM

5-1(O).   Name the six simple machines.

5-2(O).   Explain resonance and how it can be hazardous to aircraft.

5-3(O).   Explain the relationship between the density of a fluid and specific gravity.

5-4(O).   Explain how specific gravity of fluids can be applied to aircraft maintenance.

5-5(O).   If the temperature of a confined gas is increased, what effect does this have on its pressure?

5-6(O).   If the volume of a gas is allowed to increase, what effect does this have on its temperature if the pressure remains the same?

5-7(O).   If the pressure of a confined gas is increased, what effect does this have on its temperature?

5-8(O).   Hydraulic and pneumatic systems both use fluids, what is the difference between these fluids?

5-9(O).   Define density.

5-10(O).   Define density altitude.

5-11(O).   Name the various methods of heat transfer.

5-12(O).   What are the effects of thermal expansion on aircraft?

5-13(O).   Name the four forces acting on an aircraft in flight.

5-14(O).   Explain the four forces acting on an aircraft in flight.

5-15(O).   Name the three axes of rotation that determine movement of an airplane in flight.

5-16(O).   Where do the three axes of rotation intersect on an airplane?

5-17(O).   Name the three flight controls that provide movement around each of the three axes of rotation and on which axes they rotate the aircraft.

PHYSICS FOR AVIATION

ANSWERS

ORAL EXAM

5-1(O).   The lever, the pulley, the wheel and axle, the inclined plane, the screw, and the gear.
           [Ref: General Handbook H-8083-30A-ATB, Chapter 05 Page 8]

5-2(O).   Resonance occurs when an object is vibrated at its natural frequency, at which time it becomes relatively
           self-sustaining. Sustained vibration at this frequency can cause damage to object as well as transferring
           this energy surrounding objects that pick up their natural frequency and start to resonant. This type of
           accumulating vibration can destroy an aircraft.
           [Ref: General Handbook H-8083-30A-ATB, Chapter 05 Page 33]

5-3(O).   Specific gravity is equal to the density of a substance divided by the density of water. Water has a specific
           gravity of 1. The higher the density of the fluid the higher the specific gravity.
           [Ref: General Handbook H-8083-30A-ATB, Chapter 05 Page 2-3]

5-4(O).   Specific gravity is often used to measure the change in density. A hydrometer is used to measure the specific
           gravity of liquids, such as the electrolyte (battery liquid) in an aircraft battery or fuel to determine weight.
           [Ref: General Handbook H-8083-30A-ATB, Chapter 05 Page 2-3]

5-5(O).   Increasing the temperature of a confined gas will also increase its pressure.
           [Ref: General Handbook H-8083-30A-ATB, Chapter 05 Page 25]

5-6(O).   Allowing the volume of a gas to increase, but maintaining the same pressure its temperature will decrease.
           [Ref: General Handbook H-8083-30A-ATB, Chapter 05 Page 25]

5-7(O).   Increasing the pressure of a confined gas will cause its temperature to increase.
           [Ref: General Handbook H-8083-30A-ATB, Chapter 05 Page 25]

5-8(O).   Hydraulic fluid is a liquid and is there incompressible, while pneumatic fluid is air and therefore
           is compressible.
           [Ref: General Handbook H-8083-30A-ATB, Chapter 05 Page 26]

5-9(O).   Density is a measurement of an object's mass. It is expressed in weight per unit volume, such as pounds per
           cubic foot or grams per cubic centimeter.
           [Ref: General Handbook H-8083-30A-ATB, Chapter 05 Page 2]

5-10(O).   Density altitude is a calculated altitude obtained by correcting pressure altitude for
           non-standard temperature.
           [Ref: General Handbook H-8083-30A-ATB, Chapter 05 Page 35]

5-11(O).   The three methods of heat transfer are conduction, convection, and radiation.
           [Ref: General Handbook H-8083-30A-ATB, Chapter 05 Page 20]

5-12(O).   Metal expands when exposed to heat and if this expansion is not taken into consideration when designing
           airframes the metal would expand causing excess stresses on aircraft structures, powerplants, and
           other components.
           [Ref: General Handbook H-8083-30A-ATB, Chapter 05 Page 23]

5-13(O).   Lift, weight, thrust, and drag.
           [Ref: General Handbook H-8083-30A-ATB, Chapter 05 Page 37]

ORAL EXAM (CONTINUED)

5-18(O).   Define angle of attack.

5-19(O).   Explain a stall on an aircraft in flight.

5-20(O).   Explain the relationship between force, area, and pressure.

5-21(O).   Name the five forces or stresses that affect aircraft structures.

5-22(O).   Explain the force of tension.

5-23(O).   Explain the force of compression.

5-24(O).   Explain the force of torsion.

5-25(O).   Explain the force of bending.

5-26(O).   Explain the force of shear.

5-27(O).   Name the two forms of energy and explain each.

PHYSICS FOR AVIATION

ORAL EXAM

5-14(O).   Lift is the upward force created by the wing, weight is the pull of gravity on the airplane's mass, thrust is the force created by the airplane's propeller or turbine engine, and drag is the friction caused by the air flowing around the airplane.
[Ref: General Handbook H-8083-30A-ATB, Chapter 05 Page 37]

5-15(O).   Longitudinal, lateral, and vertical.
[Ref: General Handbook H-8083-30A-ATB, Chapter 05 Page 41]

5-16(O).   At the center of gravity (CG).
[Ref: General Handbook H-8083-30A-ATB, Chapter 05 Page 41]

5-17(O).   Ailerons rotate the aircraft around the longitudinal axis; the elevator rotates the aircraft around the lateral axis, and the rudder rotates the aircraft around the vertical axis.
[Ref: General Handbook H-8083-30A-ATB, Chapter 05 Page 41, Figure 5-60]

5-18(O).   Angle of attack is the angle between the chord line and the relative wind.
[Ref: General Handbook H-8083-30A-ATB, Chapter 05 Page 39]

5-19(O).   A stall occurs when the angle of attack becomes too great, the airflow separates from the wing and lift is destroyed.
[Ref: General Handbook H-8083-30A-ATB, Chapter 05 Page 39]

5-20(O).   Force applied to an object is the product of pressure exerted on the object multiplied by the area of the object where pressure is applied. The equation for this is Force = Pressure × Area.
[Ref: General Handbook H-8083-30A-ATB, Chapter 05 Page 29]

5-21(O).   Tension, compression, torsion, bending, and shear.
[Ref: General Handbook H-8083-30A-ATB, Chapter 05 Page 14-15]

5-22(O).   Tension is a force that tries to pull an object apart.
[Ref: General Handbook H-8083-30A-ATB, Chapter 05 Page 14]

5-23(O).   Compression is a force that tries to crush an object.
[Ref: General Handbook H-8083-30A-ATB, Chapter 05 Page 14]

5-24(O).   Torsion is the stress an object experiences when it is twisted.
[Ref: General Handbook H-8083-30A-ATB, Chapter 05 Page 14]

5-25(O).   Bending is the result of two stresses, compression and tension, acting on an object at the same time. Tension is experienced on the outside of the curve formed by the bend and compression is experienced on the inside curve of the bend.
[Ref: General Handbook H-8083-30A-ATB, Chapter 05 Page 15]

5-26(O).   Shear is the stress an object experiences when a force tries to cut or slice the object.
[Ref: General Handbook H-8083-30A-ATB, Chapter 05 Page 15]

5-27(O).   The two forms of energy are potential and kinetic. Potential energy is energy at rest, or energy that is stored. Kinetic energy is energy in motion.
[Ref: General Handbook H-8083-30A-ATB, Chapter 05 Page 4]

PRACTICAL EXAM

5-1(P).   Given several temperatures of various scales, convert them to equivalent temperatures of a different temperature scale, e.g. Fahrenheit to Celsius.

5-2(P).   Given the required information, calculate density altitude.

5-3(P).   Given the required information, calculate pressure altitude.

5-4(P).   Given a scenario, calculate the force, area, or pressure when given two of the three.

5-5(P).   Demonstrate the mechanical advantage of the three classes of levers.

5-6(P).   Design an inclined plane on paper, indicating the mechanical advantage.

5-7(P).   Given a picture of a venturi, identify the changes in pressure and velocity as a fluid passes through the venturi.

5-8(P).   Design a mechanical pulley system.

5-9(P).   Given an object's specific gravity that is less than one, determine its density.

5-10(P).   Given a scenario, calculate the horsepower for a given weight, distance, and time.

5-11(P).   Given a scenario, calculate expansion due to temperature change.

PAGE LEFT BLANK INTENTIONALLY

AIRCRAFT WEIGHT AND BALANCE

Terminology, Weighing Procedures, Weight and Balance Equipment, Loading for Flight, Extreme Conditions, Equipment Change

QUESTIONS

Note: References in this section have also been taken from FAA-H-8083-1 Aircraft Weight and Balance Handbook.
It is an excellent supplement to this chapter and can be purchased in Print or eBook formats at *www.actechbooks.com*

6-1 AMG069
Which one of the following can provide the empty weight of an aircraft if the aircraft's weight and balance records become lost, destroyed, or otherwise inaccurate?
- A. Reweighing the aircraft with the proper configuration for determining weight.
- B. The applicable Aircraft Specification or Type Certificate Data Sheets.
- C. The applicable flight manual or pilot's operating handbook.

6-2 AMG069
1. Private aircraft are required by regulations to be weighed periodically.
2. Private aircraft are required to be weighed after making any alteration.

Regarding the above statements:
- A. Neither #1 nor #2 are true
- B. Only # 1 is true
- C. Only #2 is true

6-3 AMG003
In the theory of weight and balance, what is the name of the distance from the fulcrum to an object?
- A. Arm
- B. Datum
- C. Moment

6-4 AMG003
What type of measurement is used to designate arm in weight and balance computation?
- A. Distance
- B. Weight
- C. Weight/distance

6-5 AMG003
A 7 pound component located at an arm of +146 is replaced with a 4 pound component at the same location, how does this effect the overall CG of the aircraft?
- A. The center of gravity moves rearward.
- B. The center of gravity moves forward.
- C. Not enough information is given to determine.

6-6 AMG003
The major source of weight change for most aircraft as they age is caused by?
- A. Accumulation of grime and debris and moisture absorption in cabin insulation.
- B. Repairs and alterations made to the aircraft over time.
- C. Installation of hardware and safety wire and added layers of paint to the structure.

AIRCRAFT WEIGHT AND BALANCE

ANSWERS

6-1 Answer A.
If the weight and balance report for an aircraft is lost, the aircraft must be weighed and a new report must be created.
[Ref: General Handbook H-8083-30A-ATB, Chapter 06 Page 2]

6-2 Answer A.
Statement #1 is false. For a small general aviation airplane, being used privately, such as a Cessna 172, there is no FAA requirement that it be periodically reweighed. There is, however, an FAA requirement that the airplane always has a current and accurate weight and balance report. Statement #2 is false. If the airplane has new equipment installed, such as a radio or a global positioning system, a new weight and balance report must be created. If the installer of the equipment wants to place the airplane on scales and weigh it after the installation that is a perfectly acceptable way of creating the new report. If the installer knows the exact weight and location of the new equipment, it is also possible to create a new report by doing a series of mathematical calculations.
[Ref: General Handbook H-8083-30A-ATB, Chapter 06 Page 2]

6-3 Answer A.
This question refers to a "fulcrum", a fulcrum is the point where an object will balance. In aviation, the fulcrum of an aircraft is also the center of gravity. The arm is the horizontal distance that a part of the aircraft or a piece of equipment is located from the fulcrum. However, to make weight and balance calculation easier, the use of a datum is employed. In weight and balance theory, the datum is a reference point only and can be placed anywhere on or even in front of the airplane. The datum is often placed at the nose of the aircraft or even at a spot measured forward from a specific location on the aircraft, such as the nose, to allow for all weight and balance calculations to be positive. Thus, the arm can be defined as the horizontal distance that a part of the aircraft or a piece of equipment is located from the datum, remembering that the center of gravity does not change.
[Ref: General Handbook H-8083-30A-ATB, Chapter 06 Page 3]

6-4 Answer A.
The arm's distance is always given or measured in inches from the datum. Distances to the right (aft) of the datum are positive and to the left (forward) of the datum are negative.
[Ref: General Handbook H-8083-30A-ATB, Chapter 06 Page 3]

6-5 Answer C.
This can not be determined with the given information because we do not know if position +146 in located in front of or behind the previous center of gravity. If +146 is located in front of the CG, the weight reduction will move the CG rearward. If +146 is located behind the CG, the reduction will move the CG forward.
[Ref: General Handbook H-8083-30A-ATB, Chapter 06 Page 3-4]

6-6 Answer B.
Over time, almost all aircraft have a tendency to gain weight. Examples of how this can happen include all of the answers provided however, the greatest source of weight change is from repairs and alterations.
[Ref: General Handbook H-8083-30A-ATB, Chapter 06 Page 2]

6-7 AMG003

What determines whether the value of a moment is preceded by a plus (+) or minus (-) sign in aircraft weight and balance?
- A. The location of the weight in reference to the datum.
- B. The result of a weight being added or removed and its location relative to the datum.
- C. The location of the datum in reference to the aircraft CG.

6-8 AMG003

In the process of weighing an airplane to obtain the CG, the arms from the weighing points always extend
- A. parallel to the centerline of the airplane.
- B. straight forward from each of the landing gear.
- C. directly from each weighing point to the others.

6-9 AMG003

When dealing with weight and balance of an aircraft, the term "maximum weight" is interpreted to mean the maximum
- A. weight of the empty aircraft.
- B. weight of the useful load.
- C. authorized weight of the aircraft and its contents.

6-10 AMG003

The useful load of an aircraft consists of the
- A. crew, usable fuel, passengers, and cargo.
- B. crew, usable fuel, oil, cargo, and fixed equipment.
- C. crew, passengers, usable fuel, oil, cargo, and fixed equipment.

6-11 AMG003

The amount of fuel used for computing empty weight and corresponding CG is?
- A. Empty fuel tanks.
- B. Unusable fuel.
- C. The amount of fuel necessary for 1/2 hour of operation.

6-12 AMG003

The useful load of an aircraft is the difference between
- A. The maximum takeoff weight and the basic empty weight.
- B. Maximum ramp or takeoff weight as applicable and zero fuel weight.
- C. The weight of an aircraft filled, and full fuel, and weight empty with minimum fuel.

AIRCRAFT WEIGHT AND BALANCE

ANSWERS

6-7 Answer A.

The algebraic sign of the moment is determined based on the datum location and whether weight is added or removed, and would be as follows:

- Weight added aft of the datum produces a positive moment (+ weight, + arm)
- Weight added forward of the datum produces a negative moment (+ weight, - arm)
- Weight removed aft of the datum produces a negative moment (- weight, + arm)
- Weight removed forward of the datum produces a positive moment (- weight, - arm)

[Ref: General Handbook H-8083-30A-ATB, Chapter 06 Page 4]

6-8 Answer A.

When weighing an aircraft, the arm of an object is always parallel to the centerline of the aircraft.

[Ref: General Handbook H-8083-30A-ATB, Chapter 06 Page 3, 6]

6-9 Answer C.

The maximum weight is the maximum authorized weight of the aircraft and its contents, and is indicated in the Aircraft Specifications or Type Certificate Data Sheet.

[Ref: General Handbook H-8083-30A-ATB, Chapter 06 Page 4]

6-10 Answer A.

The useful load consists of fuel, any other fluids that are not part of empty weight, passengers, baggage, pilot, copilot, and crew members.

[Ref: General Handbook H-8083-30A-ATB, Chapter 06 Page 5]

6-11 Answer B.

Unusable fuel is defined as the fuel remaining after a runout test has been completed in accordance with governmental regulations.

[Ref: General Handbook H-8083-30A-ATB, Chapter 06 Page 5]

6-12 Answer A.

Useful load is defined as the difference between take off weight, or ramp weight if applicable, and basic empty weight.

[Ref: General Handbook H-8083-30A-ATB, Chapter 06 Page 5]

6-13 AMG003
When determining the empty weight of an aircraft certificated under current airworthiness standards (FAR 23), the oil contained in the supply tank is considered
A. a part of the empty weight.
B. a part of the useful load.
C. the same as the fluid contained in the water injection reservoir.

6-16 AMG002
To determine center of gravity, which of the following formulas is used?
A. total arm × total weight
B. total moment / total weight
C. total moment × total weight

6-14 AMG003
What is meant by the term "residual fuel"?
A. A known amount of fuel left in the tanks, lines, and engine.
B. The fuel remaining in the tanks, lines, and engine after draining.
C. The fuel remaining in the tanks, lines, and engine before draining.

6-17 AMG069
The maximum weight as used in the weight and balance control of a given aircraft can normally be found
A. by adding the fuel, passengers and baggage to the empty weight.
B. in the Aircraft Specification or Type Data Sheets.
C. by adding the empty weight and payload.

6-15 AMG003
Zero fuel weight is the
A. dry weight plus the weight of full crew, passengers, and cargo.
B. basic operating weight without crew, fuel, and cargo.
C. maximum permissible weight of a loaded aircraft (passengers, crew, cargo) without fuel.

6-18 AMG003
Load cell scales are commonly found to be the platform type and placed on top of the aircraft
A. fuselage.
B. wing.
C. jacks.

AIRCRAFT WEIGHT AND BALANCE

ANSWERS

6-13 Answer A.
Empty weight is defined as the weight of the airframe, engines, all permanently installed equipment and unusable fuel. For most aircraft certified after 1978, a full reservoir of oil is to be included in the empty weight. Always check the Aircraft Specifications or Type Certificate Data Sheet to determine if a full oil reservoir is required.
[Ref: General Handbook H-8083-30A-ATB, Chapter 06 Page 5]

6-14 Answer B.
Residual fuel, (also called unusable fuel) is the small amount of fuel within the aircraft that can not be drawn by the engine during operations as it is below the level of the fuel intake. Because the fuel is there but can not be used, it is considered as a part of the empty airframe itself. It also includes undrainable fuel in the fuel lines, carburetor, and other engine parts.
[Ref: General Handbook H-8083-30A-ATB, Chapter 06 Page 4]

6-15 Answer C.
Maximum Zero Fuel Weight is defined as the maximum authorized weight of an aircraft without fuel. This is the sum of basic operating weight (BOW) and payload (weight of occupants, cargo, and baggage).
[Ref: General Handbook H-8083-30A-ATB, Chapter 06 Page 4]

6-16 Answer B.
Center of Gravity = Total Moment ÷ Total Weight. This calculation will provide the point at which an airplane would balance if suspended.
[Ref: General Handbook H-8083-30A-ATB, Chapter 06 Page 7]

6-17 Answer B.
Maximum weight, as well other important weight and balance information found in the Aircraft Specification or Type Certificate Data Sheet.
[Ref: General Handbook H-8083-30A-ATB, Chapter 06 Page 8]

6-18 Answer C.
Load cells are defined as a component in an electronic weighing system that is placed between the jack and the jack pad on the aircraft. The load cell contains strain gauges whose resistance changes with the weight on the cell.
[Ref: General Handbook H-8083-30A-ATB, Chapter 06 Page 8]

6-19 AMG003
Use of which of the following generally yields the highest degree of aircraft leveling accuracy?
   A. electronic load cell(s)
   B. spirit level(s)
   C. plumb bob and chalk line

6-20 AMG003
When an aircraft is weighed with full fuel tanks, which device is used to determine the weight of the fuel?
   A. A calculator
   B. A thermometer
   C. A hydrometer

6-21 AMG003
What tasks are completed prior to weighing an aircraft to determine empty weight?
   A. Remove all items except those on the aircraft equipment list; drain fuel and hydraulic fluid.
   B. Remove all items on the aircraft equipment list; drain fuel, compute oil and hydraulic fluid weight.
   C. Remove all items except those on the aircraft equipment list; drain fuel and fill hydraulic reservoir.

6-22 AMG003
To obtain useful weight data for purposes of determining the CG, it is necessary that an aircraft be weighed
   A. in a level flight attitude.
   B. with all items of useful load installed.
   C. with at least minimum fuel (1/2 gallon per METO horsepower) in the fuel tanks.

6-23 AMG003
When an aircraft is positioned for weighing on scales located under each landing gear wheel, which of the following may cause erroneous scale readings?
   A. gear downlocks installed
   B. parking brakes set
   C. parking brakes not set

6-24 AMG003
The standard weight of a person, for the purposes of weight and balance calculations, is
   A. 180 pounds.
   B. 170 pounds.
   C. 75 kilos.

AIRCRAFT WEIGHT AND BALANCE

ANSWERS

6-19 Answer B.

The leveling method that yields the highest degree of accuracy is achieved using a spirit level, sometimes thought of as a carpenter's level, by placing it on or against a specified place on the aircraft. Spirit levels consist of a vial full of liquid, except for a small air bubble. When the air bubble is centered between the two black lines, a level condition is indicated.

[Ref: General Handbook H-8083-30A-ATB, Chapter 06 Page 15]

6-20 Answer C.

A hydrometer measures the specific gravity of a liquid and will give you the unit of pounds per gallon of the fuel to be used to calculate the total weight of the fuel.

[Ref: General Handbook H-8083-30A-ATB, Chapter 06 Page 13]

6-21 Answer C.

Empty weight is defined as the weight of the airframe, engines, all permanently installed equipment and unusable fuel. Therefore, all items not listed on the aircraft equipment list must be removed including fuel and most likely, per the Type Certificate Date Sheet, servicing of the hydraulic reservoir must be accomplished before the aircraft can be weighed.

[Ref: General Handbook H-8083-30A-ATB, Chapter 06 Page 4]

6-22 Answer A.

Before an aircraft can be weighed and reliable readings obtained, it must be in a level flight attitude.

[Ref: General Handbook H-8083-30A-ATB, Chapter 06 Page 15]

6-23 Answer B.

When weighing an aircraft with the wheels placed on the scales, release the parking brakes to reduce the possibility of incorrect readings caused by side loads on the scales.

[Ref: General Handbook H-8083-30A-ATB, Chapter 06 Page 15]

6-24 Answer B.

The standard weight for crew members and passengers is 170 lb. per person.

[Ref: General Handbook H-8083-30A-ATB, Chapter 06 Page 17]

6-25 AMG002
As weighed, the total empty weight of an aircraft is 5,862 pounds with a moment of 885,957. However, when the aircraft was weighed, 20 pounds of potable water were on board at +84, and 23 pounds of hydraulic fluid were in the tank located at +101. What is the empty weight CG of the aircraft?
   A. 150.700
   B. 151.700
   C. 151.360

6-26 AMG002
Two boxes which weigh 10 pounds and 5 pounds are placed in an airplane so their distance aft from the CG are 4 feet and 2 feet respectively. How far forward of the CG should a third box weighing 20 pounds be placed so that the CG will not be changed?
   A. 3 feet
   B. 2.5 feet
   C. 8 feet

6-27 AMG002
In a balance computation of an aircraft from which an item located aft of the datum was removed, use
   A. (-) weight × (+) arm (-) moment.
   B. (-) weight × (-) arm (+) moment.
   C. (+) weight × (-) arm (-) moment.

6-28 AMG002
Consider the specifications of the following aircraft:
   The datum is 30.24" forward of the main gear
   The distance from the main gear to the tail gear is 360.26"
   The weight measured on the right main gear is 9,980 lbs
   The weight measured on the left main gear is 9,770 lbs
   The weight measured on the tail wheel is 1,970 lbs

The following items were in the aircraft when weighed:
   Lavatory water weighing 34 lbs at an arm of +352
   Ballast weighing 146 lbs at an arm of +380
   Hydraulic fluid weighing 22 lbs at an arm of +8

What is the empty weight CG of the aircraft described?
   A. 62.92"
   B. 60.31"
   C. 58.54"

6-29 AMG002
When an aircraft is weighed, the combined net weight at the main gear is 3540 pounds with an arm of 195.5". At the nose gear, the net weight is 2322 pounds with an arm of 83.5". The datum line is forward of the nose of the aircraft. What is the empty CG of the aircraft?
   A. 151.1
   B. 155.2
   C. 146.5

AIRCRAFT WEIGHT AND BALANCE

ANSWERS

6-25 Answer C.
Empty weight is defined as the weight of the airframe, engines, all permanently installed equipment and unusable fuel. Therefore, all items not listed on the aircraft equipment list must be removed including usable fuel. Hydraulic fluid is a part of the aircraft empty weight and can be ignored.

Beginning weight: 5862 lbs.
Beginning moment: 885,957
Water moment (weight × arm): 20 × 84 = 1680
Adjusted weight: 5862 – 20 = 5842 lbs.
Adjusted moment: 885,957 – 1680 = 884,277
Moment divided by weight = CG 881,954/5862 = 151.36
[Ref: General Handbook H-8083-30A-ATB, Chapter 06 Page 18-20]

6-26 Answer B.
The center of gravity can be thought of as a fulcrum (datum) and the aircraft as a board balanced on this fulcrum (datum). If we change one side, we have to change the other side to maintain a balanced board. Here are the mathematical equations to determine the arm of the third box.
Remember: Moment = weight × Arm
Moment of 10-pound box: 10 × 4 = 40
Moment of 5-pound box: 5 × 2 = 10
Total change in moments: 40 + 10 = 50
Note: The added weight changed on the aft or positive side of the CG, therefore we have to offset the weight change on the forward or negative side of the CG to maintain balance. We know the weight but we need to determine where to place the weight, in other words its arm. Arm of 20-pound weight: 50 / 20 = 2.5. The 20-pound weight needs to be added 2.5 feet forward of the CG of the aircraft.
[Ref: General Handbook H-8083-30A-ATB, Chapter 06 Page 18-20]

6-27 Answer A.
What the question is asking is a bit confusing. What needs to be determined is whether the moment is positive or negative based on the data provided. Remembering the datum is the point where the aircraft balances; objects to the aft or right of the datum have positive moments and objects forward or left of the datum have negative moments. A moment equals an object's weight and arm (distance from datum). In the question an item is being removed (a negative weight) from aft of the datum (a positive arm) which mathematical would give a negative (-) moment.
[Ref: General Handbook H-8083-30A-ATB, Chapter 06 Page 18-20]

6-28 Answer B.
To answer this question you will need to do several mathematical computations. To help organize the data and quickly determine the answer use the following table. Scratch paper is allowed in the testing environment.

ITEM	WEIGHT	**ARM	MOMENT
Right Main	9,980	30.24	301,795.20
Left Main	9,770	30.24	295,444.80
Tall Wheel	1,970	*390.50	769,285.00
Totals	21,720	62.92	1,366,525.00

*Main gear arm (30.24) plus distance from main gear to tail gear (360.26).

ITEM	WEIGHT	**ARM	MOMENT
Aircraft	21,720	62.91	1,366,525
Water	-34	352	-11,968
Ballast	-146	380	-55,480
Totals	21,540	60.31	1,299,077

Note: Hydraulic fluid is included with the empty weight.
**Note: Arm = moment / weight
[Ref: General Handbook H-8083-30A-ATB, Chapter 06 Page 18-20]

6-29 Answer A.
To answer this question you will need to do several mathematical computations. To help organize the data and quickly determine the answer use the following table. Scratch paper is allowed in the testing environment.

ITEM	WEIGHT	**ARM	MOMENT
Main	3540	195.5	692,070
Nose	2322	83.5	193.887
Totals	5,862	151.1	885,957

**Note: Arm = moment / weight
[Ref: General Handbook H-8083-30A-ATB, Chapter 06 Page 18-20]

6-30 AMG002
Find the empty weight CG location for the following aircraft. Each main wheel weighs 753 pounds, nose wheel weighs 22 pounds, distance between nose wheel and main wheels is 87.5", nose wheel location is +9.875" from datum, with 1 gallon of hydraulic fluid at -2.10" included in the weight.
  A. +97.375"
  B. +95.61"
  C. +96.11"

6-31 AMG002
An aircraft with an empty weight of 2100 pounds and an empty weight CG of +32.5 was altered as follows:
  • Two 18 pound seats located at +73 were removed;
  • Structural modifications were made at +77 increasing weight by 17 pounds;
  • A seat and safety belt weighing 25 pounds were installed at +74.5;
  • Radio equipment weighing 35 pounds was installed at +95

What is the new CG of the aircraft?
  A. +34.01
  B. +33.68
  C. +34.65

6-32 AMG003
You must weigh an aircraft with full fuel tanks in order to document its current CG point. After the total weight has been determined, what must be done?
  A. Subtract the weight of unusable fuel.
  B. Subtract the weight of usable fuel.
  C. Nothing. The weight you have determine is correct.

6-33 AMG002
When accomplishing loading computation for a small aircraft, necessary information obtained from the weight and balance records would include
  A. unusable fuel weight and distance from datum.
  B. weight and location of permanent ballast.
  C. current empty weight and empty weight CG.

6-34 AMG002
All other things being equal, if an item of useful load located aft of an aircraft's CG is removed, the aircraft's CG will be
  A. aft in proportion to the weight of the item and its location in the aircraft.
  B. forward in proportion to the weight of the item and its location in the aircraft.
  C. forward in proportion to the weight of the item, regardless of its location in the aircraft.

6-35 AMG002
When making a rearward (aft) weight and balance check to determine that the CG will not exceed the rearward limit during extreme conditions, the items of useful load which should be computed at their minimum weights are those located forward of the
  A. forward CG limit.
  B. datum.
  C. rearward CG limit.

AIRCRAFT WEIGHT AND BALANCE

ANSWERS

6-30 Answer C.
To answer this question you will need to do several mathematical computations. To help organize the data and quickly determine the answer use the following table. Scratch paper is allowed in the testing environment.

ITEM	WEIGHT	**ARM	MOMENT
Main	3540	195.5	692,070
Nose	2322	83.5	193.887
Totals	5,862	151.1	885,957

Note: Hydraulic fluid is included with the empty weight.
**Note: Arm = moment ÷ weight
         Main wheel arm = 87.5" + 9.875"
[Ref: General Handbook H-8083-30A-ATB, Chapter 06 Page 18-20]

6-31 Answer B.
To answer this question you will need to do several mathematical computations. To help organize the data and quickly determine the answer use the following table. Scratch paper is allowed in the testing environment.

ITEM	WEIGHT	**ARM	MOMENT
Aircraft	2100	32.5	68,250.0
Seats (Removed)	-36	73.0	-2,628.0
Modification	17	77.0	1,309.0
Seat	25	74.5	1,826.5
Radio	35	95.0	3,325.0
Totals	2141	33.68	72,118.5

**Note: Arm = moment ÷ weight
[Ref: General Handbook H-8083-30A-ATB, Chapter 06 Page 18-20]

6-32 Answer B.
Empty weight is defined as the weight of the airframe, engines, all permanently installed equipment and unusable fuel. Because the airplane was weighed with the fuel tanks full, the full weight of the fuel must be subtracted and the unusable fuel added back in. The weight of the fuel being subtracted is based on the pounds per gallon determined by the hydrometer check.
[Ref: General Handbook H-8083-30A-ATB, Chapter 06 Page 15-19]

6-33 Answer C.
To properly calculate loading information, the current empty weight and the empty weight center of gravity must be known.
[Ref: General Handbook H-8083-30A-ATB, Chapter 06 Page 20]

6-34 Answer B.
The center of gravity can be thought of as a fulcrum (datum) and the aircraft as a board balanced on this fulcrum (datum). If one-side changes, the board is no longer balanced. In this example weight is removed from the right side of the fulcrum (datum) or aft of the aircraft. This would make the aircraft nose heavy (the left side of the board would move down). To rebalance the aircraft (board) the datum (fulcrum) would have to be moved to the left or forward of its current location in proportion (moment) of the item removed to maintain its balance.
[Ref: General Handbook H-8083-30A-ATB, Chapter 06 Page 20]

6-35 Answer C.
On an aft extreme condition check, all useful load items behind the aft CG limit are loaded and all useful load items in front of the aft CG limit are left empty. Even though the pilot's seat will be located in front of the aft CG limit, the pilot's seat cannot be left empty. If the fuel tank is located forward of the aft CG limit, minimum fuel will be shown.
[Ref: General Handbook H-8083-30A-ATB, Chapter 06 Page 21]

6-36 AMG002
When computing the maximum forward loaded CG of an aircraft, minimum weights, arms, and moments should be used for items of useful load that are located aft of the
A. rearward CG limit.
B. forward CG limit.
C. datum.

6-37 AMG002
An aircraft as loaded weighs 4,954 pounds at a CG of +30.5 inches. The CG range is +32.0 to +42.1. Find the minimum weight of the ballast necessary to bring the CG within the CG range. The ballast arm is +162 inches.
A. 61.98 pounds
B. 30.58 pounds
C. 57.16 pounds

6-38 AMG002
When computing weight and balance, an airplane is considered to be in balance when?
A. the average moment arm of the loaded airplane falls within its cg range.
B. all moment arms of the plane fall within CG range.
C. the movement of the passengers will not cause the moment arm to fall outside the CG range.

6-39 AMG002
Which statement is true regarding helicopter weight and balance?
A. Regardless of internal or external loading, lateral CG control is ordinarily not a factor in maintaining helicopter weight and balance.
B. The moment of tail-mounted components is subject to constant change.
C. Weight and balance procedures for airplanes generally also apply to helicopters.

6-40 AMG002
Improper loading of a helicopter which results in exceeding either the fore and aft CG limits is hazardous due to the
A. reduction or loss of effective cyclic pitch control.
B. coriolis effect being translated to the fuselage.
C. reduction or loss of effective collective pitch control.

6-41 AMG002
Where do you look to determine the operating CG range when calculating a new aircraft weight and balance document?
A. It is found on the airframe data plate.
B. It is found in the type certificate data sheet.
C. It is found in the pilot's aircraft information manual.

AIRCRAFT WEIGHT AND BALANCE

ANSWERS

6-36 Answer B.
On what is called a forward extreme condition check, all useful load items in front of the forward CG limit are loaded, and all useful load items behind the forward CG limit are left empty.
[Ref: General Handbook H-8083-30A-ATB, Chapter 06 Page 21]

6-37 Answer C.
Ballast Needed = Loaded weight of aircraft (distance CG is out of limits) ÷ Arm from ballast location to affected limit.
[Ref: General Handbook H-8083-30A-ATB, Chapter 06 Page 23]

6-38 Answer B.
For an aircraft to be balanced, the sum of the moment arms must fall within the CG range, represented on a graph provided with the aircraft documentation. Remembering the fulcrum example: even though the weights on either side of the fulcrum are not equal, and the distances from each weight to the fulcrum are not equal, when the product of the weights and arms (moments) are equal a balanced condition is achieved. In order to fly legally, the center of gravity for the aircraft must fall within the CG limits.
[Ref: General Handbook H-8083-30A-ATB, Chapter 06 Page 13-16]

6-39 Answer C.
All of the terminology and concepts that apply to airplane weight and balance also apply generally to helicopter weight and balance; however most have much more restricted CG ranges than airplanes.
[Ref: General Handbook H-8083-30A-ATB, Chapter 06 Page 27]

6-40 Answer A.
Cyclic pitch control is defined as the control for changing the pitch of each rotor blade individually as it rotates through one cycle to govern the tilt of the rotor disk and, consequently, the direction and velocity of horizontal movement (left/right/forward/aft). If the CG location is too extreme, in either direction, it may not be possible to keep the fuselage horizontal or maintain control of the helicopter.
[Ref: General Handbook H-8083-30A-ATB, Chapter 06 Page 27]

6-41 Answer B.
Acceptable weight and balance ranges or each individual model of an aircraft are provided on the Type Certificate Data Sheet. Minimum equipment lists including their location and arms are given in the Aircraft Information Manual and so can be notated if a change occurs.
[Ref: General Handbook H-8083-30A-ATB, Chapter 06 Page 9]

AIRCRAFT WEIGHT AND BALANCE

QUESTIONS

6-42 AMG069
The FAA mandates the same weight and balance requirements for weight-shift control aircraft and powered parachutes as it does for certified airplanes and helicopters.
A. True, the regulations are the same.
B. False, the regulations are not the same.
C. False, the regulations are the same for weight-shift control aircraft but not for powered parachutes.

6-43 AMG002
If an aircraft CG is found to be at 24% of MAC, that 24% is an expression of the?
A. Distance from the TEMAC.
B. Distance from the LEMAC.
C. Average distance from the LEMAC to the wing center of lift.

6-44 AMG002
An aircraft's LEMAC and TEMAC are defined in terms of distance?
A. From the datum.
B. From each other.
C. Ahead of and behind center of lift.

6-45 AMG002
Consider the following on a large aircraft, and convert the CG location from inches to percent of MAC.
• The CG is located at 283 inches behind the datum.
• LEMAC is located at 270 inches behind the datum.
• TEMAC is located at 324 inches behind the datum.
A. 24%
B. 17%
C. 21%

8083-30A-ATB General Test Guide

6-15

ANSWERS

6-42 Answer B.
Weight-shift control aircraft and powered parachutes do not fall under the same Code of Federal Regulations that govern certified airplanes and helicopters and, therefore, do not have Type Certificate Data Sheets or the same type of FAA mandated weight and balance reports.
[Ref: General Handbook H-8083-30A-ATB, Chapter 06 Page 28]

6-44 Answer A.
- LEMAC is an acronym for the Leading Edge of the Mean Aerodynamic Chord.
- TEMAC is an acronym for the Trailing Edge of the Mean Aerodynamic Chord.
- Both the LEMAC and TEMAC are given in distance (inches) from the datum of the aircraft.

[Ref: General Handbook H-8083-30A-ATB, Chapter 06 Page 31]

6-43 Answer B.
On larger airplanes, the CG is identified as being at a location that is a specific percent of the mean aerodynamic chord (% MAC). For example, imagine that the MAC on a particular airplane is 100", and the CG falls 20" behind the leading edge of the MAC. That means it falls one-fifth of the way back, or at 20% of the MAC.
[Ref: General Handbook H-8083-30A-ATB, Chapter 06 Page 30-31]

6-45 Answer B.
To convert from inches to percent MAC, use the formula: Percent of MAC = (CG – LEMAC) / MAC × 100. So; 283 – 270 = 13. Divided by MAC which is 54 = .241 × 100 = 24%
[Ref: General Handbook H-8083-30A-ATB, Chapter 06 Page 31]

ORAL EXAM

6-1(O).   What is the purpose of weighing an aircraft?

6-2(O).   Define the following terms: datum, arm, moment, tare, ballast, residual fuel/oil, and moment index.

6-3(O).   Explain when a moment is positive or negative.

6-4(O).   When does an aircraft have to be reweighed?

6-5(O).   What are the two primary reasons for an aircraft to be weighed and balanced?

6-6(O).   When preparing to weigh an aircraft where will you find the "leveling means" for the aircraft?

6-7(O).   How is tare weight dealt with once the aircraft is weighed?

6-8(O).   Define MAC and when is it used.

6-9(O).   How are the center of gravity and the center of lift of an aircraft related?

6-10(O). What is an adverse loaded CG check?

AIRCRAFT WEIGHT AND BALANCE

ORAL EXAM

6-1(O). To determine its empty weight and the center of gravity for safe and efficient operations.
[Ref: General Handbook H-8083-30A-ATB, Chapter 06 Page 1]

6-2(O).
- Datum – The imaginary vertical plane from which all horizontal distances are measured for balance purposes. Also referred to as a reference datum.
- Arm – The horizontal distance from the reference datum to center of gravity (CG) of an item.
- Moment – the product of the weight of an item multiplied by its arm.
- Tare – are those items, such as chocks, that are used to hold an aircraft on the scales when it is weighed.
- Ballast – a weight installed or carried in an aircraft to move the center of gravity to a location within its allowable limits.
- Residual fuel/oil – fuel that remains in the sumps and fuel lines when the fuel system is drained from the inlet to the fuel metering system, with the aircraft in level flight attitude. The weight of the residual fuel is part of the empty weight of the aircraft.
- Moment index the moment (weight times arm) divided by a reduction factors such as 100 or 1,000 to make the number smaller and reduce the chance of mathematical errors in computing the center of gravity.
[Ref: General Handbook H-8083-30A-ATB, Glossary]

6-3(O). The algebraic sign of the moment is determined based on the location of the datum.
[Ref: General Handbook H-8083-30A-ATB, Chapter 06 Page 3]

6-4(O). When required by a maintenance program (usually under FAR Part 121), when there is change in equipment or the aircraft is modified (if the calculation method is not used), or if the weight and balance report is lost, destroyed, or otherwise inaccurate.
[Ref: General Handbook H-8083-30A-ATB, Chapter 06 Page 2]

6-5(O). Safety is the primary reason. A secondary reason is for the efficiency of the aircraft.
[Ref: General Handbook H-8083-30A-ATB, Chapter 06 Page 2]

6-6(O). In the Type Certificate Data Sheet for the aircraft.
[Ref: General Handbook H-8083-30A-ATB, Chapter 06 Page 7]

6-7(O). Tare weight must be subtracted from the total weight to find the correct weight of the aircraft.
[Ref: General Handbook H-8083-30A-ATB, Chapter 06 Page 6]

6-8(O). Mean Aerodynamic Chord and is an imaginary airfoil that has the same aerodynamic characteristics as the actual airfoil. The center of gravity on large aircraft is given in a percent of the MAC.
[Ref: General Handbook H-8083-30A-ATB, Chapter 06 Page 30 and FAA-H-8083-1, Chapter 03 Page 7]

6-9(O). The most efficient condition for an aircraft is to have the point where it balances fall very close to, or perhaps exactly at, the aircraft's center of lift. If this were the case, little or no flight control force would be needed to keep the aircraft flying straight and level. In terms of stability and safety, however, this perfectly balanced condition might not be desirable and these conditions are taken into consideration during the design phase of the aircraft.
[Ref: General Handbook H-8083-30A-ATB, Chapter 06 Page 2]

6-10(O). An adverse loaded CG check is a weight and balance check to determine that no condition of legal loading of an aircraft can move the CG outside of its allowable limits.
[Ref: General Handbook H-8083-30A-ATB, Chapter 06 Page 21 and FAA-H-8083-1, Glossary Page 1]

PRACTICAL EXAM

6-1(P).   Given a specified aircraft, locate the datum using the appropriate Type Certificate Data Sheet.

6-2(P).   Given the basic required information from an aircraft weighing, calculate the new empty weight and center of balance for the aircraft.

6-3(P).   Given loading graphs and CG Envelops, answer specified questions about the aircraft.

6-4(P).   Given an actual or hypothetical equipment change on an aircraft, calculate the weight and location of required ballast to maintain the aircraft's center of gravity.

6-5(P).   Given a specific aircraft, prepare an aircraft for weighing per the manufacturer's instructions.

6-6(P).   Given a specific aircraft, calculate the center of gravity for a fully loaded aircraft.

PAGE LEFT BLANK INTENTIONALLY

AIRCRAFT MATERIALS, HARDWARE, AND PROCESSES

Aircraft Metals, Forging, Nonmetallic Aircraft Materials, Packings, Seals, Aircraft Hardware, Rivets, Fasteners, Screws, and Sleeves

CHAPTER
07

QUESTIONS

7-1 AMG019
Aircraft metals must be _____ so they can be formed and shaped without detrimental effect.
A. malleable
B. elastic
C. dense

7-2 AMG019
In the material designation number "4130" for chromium molybdenum steel what does the first digit (4) of the number indicate?
A. The main alloying ingredient.
B. The percentage of the main alloying ingredient.
C. The hardness state of the material.

7-3 AMG019
What is generally used in the construction of aircraft engine firewalls?
A. Stainless steel
B. Chrome-molybdenum alloy steel
C. Titanium nickel alloy

7-4 AMG019
Aircraft aluminum skin is easily worked because it possesses these two characteristics:
A. It's malleable and ductile.
B. It's elastic and strong.
C. It's permeable and hard.

7-5 AMG019
The aluminum code number 1100 identifies what type of aluminum?
A. Aluminum alloy containing 11 percent pure copper
B. Aluminum alloy containing zinc
C. 99% commercially pure aluminum

7-6 AMG019
Which is the main alloying ingredient of 2024 aluminum?
A. Zinc.
B. Copper.
C. Magnesium.

AIRCRAFT MATERIALS, HARDWARE, AND PROCESSES

ANSWERS

7-1 Answer A.
Malleable metal can be hammered, rolled, or pressed into various shapes without cracking, breaking, or otherwise weakening the metal.
[Ref: General Handbook H-8083-30A-ATB, Chapter 07 Page 1]

7-2 Answer A.
In this system, a four-numeral series designates the plain carbon and alloy steels; five numerals designate certain types of alloy steels. The first digit indicates the type of steel, the second digit also generally (but not always) gives the approximate amount of the major alloying element, and the last two (or three) digits are intended to indicate the approximate middle of the carbon range.
[Ref: General Handbook H-8083-30A-ATB, Chapter 07 Page 3]

7-3 Answer A.
Partly due to its corrosion resistant characteristics, some common applications for stainless steel are in the fabrication of firewalls, exhaust collectors, stacks, and manifolds, where both temperatures are high and the presence of corrosive agents may be common.
[Ref: General Handbook H-8083-30A-ATB, Chapter 07 Page 3]

7-4 Answer A.
Aluminum alloys, although strong, are easily worked because they are malleable and ductile.
[Ref: General Handbook H-8083-30A-ATB, Chapter 07 Page 6]

7-5 Answer C.
1100 is the code number used to represent aluminum that is 99.00 percent pure aluminum. The last 2 digits of the 1xxx are used to indicate the hundredths of 1% above the original 99%.
[Ref: General Handbook H-8083-30A-ATB, Chapter 07 Page 7]

7-6 Answer B.
The first number 2 off 2xxx aluminum alloys denotes that the main alloying ingredient is copper.
[Ref: General Handbook H-8083-30A-ATB, Chapter 07 Page 8]

7-7 AMG019
What aluminum alloy designation indicates that the metal has received no hardening or tempering treatment?
  A. 3003-F
  B. 5052-H36
  C. 6061-O

7-8 AMG019
The metal Titanium, when moistened and drawn across glass, will produce a pencil like line.
  A. True
  B. False
  C. Cannot be determined

7-9 AMG019
Iron Constantan thermocouples function primarily by measuring the
  A. hardness of a metal as it changes temperature.
  B. electrical conductivity of a metal as it changes temperature.
  C. expansion of a metal as it changes temperature.

7-10 AMG019
The cast housing of a turbine engine gearbox must be quenched during the heat treatment process. Which of the following has the slowest cooling potential?
  A. Oil
  B. Water
  C. Brine (salt water)

7-11 AMG019
Parts are rinsed thoroughly in hot water after they have been heat treated in a sodium and potassium nitrate bath to
  A. prevent corrosion.
  B. prevent surface cracking.
  C. retard discoloration.

7-12 AMG019
When quenching a heated piece of steel, the proper procedure is to
  A. quickly drop the part in the quenching solution tank and allow it to soak.
  B. agitate the part vigorously as it is placed in the quenching solution.
  C. immerse irregular parts so the light end enters the solution first.

AIRCRAFT MATERIALS, HARDWARE, AND PROCESSES

ANSWERS

7-7 Answer A.
The various designations are as follows:
- F — as fabricated.
- O — annealed, recrystallized (wrought products only).
- H — strain hardened.
- H1 (plus one or more digits) — strain hardened only.
- H2 (plus one or more digits) — strain hardened and partially annealed.
- H3 (plus one or more digits) — strain hardened and stabilized.

[Ref: General Handbook H-8083-30A-ATB, Chapter 07 Page 8]

7-8 Answer A.
Titanium resembles stainless steel in appearance. A quick method used to identify titanium is the spark test. Titanium gives off a brilliant white trace ending in a brilliant white burst. It can also be identified by moistening the titanium and using it to draw a line on a piece of glass. This will leave a dark line similar in appearance to a pencil mark.

[Ref: General Handbook H-8083-30A-ATB, Chapter 07 Page 9]

7-9 Answer B.
Thermocouples provide an accurate temperature measurement. Thermocouples are usually encased in metallic or ceramic tubes closed at the hot end to protect them from the furnace gases. A necessary attachment is an instrument, such as a millivoltmeter or potentiometer, for measuring the electromotive force generated by the thermocouple.

[Ref: General Handbook H-8083-30A-ATB, Chapter 07 Page 16]

7-10 Answer A.
Various solutions are used in the quenching process and the rate of cooling depends on the solution used. Cooling is relatively rapid during quenching in brine, somewhat less rapid in water, and slow in oil.

[Ref: General Handbook H-8083-30A-ATB, Chapter 07 Page 17]

7-11 Answer A.
Sodium and Potassium Nitrate are salts which are highly corrosive. Thus any metal part immersed in these or any other salt must be rinsed properly to avoid corrosion.

[Ref: General Handbook H-8083-30A-ATB, Chapter 07 Page 17-19]

7-12 Answer B.
Agitating the part as it is placed in solution will dislodge vapor and air bubbles from the part allowing it to cool more evenly. Do not just drop the part in the container as allowing it to lie on the bottom will affect the rate of cooling between the top and bottom causing it to warp. Immersing the heavy end of an object first will begin the cooling process on the denser end earlier, thus allowing a more even cooling.

[Ref: General Handbook H-8083-30A-ATB, Chapter 07 Page 19]

7-13 AMG019
What is meant by a metal's critical temperature range?
  A. The temperature at which hardening of a metal begins.
  B. The metal's melting point.
  C. The temperature at which carbon particles dissolve in steel.

7-14 AMG019
Which of the following is an effect of annealing steel and aluminum alloys?
  1. A decrease in internal stress.
  2. A softening of the metal.
  3. Improved corrosion resistance.
  A. #1 and #2
  B. #1 and #3
  C. #2 and #3

7-15 AMG019
Which heat treating operation would be performed when the surface of the metal is changed chemically by introducing a high carbide or nitride content?
  A. Tempering
  B. Normalizing
  C. Case hardening

7-16 AMG019
Normalizing is a process of heat treating for
  A. Aluminum alloys only.
  B. Iron-base metals only.
  C. Both aluminum alloys and iron base metals.

7-17 AMG019
Why is steel tempered after being hardened?
  A. To increase its hardness and ductility.
  B. To increase its strength and decrease its internal stresses.
  C. To relieve its internal stresses and reduce brittleness.

7-18 AMG019
Case hardening may be in the form of
  A. carburizing, nitriding, or cyaniding.
  B. nitrating, cycling, or quenching.
  C. carburizing, neutralizing, or sanitizing.

AIRCRAFT MATERIALS, HARDWARE, AND PROCESSES

ANSWERS

7-13 Answer C.
Critical temperature is the point at which carbon molecules begin to dissolve in steel. At this point, the rate of the subsequent cooling can alter and determines the metal's hardness.
[Ref: General Handbook H-8083-30A-ATB, Chapter 07 Page 20]

7-14 Answer A.
Annealing of steel produces a fine grained, soft, ductile metal without internal stresses or strains. In the annealed state, steel is at its weakest. In general, annealing is the opposite of hardening.
[Ref: General Handbook H-8083-30A-ATB, Chapter 07 Page 21]

7-15 Answer C.
Case hardening produces a hard wear-resistant surface or case over a strong, tough core. In case hardening, the surface of the metal is changed chemically by introducing a high carbide or nitride content. The core is unaffected chemically.
[Ref: General Handbook H-8083-30A-ATB, Chapter 07 Page 21]

7-16 Answer B.
Normalizing is the process of heating a ferrous part to a proper temperature until it is uniformly heated and then cooling it slowly in still air.
[Ref: General Handbook H-8083-30A-ATB, Chapter 07 Page 21]

7-17 Answer C.
Rapid quenching creates stress within the steel. Tempering reheats the metal to just below its critical temperature to relieve internal stress and draw out some of its brittleness.
[Ref: General Handbook H-8083-30A-ATB, Chapter 07 Page 21]

7-18 Answer A.
Case hardening produces a hard, wear resistant surface over a strong core. It can be accomplished through several processes. Carburizing adds a controlled amount of carbon to the steel surface to form carbides. Nitriding introduces nitrogen to the surface of the steel. Cyaniding is a third method, however it isn't used in aircraft work.
[Ref: General Handbook H-8083-30A-ATB, Chapter 07 Page 21]

7-19 AMG019

The core material of Alclad 2024-T4 is
 A. heat treated aluminum alloy, and the surface is commercially pure aluminum.
 B. commercially pure aluminum, and the surface material is heat treated aluminum alloy.
 C. strain hardened aluminum alloy, and the surface material is commercially pure aluminum.

7-20 AMG019

Which material cannot be heat treated repeatedly without harmful effects?
 A. Unclad aluminum alloy in sheet form
 B. 6061-T9 stainless steel
 C. Clad aluminum alloy

7-21 AMG019

At what point does an aircraft alloy 2017 aluminum rivet obtain its maximum strength?
 A. When it is mechanically set with a squeezer or rivet gun
 B. When it is heat treated prior to installation
 C. Approximately 9 days after installation

7-22 AMG019

What type of testing best determines a non-ferrous metal's heat treatment condition?
 A. Rockwell testing
 B. Brinell testing
 C. Barcol testing

7-23 AMG019

Which of the following occurs when a mechanical force is repeatedly applied to most metals at room temperature, such as rolling, hammering, or bending?
 1. The metals become artificially aged.
 2. The metals become stress-corrosion cracked.
 3. The metals become cold worked, strained, or work hardened.
 A. #2
 B. #1 and #3
 C. #3

7-24 AMG037

Composite aircraft structures can reach up to _____ the tensile strength of steel or aluminum.
 A. 10 times
 B. 100 times
 C. 4-6 times

AIRCRAFT MATERIALS, HARDWARE, AND PROCESSES

ANSWERS

7-19 Answer A.
The terms "Alclad and Pureclad" are used to designate sheets that consist of an aluminum alloy core coated with a layer of pure aluminum to a depth of approximately 5 1/2 percent on each side.
[Ref: General Handbook H-8083-30A-ATB, Chapter 07 Page 23]

7-20 Answer C.
The treatment of material which has been previously heat treated is considered a reheat treatment. Unclad heat-treatable alloys can be solution heat treated repeatedly without harmful effects. The number of solution heat treatments allowed for clad sheet is limited due to increased diffusion of core and cladding with each reheating. Existing specifications allow one to three reheat treatments of clad sheet depending upon cladding thickness.
[Ref: General Handbook H-8083-30A-ATB, Chapter 07 Page 24]

7-21 Answer C.
The heat treatment of alloy 2017 rivets consists of subjecting the rivets to a temperature between 930 °F to 950 °F for approximately 30 minutes, and immediately quenching in cold water. These rivets reach maximum strength in about 9 days after being driven.
[Ref: General Handbook H-8083-30A-ATB, Chapter 07 Page 26]

7-22 Answer C.
A Barcol tester measures heat treatment condition in Brinell units by measuring the force of pressing a spring loaded indenter into a soft metal being tested such as aluminum, brass, or copper.
[Ref: General Handbook H-8083-30A-ATB, Chapter 07 Page 29-30]

7-23 Answer B.
Work hardening and strain result when metals are mechanically worked at temperatures below their critical range. While hardening reduces a metal's flexibility, strain hardening increases its strength and hardness. Artificial age hardening can also be accelerated by reheating and soaking for a specified period of time.
[Ref: General Handbook H-8083-30A-ATB, Chapter 07 Page 31]

7-24 Answer C.
Composite aircraft structures have a longer life, greater flexibility, higher corrosion resistance, are 3-5 times stiffer, and have a tensile strength 4 to 6 times that of steel or aluminum.
[Ref: General Handbook H-8083-30A-ATB, Chapter 07 Page 33]

7-25 AMG037
Regarding the use of respirators when working with composite material; which is the best indication that the mask's filters need to be replaced?
A. You can smell resin with the mask on.
B. The mask is clogged with debris, making breathing more difficult.
C. The expiration date of the mask has passed.

7-26 AMG037
Honeycomb composite construction for aircraft consist of
A. core, face sheets, and adhesive.
B. core, beeswax, and resin.
C. face sheet, resin, and fiberglass.

7-27 AMG017
What type of synthetic rubber offers the best resistance to aviation fuels and oils and is therefore used for fuel hoses, fuel tank linings, and gaskets?
A. Buna-N
B. Buna-S
C. Neoprene

7-28 AMG017
Selecting the O-ring most compatible with the type of fluid being sealed should be done with reference to
A. the factory color coding on the ring.
B. numerical coding etched on the inside of the ring surface.
C. the labeling on the package.

7-29 AMG017
The advantages of MS28782 Teflon backup rings include:
1. They are unaffected by age.
2. They are unaffected by fluid or vapor.
3. They are interchangeable with any other MS28782 ring of equal size.
4. They can tolerate extreme temperatures.
A. Only 1 and 2 above
B. Only 3 and 4 above
C. All of the above

7-30 AMG017
A class three bolt thread is
A. a tight fit.
B. a loose fit.
C. a medium fit.

AIRCRAFT MATERIALS, HARDWARE, AND PROCESSES

ANSWERS

7-25 Answer A.
When working with resins, it is important to use vapor protection. Charcoal filters within a respirator remove the vapors for a period of time. When removing the respirators for breaks, and upon placing it back on, if you can smell the resin vapors, replace the filters immediately.
[Ref: General Handbook H-8083-30A-ATB, Chapter 07 Page 32]

7-26 Answer A.
Honeycomb core is made from paper, Nomex, carbon, fiberglass or metal. The core is sandwiched together between a high-density laminate or solid face and back and held together with an adhesive.
[Ref: General Handbook H-8083-30A-ATB, Chapter 07 Page 34]

7-27 Answer C.
Neoprene has superior resistance to oil. It is a good material for use in non-aromatic gasoline systems but it has poor resistance to aromatic gasoline.
[Ref: General Handbook H-8083-30A-ATB, Chapter 07 Page 35]

7-28 Answer C.
The part number on the sealed envelope provides the most reliable identification of an O-ring's type and characteristics. While manufacturers provide color coding on some O-rings, the color stain is not permanent and may be omitted due to manufacturing limitations.
[Ref: General Handbook H-8083-30A-ATB, Chapter 07 Page 37]

7-29 Answer C.
Characteristics of Teflon rings include all of the advantages listed and are suitable for use in extreme situations, such as high pressure hydraulic systems. The primary purpose of inspecting a Teflon ring is to ensure the surfaces are free from dirt or irregularities and to verify the edges are clean cut and sharp.
[Ref: General Handbook H-8083-30A-ATB, Chapter 07 Page 37-38]

7-30 Answer C.
The Class of a thread indicates the tolerance allowed in manufacturing. Class 1 is a loose fit, Class 2 is a free fit, Class 3 is a medium fit, and Class 4 is a close fit. Aircraft bolts are usually manufactured in the Class 3, medium fit. A Class 4 fit requires a wrench to turn the nut onto a bolt, whereas a Class 1 fit can easily be turned with the fingers. Generally, aircraft screws are manufactured with a Class 2 thread fit for ease of assembly.
[Ref: General Handbook H-8083-30A-ATB, Chapter 07 Page 40]

7-31 AMG017
An AN-73 bolt has the head drilled for insertion of safety wire.
- A. True
- B. False
- C. Cannot be determined

7-34 AMG017
When is a AN clevis bolt used in an airplane?
- A. For tension and shear load conditions.
- B. For areas where external tension loads are applied.
- C. Only for shear load applications.

7-32 AMG017
A bolt with a raised or recessed triangle on the head is classified as a
- A. NAS standard aircraft bolt.
- B. NAS close tolerance bolt.
- C. AN corrosion resistant steel bolt.

7-35 AMG017
A clevis bolt used with a fork-end cable terminal and is secured with a
- A. castellated shear nut tightened with no strain imposed and safetyed with a cotter pin.
- B. castle nut tightened until slight binding occurs between the fork and the fitting to which it is being attached.
- C. castellated shear nut and cotter pin or a thin self-locking nut tightened to prevent rotation of the bolt in the fork.

7-33 AMG017
Which of the bolt head code markings shown below identifies a corrosion resistant AN standard steel bolt? Refer to Figure 7-1 below.
- A. 1
- B. 2
- C. 3

7-36 AMG017
Which statements regarding aircraft bolts is correct?
1. Alloy bolts smaller than 1/4" diameter should not be used in primary structures.
2. When tightening castellated nuts, it is permissible to tighten the nut up to 10% over the recommended torque to permit alignment.
3. In general, bolt grip lengths should equal the material thickness.
- A. #1 and #2 are correct.
- B. #1 and #3 are correct.
- C. All are correct.

Figure 7-1. Aircraft hardware.

AIRCRAFT MATERIALS, HARDWARE, AND PROCESSES

ANSWERS

7-31 Answer A.
The AN-73 drilled head bolt is similar to the standard hex bolt, but has a deeper head drilled to receive wire for safe tying.
[Ref: General Handbook H-8083-30A-ATB, Chapter 07 Page 41]

7-32 Answer B.
Close tolerance NAS bolts are marked with either a raised or recessed triangle. The material markings for NAS bolts are the same as those for AN bolts, except that they may be either raised or recessed.
[Ref: General Handbook H-8083-30A-ATB, Chapter 07 Page 42]

7-33 Answer C.
All aircraft grade bolts are marked with an identifying symbol on their head. A cross indicates a standard steel AN bolt. An "X" in a triangle indicates a close tolerance bolt. A single line indicates a corrosion resistant AN steel bolt.
[Ref: General Handbook H-8083-30A-ATB, Chapter 07 Page 42]

7-34 Answer C.
The head of a clevis bolt is round and is either slotted to receive a common screwdriver or recessed to receive a crosspoint screwdriver. This type of bolt is used only where shear loads occur and never in tension. It is often inserted as a mechanical pin in a control system.
[Ref: General Handbook H-8083-30A-ATB, Chapter 07 Page 43]

7-35 Answer A.
The castellated shear nut, AN320, is designed for use with devices (such as drilled clevis bolts and threaded taper pins) which are normally subjected to shearing stress only. Like the castle nut, it is castellated for safetying. Note, however, that the nut is not as deep or as strong as the castle nut; also the castellations are not as deep as those in the castle nut.
[Ref: General Handbook H-8083-30A-ATB, Chapter 07 Page 43-46]

7-36 Answer B.
Grip length or grip range is determined by measuring the thickness of the material with a hook scale inserted through the hole. Once this measurement is determined, select the correct grip range by referring to the charts provided by the rivet manufacturer. Be certain that the bolt grip length is correct. Grip length is the length of the unthreaded portion of the bolt shank. The grip length should equal the thickness of the material being bolted together, however, bolts of slightly greater grip length may be used if washers are placed under the nut or the bolt head. In the case of plate nuts, add shims under the plate.
[Ref: General Handbook H-8083-30A-ATB, Chapter 07 Page 44-51]

7-37 AMG017
Aircraft nuts are made of stainless steel, anodized 2024T aluminum alloy, or
   A. copper plated carbon steel.
   B. copper plated nickel steel.
   C. cadmium plated carbon steel.

7-38 AMG017
Which of the following is true when using all AN300 series nuts (AN310, AN340, etc)?
   A. All AN300 series nuts require a secondary safetying mechanism.
   B. AN300 series nuts may not be used in high temperature applications.
   C. AN300 nuts may not be used when the components are subject to rotation.

7-39 AMG017
The locking feature of the nylon type locknut is obtained by?
   A. the use of an unthreaded nylon locking insert.
   B. a nylon insert held firmly in place at the base of the load carrying section.
   C. making the threads in the nylon insert slightly smaller than those in the load carrying section.

7-40 AMG017
Which precaution must be taken every time a self locking nut is used on an aircraft?
   A. The head of the bolt must be safety wired.
   B. A lock washer must be used with the nut.
   C. Ensure the bolt is not subject to rotation.

7-41 AMG017
Which of the following is not a benefit of AN 960 and AN 970 washers?
   A. A smooth bearing surface between the bolt and assembly.
   B. Corrosion control from contact of dissimilar metals.
   C. Increased resistance to the bolt vibrating loose.

7-42 AMG017
Unless otherwise specified or required, aircraft bolts should be installed so the bolt head is facing
   A. upward, or in a rearward direction.
   B. upward, or in a forward direction.
   C. downward, or in a forward direction.

AIRCRAFT MATERIALS, HARDWARE, AND PROCESSES

ANSWERS

7-37 Answer C.
Aircraft nuts are made of cadmium plated carbon steel, stainless steel, or anodized 2024T aluminum alloy.
[Ref: General Handbook H-8083-30A-ATB, Chapter 07 Page 45]

7-38 Answer B.
AN 300 series nuts such as wing nuts and castle nuts are non-self locking and therefore need an additional method to insure they do not rotate loose such as cotter pins or safety wire.
[Ref: General Handbook H-8083-30A-ATB, Chapter 07 Page 44]

7-39 Answer A.
A nylon type locknut is not threaded and the inside diameter is smaller than the largest diameter of the threaded portion or the outside diameter of a corresponding bolt. When the nut is screwed onto a bolt, it acts as an ordinary nut until the bolt reaches the fiber collar. When the bolt is screwed into the fiber collar, friction (or drag) causes the fiber to be pushed upward. This creates a heavy downward pressure on the load carrying part and automatically throws the load carrying sides of the nut and bolt threads into positive contact. After the bolt has been forced all the way through the fiber collar, the downward pressure remains constant. This pressure locks and holds the nut securely in place even under severe vibration.
[Ref: General Handbook H-8083-30A-ATB, Chapter 07 Page 48]

7-40 Answer C.
Do not use self locking nuts at joints which subject either the bolt or nut to rotation. They may however be used with bearings and control pulleys provided the inner race of the bearing is clamped to support the structure by the nut and bolt.
[Ref: General Handbook H-8083-30A-ATB, Chapter 07 Page 44]

7-41 Answer C.
Plain washers, such as the AN960 and AN970, are used to form a smooth bearing surface and act as a shim in obtaining correct grip length for a bolt and nut assembly, prevent damage to the surface material and provide protection of structures where corrosion caused by dissimilar metals is a factor.
[Ref: General Handbook H-8083-30A-ATB, Chapter 07 Page 50]

7-42 Answer B.
Whenever possible, place the bolt with the head on top (upward) or in the forward position. This positioning tends to prevent the bolt from slipping out if the nut is accidentally lost.
[Ref: General Handbook H-8083-30A-ATB, Chapter 07 Page 50]

7-43 AMG017
Elongated bolt holes in critical aircraft structural members may be drilled to the next larger size.
  A. True
  B. False
  C. With manufacturer's approval

7-46 AMG017
When attaching a component to the aircraft structure by way of an aircraft bolt and a castellated tension nut combination, what's an acceptable solution when the cotter pin hole does not align within the recommended torque range?
  A. Exceed the torque range
  B. Tighten below the torque range
  C. Change washers and try again

7-44 AMG017
A helicoil insert is used
  A. to replace damaged rivets in aircraft structures.
  B. to replace damaged threads in aircraft structures.
  C. when the next smaller size bolt is desired.

7-47 AMG017
When the specific torque value for nuts is not given, where can the recommended torque value be found?
  A. AC43.13-2B
  B. Technical Standard Order
  C. AC43.13-1B

7-45 AMG017
Unless otherwise specified, torque values for tightening aircraft nuts and bolts relate to
  A. clean, dry threads.
  B. clean, lightly oiled threads.
  C. both dry and lightly oiled threads.

7-48 AMG020
An 1100 aluminum alloy rivet is a soft rivet not suitable for high strength applications.
  A. True
  B. False
  C. Cannot be determined

AIRCRAFT MATERIALS, HARDWARE, AND PROCESSES

ANSWERS

7-43 Answer C.
In cases of oversized or elongated holes in critical members, obtain advice from the aircraft or engine manufacturer before drilling or reaming the hole to take the next larger bolt. Usually, such factors as edge distance, clearance, or load factor must be considered. Oversized or elongated holes in noncritical members can usually be drilled or reamed to the next larger size.
[Ref: General Handbook H-8083-30A-ATB, Chapter 07 Page 51]

7-46 Answer C.
Nuts should never be over torqued. To help a hole line up with the castellation add washers under the nut until the cotter key aligns.
[Ref: General Handbook H-8083-30A-ATB, Chapter 07 Page 54]

7-44 Answer B.
A helicoil is a formed screw threaded coil with a diamond shaped cross section used as a replacement screw thread bushing when the original threaded area is stripped or otherwise damaged.
[Ref: General Handbook H-8083-30A-ATB, Chapter 07 Page 52]

7-47 Answer C.
AC43.13-1B includes a torque value table which can be used as a guide when tightening nuts, bolts, studs, screws, etc., whenever a specific torque setting is not called for by the manufacturer.
[Ref: AC43.13-1B, Table 7-1 Pages 7-9]

7-45 Answer A.
Unless a torque table or manufacturer's instruction specifies otherwise, torque values are always given for clean dry threads. Do not lubricate nuts or bolts except for corrosion resistant steel parts or when instructed to do so.
[Ref: General Handbook H-8083-30A-ATB, Chapter 07 Page 53-54]

7-48 Answer A.
The 1100 rivet, which is composed of 99.00 percent pure aluminum, is very soft. It is for riveting the softer aluminum alloys, which are used for nonstructural parts (parts where strength is not a factor).
[Ref: General Handbook H-8083-30A-ATB, Chapter 07 Page 56]

7-49 AMG020
A damaged aluminum wing skin is repaired with copper rivets. This repair is done without consulting the manufacturer of the aircraft. What is one problem this may cause?
  A. Dissimilar metal corrosion
  B. Inadequate rivet-hole clearance
  C. Inadequate strength

7-50 AMG020
Self-plugging (friction lock) rivets are typically used when access to both sides of an aircraft surface is difficult or impossible.
  A. True
  B. False
  C. Never

7-51 AMG020
Which rivet type is the only blind rivet considered to be interchangeable with a solid rivet?
  A. Wiredraw Cherrylock rivets
  B. Huck Mechanical locked rivets
  C. Bulbed Cherrylock rivets

7-52 AMG017
Which type of specialty fastener would be best suited to secure an aircraft cowling?
  A. Camloc fasteners
  B. Dzus fasteners
  C. Turnlock fasteners

7-53 AMG017
What is the primary benefit of an MS33737 instrument nut?
  A. It pulls the instrument tightly against the instrument panel.
  B. It provides a shock absorbing surface to minimize vibration to the instrument.
  C. It reduces magnetic influences in the cockpit, which can affect the accuracy of the instrument.

7-54 AMG017
One of the most common aircraft cables is a 7×19. What does the "7×19" indicate?
  A. The cable's tensile strength is the product of 7 and 19.
  B. The cable is made up of 19 strands of wire, which contains 7 wires in each strand.
  C. The cable is made up of 7 strands of wire, which contains 19 wires in each strand.

AIRCRAFT MATERIALS, HARDWARE, AND PROCESSES

ANSWERS

7-49 Answer A.
The use of copper rivets in aircraft repair is limited. Copper rivets can be used only on copper alloys or nonmetallic materials such as leather. If a copper rivet is inserted into an aluminum alloy two dissimilar metals are brought in contact with each other. As all metals possess a small electrical potential, dissimilar metals in the presence of moisture will cause an electrical current to flow between them and corrosion will result.
[Ref: General Handbook H-8083-30A-ATB, Chapter 07 Page 57]

7-50 Answer A.
Self-plugging (friction lock) rivets are designed so that installation requires only one person; it is not necessary to have the work accessible from both sides.
[Ref: General Handbook H-8083-30A-ATB, Chapter 07 Page 60]

7-51 Answer C.
The large blind head of the bulbed cherrylock rivets introduced the word "bulb" to blind rivet terminology. In conjunction with the unique residual preload developed by the high stem break load, its proven fatigue strength makes it the only blind rivet interchangeable structurally with solid rivets.
[Ref: General Handbook H-8083-30A-ATB, Chapter 07 Page 62]

7-52 Answer A.
The Camloc fastener is typically a non-structural fastener containing 3 parts, a stud assembly, a grommet, and a receptacle. It is commonly used to secure aircraft cowlings, fairings, and other frequently removable parts of an aircraft.
[Ref: General Handbook H-8083-30A-ATB, Chapter 07 Page 69]

7-53 Answer C.
The MS33737 instrument nut reduces magnetic influences in the cockpit, while nonmagnetic mounting nuts secure instruments in a control panel.
[Ref: General Handbook H-8083-30A-ATB, Chapter 07 Page 72]

7-54 Answer C.
The most common aircraft cables are the 7 × 7 and 7 × 19. The 7 × 19 cable is constructed of seven strands of 19 wires each. Six of these strands are laid around the center strand. This cable is extra flexible and is used in primary control systems and in other places where operation over pulleys is frequent.
[Ref: General Handbook H-8083-30A-ATB, Chapter 07 Page 75]

ORAL EXAM

7-1(O).   What does the code "1100" tell us about aluminum?

7-2(O).   If given an unknown piece of metal, how can you tell if it is titanium or stainless steel?

7-3(O).   Explain case hardening.

7-4(O).   Name the three methods of case hardening.

7-5(O).   Explain the special characteristics of Alclad 2024-T4.

7-6(O).   Explain the construction of a honeycomb composite material.

7-7(O).   Compare the tensile strength of composite aircraft structures and those made of steel or aluminum.

7-8(O).   Explain the term "ice box rivets".

7-9(O).   When are "ice box rivets" used?

7-10(O).   Name the two types of heat treatments applicable to aluminum alloys.

7-11(O).   Artificial aging is another term for what type of heat treatment?

7-12(O).   Why are cork gaskets the best choice for mating rough surfaces?

7-13(O).   Name the classes of bolt threads and explain what the differences are between them.

7-14(O).   When are self-locking nuts used on aircraft?

7-15(O).   What are AN960 and AN970 washers used for?

7-16(O).   Explain the correct way to line up a hole for use with a cotter pin.

7-17(O).   Define grip length or range.

5-18(O).   Explain how to determine the correct grip length or range when selecting a bolt.

7-19(O).   Explain the standard positioning for aircraft bolts when installed on an aircraft and why.

7-20(O).   Explain the use of helicoils.

7-21(O).   What specialty fastener is best suited to secure an aircraft cowling?

7-22(O).   Explain the primary benefit of an MS33737 instrument nut.

7-23(O).   Explain the industry standard for securing fasteners with safety wire.

AIRCRAFT MATERIALS, PROCESSES, & HARDWARE

ANSWERS

ORAL EXAM

7-1(O). The code 1100 is given to aluminum that is 99.00 percent pure aluminum.
[Ref: General Handbook H-8083-30A-ATB, Chapter 07 Page 7]

7-2(O). Two methods can be used. One is the spark test; titanium will give off a brilliant white trace ending in a brilliant white burst. The other is by moistening the titanium and using it to draw a line on a piece of glass. This will leave a dark line similar in appearance to a pencil mark.
[Ref: General Handbook H-8083-30A-ATB, Chapter 07 Page 9]

7-3(O). It is a heat-treating operation where the surface of the metal is changed chemically by introducing a high carbide or nitride content producing a hard wear-resistant surface or case over a strong, tough core.
[Ref: General Handbook H-8083-30A-ATB, Chapter 07 Page 21]

7-4(O). The common forms of case hardening are carburizing, cyaniding, and nitriding.
[Ref: General Handbook H-8083-30A-ATB, Chapter 07 Page 21]

7-5(O). "Alclad and Pureclad" are used to designate sheets that consist of an aluminum alloy core coated with a layer of pure aluminum to a depth of approximately 5 1/2 percent on each side.
[Ref: General Handbook H-8083-30A-ATB, Chapter 07 Page 23]

7-6(O). Honeycomb's core is made from paper, Nomex, carbon, fiberglass or metal. The core is sandwiched together between a high-density laminate or solid face and back and held together with an adhesive.
[Ref: General Handbook H-8083-30A-ATB, Chapter 07 Page 34]

7-7(O). Composite aircraft structures have a tensile strength 4 to 6 times that of steel or aluminum.
[Ref: General Handbook H-8083-30A-ATB, Chapter 07 Page 33]

7-8(O). "Ice box rivets," are 2017-T and 2024-T rivets that have been annealed, and must be kept refrigerated until they are to be driven. This refrigeration delays the hardening of the rivets.
[Ref: General Handbook H-8083-30A-ATB, Chapter 07 Page 56]

7-9(O). The 2017-T and 2024-T rivets are used in aluminum alloy structures where more strength is needed than is obtainable with the same size 2217-T rivet.
[Ref: General Handbook H-8083-30A-ATB, Chapter 07 Page 56]

7-10(O). One is called solution heat treatment, and the other is known as precipitation heat treatment.
[Ref: General Handbook H-8083-30A-ATB, Chapter 07 Page 23]

7-11(O). Precipitation heat treatment.
[Ref: General Handbook H-8083-30A-ATB, Chapter 07 Page 23]

7-12(O). A cork gasket best conforms to the uneven or varying space.
[Ref: General Handbook H-8083-30A-ATB, Chapter 07 Page 38]

7-13(O). The Class of a thread indicates the tolerance allowed in manufacturing. Class 1 is a loose fit, Class 2 is a free fit, Class 3 is a medium fit, and Class 4 is a close fit.
[Ref: General Handbook H-8083-30A-ATB, Chapter 07 Page 40]

PRACTICAL EXAM

7-1(P).   Given an actual aircraft or mock-up, torque a series of bolts per specifications.

7-2(P).   Given an actual aircraft or mock-up, use industry standards and properly safety-wire a series of bolts per specifications.

7-3(P).   Given an actual aircraft or mock-up, select the appropriate hardware and install a specified component. NOTE: Be prepared to select and install all standard aircraft hardware including, but not limited to, screws, bolts, nuts (including self-locking), cotter pins, and washers.

7-4(P).   Given an actual aircraft or mock-up, select, install, and secure a clevis bolt and associated hardware per industry standards.

7-5(P).   Given an actual aircraft or mock-up, properly install and safety a turnbuckle per industry standards. 5-6(P). Given various standard aviation rivets, identify them by physical characteristics.

AIRCRAFT MATERIALS, PROCESSES, & HARDWARE

ANSWERS

ORAL EXAM

7-14(O).   Self-locking nuts are used on aircraft to provide tight connections, which will not shake loose under severe vibration.
[Ref: General Handbook H-8083-30A-ATB, Chapter 07 Page 46]

7-15(O).   Plain washers, such as the AN960 and AN970, are used to form a smooth bearing surface and act as a shim in obtaining correct grip length for a bolt and nut assembly, prevent damage to the surface material and provide protection of structures where corrosion caused by dissimilar metals is a factor.
[Ref: General Handbook H-8083-30A-ATB, Chapter 07 Page 50]

7-16(O).   If the cotter pin hole does not align within the recommended torque range, the acceptable practice is to change washers and try realigning the holes again.
[Ref: General Handbook H-8083-30A-ATB, Chapter 07 Page 54]

7-17(O).   Grip length is the length of the unthreaded portion of the bolt shank.
[Ref: General Handbook H-8083-30A-ATB, Chapter 07 Page 51]

7-18(O).   In general, bolt grip lengths should equal the material thickness. To determine grip length or grip range measure the thickness of the material with a hook scale inserted through the hole. Once this measurement is determined, select the correct grip range by referring to the charts provided by the manufacturer.
[Ref: General Handbook H-8083-30A-ATB, Chapter 07 Page 44, 51]

7-19(O).   Unless otherwise specified or required, aircraft bolts should be installed so the bolt head is facing upward or in a forward direction. This positioning tends to prevent the bolt from slipping out if the nut is accidentally lost.
[Ref: General Handbook H-8083-30A-ATB, Chapter 07 Page 51]

7-20(O).   Helicoils can be used to restore damaged threads.
[Ref: General Handbook H-8083-30A-ATB, Chapter 07 Page 52]

7-21(O).   Camloc fasteners are used to secure aircraft cowlings and fairings.
[Ref: General Handbook H-8083-30A-ATB, Chapter 07 Page 69]

7-22(O).   The MS33737 instrument nut reduces magnetic influences in the cockpit.
[Ref: General Handbook H-8083-30A-ATB, Chapter 07 Page 72]

7-23(O).   In safetying, arrange the wire so that if the bolt or screw begins to loosen, the force applied to the wire is in the tightening direction.
[Ref: General Handbook H-8083-30A-ATB, Chapter 07 Page 80]

AIRCRAFT CLEANING AND CORROSION CONTROL

Forms of Corrosion, Factors Affecting Corrosion, Preventing Corrosion, Corrosion-prone Areas, Inspection, and Removal

CHAPTER 08

QUESTIONS

8-1 AMG012
Which of the listed conditions is NOT one of the requirements for corrosion to occur?
- A. The presence of an electrolyte.
- B. Electrical contact between an anodic area and a cathodic area.
- C. The presence of a passive oxide film.

8-2 AMG012
Caustic cleaning products used on aluminum structures have the effect of producing
- A. passive oxidation.
- B. improved corrosion resistance.
- C. corrosion.

8-3 AMG012
Which of these materials is the most cathodic?
- A. Zinc
- B. 2024 aluminum alloy
- C. Stainless steel

8-4 AMG012
Which of these materials is the most anodic?
- A. cadmium
- B. aluminum (1100)
- C. magnesium

8-5 AMG012
Regarding the below statements:
1. In the corrosion process, it is the cathodic area or dissimilar cathodic material that corrodes.
2. In the galvanic or electro-chemical series for metals, the most anodic metals are those that will give up electrons most easily.
- A. Only #1 is true.
- B. Only #2 is true.
- C. Both #1 and #2 are true.

8-6 AMG012
Of the following, when and/or where is galvanic corrosion most likely to occur?
- A. When an electrolyte (water) covers the surface of an aluminum skin, seeps into the cracks between lap joints, and oxygen is excluded from the area.
- B. At the interface of a steel fastener and aluminum alloy inspection plate in the presence of an electrolyte.
- C. In an area of unprotected metal exposed to an atmosphere containing battery fumes, exhaust gases, or industrial contaminants.

AIRCRAFT CLEANING AND CORROSION CONTROL

ANSWERS

8-1 Answer C.
The corrosion process always involves two simultaneous changes: The metal that is attacked or oxidized suffers what may be called anodic change, and the corrosive agent is reduced and may be considered as undergoing cathodic change.
[Ref: General Handbook H-8083-30A-ATB, Chapter 08 Page 4]

8-2 Answer C.
Caustic cleaning solutions in concentrated form should be kept tightly capped and as far from aircraft as possible. Some cleaning solutions used in corrosion removal are, in themselves, potentially corrosive agents; therefore, particular attention should be directed toward their complete removal after use on aircraft. Where entrapment of the cleaning solution is likely to occur, use a noncorrosive cleaning agent, even though it is less efficient.
[Ref: General Handbook H-8083-30A-ATB, Chapter 08 Page 5]

8-3 Answer C.
All metals are electrically active and have potential "nobility" in a chemical environment. The more noble a metal is the more cathodic it is and will less easily corrode. Platinum is the most noble metal. Stainless steel is more noble and cathodic than zinc or aluminum alloys.
[Ref: General Handbook H-8083-30A-ATB, Chapter 08 Page 5]

8-4 Answer C.
All metals are electrically active and have potential "nobility" in a chemical environment. The less noble, or more anodic a metal is the more easily it will corrode. Magnesium is the least noble of all metals and so the most anodic.
[Ref: General Handbook H-8083-30A-ATB, Chapter 08 Page 6]

8-5 Answer B.
The corrosion process always involves two simultaneous changes: The metal that is attacked or oxidized suffers what may be called anodic change; and the corrosive agent is reduced and may be considered as undergoing cathodic change. During an electro-chemical attack, the quantity of corrosive agent is reduced and, if not renewed or removed, may completely react with the metal, becoming neutralized.
[Ref: General Handbook H-8083-30A-ATB, Chapter 08 Page 5]

8-6 Answer B.
Galvanic action, not unlike electroplating, occurs at the points or areas of contact where the insulation between the surfaces has broken down or been omitted. This electrochemical attack can be very serious because in many instances the action is taking place out of sight, and the only way to detect it prior to structural failure is by disassembly and inspection.
[Ref: General Handbook H-8083-30A-ATB, Chapter 08 Page 6]

8-7 AMG012
Corrosion caused by galvanic action is the result of
A. excessive anodation.
B. contact between two unlike metals.
C. excessive etching

8-8 AMG012
Galvanic corrosion is most likely to be most rapid and severe when the surface area of the
A. cathodic metal is smaller than the surface area of the anodic metal.
B. anodic and cathodic metals are approximately the same.
C. anodic metal is smaller than the surface area of the cathodic metal.

8-9 AMG012
Which of the following may not be detectable even by careful visual inspection of the surface of aluminum alloy parts or structures?
A. Filiform corrosion
B. Intergranular corrosion
C. Uniform etch corrosion

8-10 AMG012
Which is the best method to detect intergranular corrosion?
A. Magnetic particle inspection.
B. Ultrasonic inspection.
C. Liquid penetrant.

8-11 AMG012
Which is the most likely cause of type of corrosion shown in the picture?
A. a caustic chemical which has dripped onto the surface.
B. dissimilar metal contact.
C. irregularities during the metal's initial manufacturing.

8-12 AMG012
The form of corrosion pictured below is most likely caused by
A. poor cleaning processes prior to painting.
B. slight relative movement between this and another metallic surface.
C. presence of caustic substance such as battery acid.

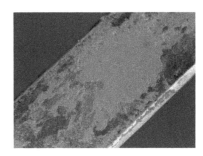

AIRCRAFT CLEANING AND CORROSION CONTROL

ANSWERS

8-7 Answer B.
Galvanic action, not unlike electroplating, occurs at the points or areas of contact where the insulation between the surfaces has broken down or been omitted. This electrochemical attack can be very serious because in many instances the action is taking place out of sight, and the only way to detect it prior to structural failure is by disassembly and inspection.
[Ref: General Handbook H-8083-30A-ATB, Chapter 08 Page 7]

8-8 Answer C.
During an electro-chemical attack, the quantity of corrosive agent is reduced. With a smaller area this reduction will be increased and thus more severe.
[Ref: General Handbook H-8083-30A-ATB, Chapter 08 Page 5]

8-9 Answer B.
Light to moderate intergranular corrosion is an attack along the grain boundaries of an alloy and may exist without visible evidence. Extreme intergranular corrosion is visibly evident as it may cause the surface to exfoliate, or delaminate along the grain boundaries.
[Ref: General Handbook H-8083-30A-ATB, Chapter 08 Page 9]

8-10 Answer B.
Intergranular corrosion occurs within the structure of aluminum alloys (and sometimes stainless steel). Being non-ferrous aluminum, we can rule out magnetic particle inspection. Being within the structure, as opposed to its surface, we can rule out liquid penetrants. Ultrasonic techniques excel at detecting subsurface defects of non-ferrous metals.
[Ref: General Handbook H-8083-30A-ATB, Chapter 08 Page 9 and Chapter 10 Page 23]

8-11 Answer C.
Intergranular corrosion results from a lack of uniformity caused by changes that occur in the alloy during heating and cooling during the material's manufacturing process.
[Ref: General Handbook H-8083-30A-ATB, Chapter 08 Page 11]

8-12 Answer B.
Fretting corrosion is a particularly damaging form of corrosive attack that occurs when two mating surfaces, normally at rest with respect to one another, are subject to slight relative motion.
[Ref: General Handbook H-8083-30A-ATB, Chapter 08 Page 10]

8-13 AMG012

The lifting and flaking of the metal at the surface due to delamination of grain boundaries caused by the pressure of corrosion residual product buildup is called

A. brinelling.
B. granulation.
C. exfoliation.

8-14 AMG012

Fretting corrosion is most likely to occur

A. when two surfaces fit tightly together but can move relative to one another.
B. only when two dissimilar metals are in contact.
C. when two surfaces fit loosely together and can move relative to one another.

8-15 AMG012

Stress corrosion cracking is most characteristic with which metal type?

A. Magnesium
B. Copper
C. Titanium

8-16 AMG012

Corrosion problems downstream of engine exhaust areas is caused by

A. chemical makeup of exhaust gasses.
B. heat from engine exhaust.
C. moisture mixed in the exhaust gasses.

8-17 AMG012

Minimizing corrosion related problems with piano hinges attached to control surfaces are best accomplished by

A. scheduled replacement per manufacturer's guidelines.
B. use of water displacing lubricants when servicing.
C. insure a properly painted surface between the hinge half and control surface skin.

8-18 AMG012

Which procedure is recommended to keep aircraft control cables free of corrosion?

A. Keep cables clean and dry.
B. Keep cable routing as straight as possible and free of unnecessary tension.
C. Keep cables coated with a light oil film.

AIRCRAFT CLEANING AND CORROSION CONTROL

ANSWERS

8-13 Answer C.
Very severe intergranular corrosion may sometimes cause the surface of a metal to "exfoliate." This is a lifting or flaking of the metal at the surface due to delamination of the grain boundaries caused by the pressure of corrosion residual product buildup.
[Ref: General Handbook H-8083-30A-ATB, Chapter 08 Page 9]

8-16 Answer A.
Both jet and reciprocating engine exhaust deposits are very corrosive and present particular trouble where gaps, seams, hinges, and fairings are located downstream from the exhaust pipes or nozzles.
[Ref: General Handbook H-8083-30A-ATB, Chapter 08 Page 12]

8-14 Answer A.
Fretting corrosion is a particularly damaging form of corrosive attack that occurs when two mating surfaces, normally at rest with respect to one another, are subject to slight relative motion.
[Ref: General Handbook H-8083-30A-ATB, Chapter 08 Page 10]

8-17 Answer B.
Piano-type hinges are prime spots for corrosion due to the dissimilar metal contact between the steel pin and aluminum hinge. They are also natural traps for dirt, salt, and moisture. Inspection of hinges should include lubrication and actuation through several cycles to ensure complete lubricant penetration. Use water-displacing lubricants when servicing piano hinges.
[Ref: General Handbook H-8083-30A-ATB, Chapter 08 Page 14]

8-15 Answer B.
Stress corrosion occurs as the result of the combined effect of sustained tensile stresses and a corrosive environment. Stress corrosion cracking is found in most metal systems; however, it is particularly characteristic of aluminum, copper, certain stainless steels, and high strength alloy steels (over 240,000 psi).
[Ref: General Handbook H-8083-30A-ATB, Chapter 08 Page 10]

8-18 Answer C.
A light oil coating acts as a preservative and boundary for corrosion producing oxidation.
[Ref: General Handbook H-8083-30A-ATB, Chapter 08 Page 14]

8-19 AMG012
What may be used to remove corrosion from highly stressed steel surfaces?
  A. Steel wire brushes
  B. Fine grit aluminum oxide
  C. Medium grit carborundum paper

8-20 AMG012
Ferrous oxide corrosion is typically formed by
  A. atmospheric humidity.
  B. dissimilar metal contact.
  C. exposure to a slight but constant electrical charge.

8-21 AMG012
What is the principle benefit of an Alclad aluminum surface
  A. it is easy to keep clean.
  B. pure aluminum is less susceptible to corrosion than aluminum alloys.
  C. the hardened surface protects internal structure of material.

8-22 AMG012
During inspection, you observe an oxidation layer approximately .001" thick on an aluminum wing skin. The proper action is to
  A. remove and replace the skin.
  B. remove by abrasives the oxidized layer.
  C. do nothing. The oxidation layer is actually a corrosion inhibitor.

8-23 AMG012
When an anodized surface coating is damaged in service, it can be partially restored by
  A. applying a thin coat of zinc chromate primer.
  B. chemical surface treatment.
  C. use of a suitable mild cleaner.

8-24 AMG012
Corrosion should be removed from magnesium parts with a
  A. silicon carbide brush.
  B. carborundum abrasive.
  C. stiff, hog-bristle brush.

AIRCRAFT CLEANING AND CORROSION CONTROL

ANSWERS

8-19 Answer B.
Corrosion products must be removed by careful processing, using mild abrasive papers such as rouge or fine grit aluminum oxide, or fine buffing compounds on cloth buffing wheels.
[Ref: General Handbook H-8083-30A-ATB, Chapter 08 Page 15]

8-22 Answer C.
Aluminum alloys commonly form a smooth surface oxidation that is from 0.001 to 0.0025 inch thick. This is not considered detrimental; the coating provides a hard shell barrier to the introduction of corrosive elements. Such oxidation is not to be confused with severe corrosion that can occur.
[Ref: General Handbook H-8083-30A-ATB, Chapter 08 Page 18]

8-20 Answer A.
One of the most familiar types of corrosion is ferrous oxide (rust), generally resulting from atmospheric oxidation of steel surfaces.
[Ref: General Handbook H-8083-30A-ATB, Chapter 08 Page 17]

8-23 Answer B.
When this coating is damaged in service, it can only be partially restored by chemical surface treatment. Any light corrosion removal from an anodized surface should be done very carefully to avoid removing the thin oxide film.
[Ref: General Handbook H-8083-30A-ATB, Chapter 08 Page 19]

8-21 Answer B.
Relatively pure aluminum has considerably more corrosion resistance compared with the stronger aluminum alloys. The protection obtained with the pure-aluminum clad surface (commonly called "Alclad") can be maintained if kept in a polished condition.
[Ref: General Handbook H-8083-30A-ATB, Chapter 08 Page 18]

8-24 Answer C.
Using a stiff, hog bristle brush or nonwoven abrasive pad, break loose and remove as much of the corrosion products as practicable. Steel wire brushes, carborundum abrasives, or steel cutting tools must not be used.
[Ref: General Handbook H-8083-30A-ATB, Chapter 08 Page 20]

8-25 AMG012
How may magnesium engine parts be cleaned?
  A. Soak in 20% caustic soda solution.
  B. Spray with MEK (methyl ethyl ketone).
  C. Wash with a commercial solvent, decarbonize, and scrape or grit blast.

8-28 AMG012
A nonelectrolytic chemical treatment for aluminum alloys to increase corrosion resistance and paint bonding qualities is called
  A. anodizing.
  B. alodizing.
  C. dichromating.

8-26 AMG012
If a metal joint includes contact from magnesium to another metal, the correct procedure is to:
  1. Apply at least 2 coats of epoxy primer to each mating surface.
  2. Apply vinyl tape between the mated surfaces.
  3. Apply an oil film to each mating surface.
  4. Ensure if the mating surface is aluminum, it is anodized
  A. #1 and #2
  B. # 1, 2, and 4
  C. All of the above

8-29 AMG012009
A Chromic Acid/Sulfuric Acid wash is best used to
  A. remove surface corrosion from metal components.
  B. restore a protective oxide coating on an aluminum surface.
  C. slightly etch a smooth metal surface for better paint adhesion.

8-27 AMG012
Which of the following are the desired effects of using Alodine on aluminum alloy?
1. A slightly rough surface.
2. Relieved surface stresses.
3. A smooth painting surface.
4. Increased corrosion resistance
  A. #3 and #4
  B. #1, #2, and #4
  C. #1 and #4

8-30 AMG012
Which of the following is an acceptable first step procedure to help prevent scratching when cleaning a transparent plastic surface?
  A. Gently wipe the surface with clean water.
  B. Flush the surface with clean water.
  C. Gently wipe the surface with a clean soft cloth moistened with de-mineralized or distilled water.

AIRCRAFT CLEANING AND CORROSION CONTROL

ANSWERS

8-25 Answer C.
Wash down the engine and accessories with a fine spray of kerosene or solvent. A bristle brush may be used to help clean some of the surfaces. Remember magnesium is the most chemically active of the metals used in aircraft construction and is the most difficult to protect against corrosion. The information in the text is for general reference only, always follow manufacturer's instructions for cleaning.
[Ref: General Handbook H-8083-30A-ATB, Chapter 08 Page 22-24]

8-28 Answer B.
Alodizing is a simple chemical treatment for aluminum alloys to increase their corrosion resistance and to improve their paint bonding qualities. Because of its simple application process, alodizing is quickly replacing anodizing as the preferred method of corrosion protection.
[Ref: General Handbook H-8083-30A-ATB, Chapter 08 Page 23]

8-26 Answer A.
Special care is taken with magnesium as it is the most anodic metal and will corrode quickly when in contact with any other metal. At least two coats of epoxy primer or zinc chromate must be applied to each mating surface. If spacing allows and if service temperatures are expected to be less than 250 degrees, a smooth coating of vinyl tape should also be placed between surfaces.
[Ref: General Handbook H-8083-30A-ATB, Chapter 08 Page 20]

8-29 Answer B.
Chromic Acid Inhibitor is a 10 percent solution by weight of chromic acid, activated by a small amount of sulfuric acid, and is particularly effective in treating exposed or corroded aluminum surfaces. It may also be used to treat corroded magnesium.
[Ref: General Handbook H-8083-30A-ATB, Chapter 08 Page 23]

8-27 Answer C.
Alodizing is a simple chemical treatment for all aluminum alloys to increase their corrosion resistance and to improve their paint bonding qualities.
[Ref: General Handbook H-8083-30A-ATB, Chapter 08 Page 22]

8-30 Answer B.
Before applying soap and water to plastic surfaces, flush the surfaces with fresh water to dissolve salt deposits and wash away dust particles. Plastic surfaces should be washed with soap and water, preferably by hand.
[Ref: General Handbook H-8083-30A-ATB, Chapter 08 Page 24]

8-31 AMG012
What should be done to prevent rapid deterioration when oil or grease come in contact with a tire?
A. Wipe the tire thoroughly with a dry cloth and then rinse with clean water.
B. Wipe the tire with a dry cloth followed by a washdown and rinse with soap and water.
C. Wipe the tire with a cloth dampened with aromatic naptha and then wipe dry with a clean cloth.

8-32 AMG012
When aircraft are being cleaned, which of the following safety precautions should be observed?
1. Place type ABC fire extinguishers with a booster line at each aircraft entrance.
2. Move aircraft outside if flammable liquids are used.
3. Turn off all interior electrical devices and switches.
A. All of the above
B. #2 and #3
C. #1 and #3

8-33 AMG012
Which cleaning substance is acceptable to use on oxygen system equipment?
A. Stoddard solvent
B. Methylethylketone (MEK)
C. Ethyl alcohol

8-34 AMG012
Select the solvent used to clean acrylics and rubber.
A. Aliphatic naptha
B. Methyl ethyl ketone
C. Aromatic naptha

8-35 AMG012
What is the primary disadvantage of using kerosene as a solvent?
A. It is has a low temperature flashpoint.
B. It leaves a residue which must be further cleaned with other solvents.
C. It evaporates quickly.

8-36 AMG012
Fayed surfaces cause concern in chemical cleaning because of the danger of
A. forming passive oxides.
B. entrapping corrosive materials.
C. corrosion by imbedded iron oxide.

AIRCRAFT CLEANING AND CORROSION CONTROL

ANSWERS

8-31 Answer B.
Wipe the tire with a dry cloth followed by a washdown and rinse with soap and water Surface oil, hydraulic fluid, grease, or fuel can be removed from aircraft tires by washing with a mild soap solution. After cleaning, lubricate all grease fittings, hinges, and so forth, where removal, contamination, or dilution of the grease is suspected during washing of the aircraft.
[Ref: General Handbook H-8083-30A-ATB, Chapter 08 Page 24]

8-34 Answer A.
Aliphatic Naptha can also be used for cleaning acrylics and rubber. However, because it has a low flashpoint (80 degrees), it must be used with care. Aliphatic naphtha is also recommended for wipe down of cleaned surfaces just before painting. Do not confuse this with aromatic naptha which is toxic and attacks rubber and acrylic products.
[Ref: General Handbook H-8083-30A-ATB, Chapter 08 Page 28]

8-32 Answer A.
All of these safety precautions should be observed, as appropriate, when cleaning aircraft. Again, always remember to follow published procedures.
[Ref: General Handbook H-8083-30A-ATB, Chapter 08 Page 26]

8-35 Answer B.
Kerosene does not evaporate as rapidly as dry cleaning solvent and generally leaves an appreciable film on cleaned surfaces, which may actually be corrosive. Kerosene film may be removed with safety solvent, water emulsion cleaners, or detergent mixtures.
[Ref: General Handbook H-8083-30A-ATB, Chapter 08 Page 28]

8-33 Answer C.
Only Anhydrous cleaning agents, such as ethyl alcohol, should be used to clean oxygen equipment. MEK vapor is a toxic compound which should not be breathed. Stoddard solvent and other petroleum based agents will leave an oily residue on the equipment.
[Ref: General Handbook H-8083-30A-ATB, Chapter 08 Page 28]

8-36 Answer B.
The danger of entrapping corrosive materials in faying surfaces and crevices counteracts any advantages in their speed and effectiveness.
[Ref: General Handbook H-8083-30A-ATB, Chapter 08 Page 29]

ORAL EXAM

8-1(O).   List the three methods of cleaning an aircraft exterior.

8-2(O).   Wet washing can remove accumulated dirt, oil, grease, and carbon deposits. What does it not remove?

8-3(O).   When would a dry wash be accomplished on an aircraft and what does it clean or remove?

8-4(O).   When would you polish an aircraft and what are the benefits.

8-5(O).   Why is keeping the interior of an aircraft just as important as maintaining a clean exterior?

8-6(O).   How can the accumulation of dirt and grease affect an air-cooled engine?

8-7(O).   Define metal corrosion.

8-8(O).   What are the two general classifications of corrosion?

8-9(O).   Name the five forms of corrosion.

8-10(O).   Define intergranular corrosion.

8-11(O).   Define fretting corrosion.

8-12(O).   Define stress corrosion.

8-13(O).   What form of corrosion is exfoliation and how would you describe its appearance?

8-14(O)   What is ferrous oxide?

8-15(O).   Explain the corrosion process.

8-16(O).   Name the areas of an aircraft that are prone to corrosion.

8-17(O).   Name the preventive maintenance steps that can be taken to reduce the effects caused by corrosion.

8-18(O).   Name the various components for a complete corrosion treatment (removal) program.

AIRCRAFT CLEANING AND CORROSION CONTROL

ANSWERS

ORAL EXAM

8-1(O).   Wet wash, dry wash, and polishing.
            [Ref: General Handbook H-8083-30A-ATB, Chapter 08 Page 19]

8-2(O).   Corrosion and oxide films.
            [Ref: General Handbook H-8083-30A-ATB, Chapter 08 Page 20]

8-3(O).   When the use of liquids is neither desirable nor practical and removes film, dust, and small accumulations of
            dirt and soil.
            [Ref: General Handbook H-8083-30A-ATB, Chapter 08 Page 20]

8-4(O).   Polishing is usually performed after surfaces have been cleaned. It restores luster to painted and unpainted
            surfaces of the aircraft. It is also used to remove oxidation and corrosion.
            [Ref: General Handbook H-8083-30A-ATB, Chapter 08 Page 20]

8-5(O).   Corrosion can establish itself on the inside structure to a greater degree because it is difficult to reach
            some areas for cleaning. Nuts, bolts, bits of wire, or other metal objects carelessly dropped and neglected,
            combined with moisture and dissimilar metal contact, can cause electrolytic corrosion.
            [Ref: General Handbook H-8083-30A-ATB, Chapter 08 Page 20]

8-6(O).   They provide an effective insulation against the cooling effect of air flowing over it. Such an accumulation can
            also cover up cracks or other defects.
            [Ref: General Handbook H-8083-30A-ATB, Chapter 08 Page 23]

8-7(O).   The deterioration of the metal by chemical or electrochemical attack that can occur internally as well as on the
            surface of the metal changing the smooth surface, weakening the interior, or damaging or loosening adjacent parts.
            [Ref: General Handbook H-8083-30A-ATB, Chapter 08 Page 1]

8-8(O).   Direct chemical attack and electrochemical attack.
            [Ref: General Handbook H-8083-30A-ATB, Chapter 08 Page 2]

8-9(O).   Surface, dissimilar metal, intergranular, stress, and fretting.
            [Ref: General Handbook H-8083-30A-ATB, Chapter 08 Page 4-6]

8-10(O).   Corrosion that attacks along the grain boundaries of an alloy and is commonly the results of a lack of
            uniformity caused by changes that occur in the alloy during heating and cooling during the material's
            manufacturing process.
            [Ref: General Handbook H-8083-30A-ATB, Chapter 08 Page 5]

PRACTICAL EXAM

8-1(P).   Given various samples, either actual or pictorial, identify the type of corrosion and describe the correct procedure for removing the corrosion and treating the damaged area to prevent further corrosion.

8-2(P).   Given a specific aircraft or mockup and the manufacturer's instructions, select the proper cleaning materials and remove grease that has been spilled on an aircraft tire.

8-3(P).   Given a specific aircraft or mockup and the manufacturer's instructions, select the proper cleaning material and clean a transparent plastic cockpit enclosure or windshield.

8-4(P).   Given a piece of metal commonly used on aircraft, remove any corrosion present and treat the metal to prevent further corrosion.

AIRCRAFT CLEANING AND CORROSION CONTROL

ORAL EXAM

8-11(O). Corrosion that occurs when two mating surfaces, normally at rest with respect to one another, are subject to slight relative motion.
[Ref: General Handbook H-8083-30A-ATB, Chapter 08 Page 6]

8-12(O). Corrosion that occurs by combined effect of sustained tensile stresses and a corrosive environment. *[Ref: General Handbook H-8083-30A-ATB, Chapter 08 Page 6]*

8-13(O). Exfoliation is a very severe form of intergranular corrosion and can cause lifting or flaking of the metal at the surface due to delamination of the grain boundaries caused by the pressure of corrosion residual product buildup.
[Ref: General Handbook H-8083-30A-ATB, Chapter 08 Page 5]

8-14(O). A type of surface corrosion, commonly referred to as rust, which is the result of atmospheric oxidation on the surface of steel.
[Ref: General Handbook H-8083-30A-ATB, Chapter 08 Page 11]

8-15(O). The corrosion process involves two simultaneous changes: The metal that is attacked or oxidized suffers what may be called anodic change, and the corrosive agent undergoes cathodic change.
[Ref: General Handbook H-8083-30A-ATB, Chapter 08 Page 2]

8-16(O). Exhaust trail areas, battery compartments and vent openings, bilge areas on float aircraft, wheel well and landing gear, water entrapment areas, engine frontal areas and cooling air vents, wing flap and spoiler recesses, external skin areas, helicopter rotor heads and gear boxes, and control cables.
[Ref: General Handbook H-8083-30A-ATB, Chapter 08 Page 8-10]

8-17(O).
1. Adequate cleaning
2. Thorough periodic lubrication
3. Detailed inspection for corrosion and failure of protective systems
4. Prompt treatment of corrosion and touchup of damaged paint areas
5. Keeping drain holes free of obstructions
6. Daily draining of fuel cell sumps
7. Daily wipe down of exposed critical areas
8. Sealing of aircraft against water during foul weather and proper ventilation on warm, sunny days
9. Maximum use of protective covers on parked aircraft.
[Ref: General Handbook H-8083-30A-ATB, Chapter 08 Page 7-8]

8-18(O).
1. Cleaning and stripping of the corroded area,
2. Removing as much of the corrosion products as practicable,
3. Neutralizing any residual materials remaining in pits and crevices,
4. Restoring protective surface films, and
5. Applying temporary or permanent coatings or paint finishes.
[Ref: General Handbook H-8083-30A-ATB, Chapter 08 Page 10]

FLUID LINES AND FITTINGS

Rigid Fluid Lines, Tube Bending, Flexible Hose Fluid Lines, Hose Clamps, and Flexible Hose Inspection

CHAPTER
09

QUESTIONS

9-1 AMG037
Which tubings have the characteristics of high strength and abrasion resistance, necessary for use in a high-pressure (3,000 PSI) hydraulic system for operation of landing gear and flaps?
- A. Aluminum alloy (2024-T or 5052-0)
- B. Corrosion-resistant steel (annealed CRES 304, CRE 321 or CRES 304-1/8-hard
- C. Aluminum alloy (1100-1/2H or 3003-1/2H

9-2 AMG037
Metal tubing fluid lines are sized by wall thickness and
- A. outside diameter in 1/16 inch increments.
- B. inside diameter in 1/16 inch increments.
- C. outside diameter in 1/32 inch increments.

9-3 AMG037
The material specifications for a certain aircraft require that a replacement oil line be fabricated from 3/4-inch 0.072 5052-0 aluminum alloy tubing. What is the inside dimension of this tubing?
- A. 0.606 inch
- B. 0.688 inch
- C. 0.750 inch

9-4 AMG037
The best tool for cutting aluminum tubing, or any tubing of moderately soft metal, is a
- A. hand operated wheel-type tubing cutter.
- B. fine-tooth hacksaw.
- C. circular-saw equipped with an abrasive cutting wheel.

9-5 AMG037
What is the advantage of using a fine tooth saw instead of a tube cutter when cutting rigid tubing?
- A. Decreases work hardening of the tube material.
- B. Reduces burrs inside of the tube in the cut area.
- C. A more precise cut resulting in a cleaner flaring operation.

9-6 AMG037
Which statement is true regarding flattening of tubing in bends?
- A. Flattening by a maximum of 20 percent of the original diameter is permissible.
- B. Flattening by not more than 25 percent of the original diameter is permissible.
- C. The small diameter portion in the bend cannot exceed more than 75 percent of the diameter of straight tubing

FLUID LINES AND FITTINGS

ANSWERS

9-1 Answer B.
Corrosion resistant steel tubing, annealed CRES 304, CRES 321 or CRES 304-1/8-hard, are used extensively in high pressure hydraulic systems (3,000 psi or more) for the operation of landing gear, flaps, brakes, and in fire zones.
[Ref: General Handbook H-8083-30A-ATB, Chapter 09 Page 2]

9-2 Answer A.
Rigid metal tubing is sized by outside diameter (o.d.) in 1/16" (.625") increments. Flexible fuel lines are sized by 1/16 inside diameter. No fluid lines are sized in 1/32" measurements.
[Ref: General Handbook H-8083-30A-ATB, Chapter 09 Page 2]

9-3 Answer A.
The wall thickness is typically printed on the tubing in thousands of an inch. To determine the inside diameter (i.d.) of the tube, subtract twice the wall thickness from the outside diameter.
Convert 3/4" to decimal = .75, then subtract the wall thickness 2(.072) = .144 to get 0.606 (.75-.144).
[Ref: General Handbook H-8083-30A-ATB, Chapter 09 Page 2]

9-4 Answer A.
Tubing may be cut with a tube cutter or a hacksaw. The cutter can be used with any soft metal tubing, such as copper, aluminum, or aluminum alloy.
[Ref: General Handbook H-8083-30A-ATB, Chapter 09 Page 3]

9-5 Answer A.
Use of a fine tooth saw (32 teeth per inch or more) reduces work hardening of the metal tubing, particularly when the tube is of a harder metal. However, be careful not to let the saw slip and damage the metal.
[Ref: General Handbook H-8083-30A-ATB, Chapter 09 Page 3]

9-6 Answer B.
A small amount of flattening in a bend is acceptable, but the small diameter of the flattened portion must not be less than 75% of the original outside diameter.
[Ref: General Handbook H-8083-30A-ATB, Chapter 09 Page 4]

9-7 AMG037
When bending metal tubing, what is the maximum amount of flattening permissible in the bend area of the tube?
- A. Flattened portion diameter not less than 75% of the original tube diameter
- B. Flattened portion diameter not less than 50% of the original tube diameter
- C. Flattened portion diameter not less than 2/3rds the original tube diameter

9-8 AMG036
Which is the proper flare type when fitting 3/8" OD aluminum tube with AN fittings?
- A. 37 degree double flare.
- B. 37 degree single flare.
- C. 45 degree double flare.

9-9 AMG036
Which is NOT considered an advantage of double flaring?
- A. A double flare is more resistant to shearing under stress.
- B. A double flare is smoother and seals better.
- C. A double flare is recommended for hard metal tubing when cracking may occur.

9-10 AMG036
Flexible hose used in aircraft systems is classified in size according to the
- A. outside diameter.
- B. wall thickness.
- C. inside diameter.

9-11 AMG037
Which statement is true regarding the variety of symbols utilized on the identifying color-code bands currently used on aircraft plumbing lines?
- A. Symbols are composed of various single colors according to line content.
- B. Symbols are always black against a white background regardless of line content.
- C. Symbols are composed of one to three contrasting colors according to line content.

9-12 AMG037
A gas or fluid line marked with the letters PHDAN is
- A. a dual-purpose pneumatic and/or hydraulic line for normal and emergency system use.
- B. used to carry physically dangerous materials.
- C. a pneumatic or hydraulic system drain or discharge line.

FLUID LINES AND FITTINGS

ANSWERS

9-7 Answer A.
A small amount of flattening in bends is acceptable, but the small diameter of the flattened portion must not be less than 75% of the original outside diameter.
[Ref: General Handbook H-8083-30A-ATB, Chapter 09 Page 4]

9-8 Answer A.
The flaring tool used for aircraft tubing has male and female dies ground to produce a flare of 35° to 37°. 45° is an automotive setting and should never be used on aircraft.
[Ref: General Handbook H-8083-30A-ATB, Chapter 09 Page 5]

9-9 Answer C.
A double flare folds the tube in on itself and forms an accurate flare without cracking or splitting. Double flaring is recommended with soft tubing materials on rigid tubing less than 3/8" outside diameter. When used, a double flare provides a smoother bearing surface and is less likely to form leaks. It is also more resistant to the shearing effect of torque.
[Ref: General Handbook H-8083-30A-ATB, Chapter 09 Page 6]

9-10 Answer C.
The inside diameter of the fitting is the same as the inside diameter of the hose to which it is attached.
[Ref: General Handbook H-8083-30A-ATB, Chapter 09 Page 7]

9-11 Answer B.
Identification tags are produced in two sections. The text section states the fluid in the line, and the symbol section provides a universally understood geometric symbol in black over a white background.
[Ref: General Handbook H-8083-30A-ATB, Chapter 09 Page 8]

9-12 AnswerB.
Lines containing physically dangerous materials, such as oxygen, nitrogen, or Freon™, may be marked PHDAN.
[Ref: General Handbook H-8083-30A-ATB, Chapter 09 Page 8]

9-13 AMG037
If a standard AN flared fitting is colored black, what material is in made of?
- A. Aluminum.
- B. Bronze.
- C. Steel.

9-16 AMG036
What is the procedure to remove a damaged Cryofit fitting?
- A. Apply heat directly to the fitting until the fitting slides off the tube.
- B. Cool the fitting with liquid nitrogen until the fitting slides off the tube.
- C. Cut it off at the sleeve and replace with a swaged fitting.

9-14 AMG036
When is a flareless fitting preferable over a flared fitting?
- A. In high pressure systems subjected to constant vibration and stress.
- B. When the fitting is subject to routine disconnection for service.
- C. When the hardness or brittleness of the rigid tubing would likely crack during the flaring process.

9-17 AMG037
Cryofit fittings are often used on transport category aircraft
- A. for high pressure fuel lines.
- B. when routine disconnections are not required.
- C. when the fluid lines will be subject to extremely cold temperatures.

9-15 AMG036
Which coupling nut should be selected for use with 1/2 inch aluminum oil lines to be assembled using flared tube ends and standard AN nuts,sleeves,and fittings?
- A. AN-818-5
- B. AN-818-16
- C. AN-818-8

9-18 AMG036
Which statement(s) about military standard (MS) flareless fittings is/are correct?
1. During installation, MS flareless fittings are normally tightened by turning the nut a specified amount, rather than being torqued.
2. New MS flareless tubing/fittings should be assembled clean and dry without lubrication.
3. During installation, MS flareless fittings are normally tightened by applying a specified torque to the nut.
- A. 1
- B. 1 and 2
- C. 3

FLUID LINES AND FITTINGS

ANSWERS

9-13 Answer C.
Aluminum fittings are blue, black fittings are steel, and cadmium plated bronze fittings are left a natural color. Care should be taken to use the same fitting material as the tubing to prevent dissimilar metal corrosion.
[Ref: General Handbook H-8083-30A-ATB, Chapter 09 Page 10]

9-16 Answer C.
Cryofit fittings can only be removed by cutting the tube at the sleeve and replacing it with a swaged fitting; assuming enough room remains on the line for proper routing. If insufficient line length remains, the entire line must be replaced.
[Ref: General Handbook H-8083-30A-ATB, Chapter 09 Page 11-14]

9-14 Answer A.
Flareless fittings are designed primarily for high pressure (3000 psi) hydraulic systems subject to severe vibration and fluctuating pressure.
[Ref: General Handbook H-8083-30A-ATB, Chapter 09 Page 12]

9-17 Answer B.
Many transport category aircraft use Cryofit fittings to join hydraulic lines in areas where routine disconnections are not required.
[Ref: General Handbook H-8083-30A-ATB, Chapter 09 Page 14]

9-15 Answer C.
The last dash in the designation for AN nuts is measured in 1/16-inch increments. Eight sixteenths is equal to one-half, therefore, the coupling nut that should be chosen is AN-818-8.
[Ref: General Handbook H-8083-30A-ATB, Chapter 09 Page 11]

9-18 Answer A.
Tighten the nut by hand until an increase in resistance to turning is encountered. Should it be impossible to run the nut down with the fingers, use a wrench, but be alert for the first signs of bottoming. It is important that the final tightening commence at the point where the nut just begins to bottom. Use a wrench and turn the nut one-sixth turn (one flat on a hex nut). Use a wrench on the connector to prevent it from turning while tightening the nut. After the tube assembly is installed, the system should be pressure tested. It is permissible to tighten the nut an additional one-sixth turn (making a total of one-third turn), should a connection leak.
[Ref: General Handbook H-8083-30A-ATB, Chapter 09 Page 15]

9-19 AMG036
When joining and torquing flared tubes and fittings
- A. apply sealing compound between the fitting and flare.
- B. apply lubricant between the fitting and flare.
- C. assure the connection is clean and dry.

9-20 AMG037
Hydraulic tubing, which is damaged in a localized area to such an extent that repair is necessary, may be repaired
- A. by cutting out the damaged area and utilizing a swaged tube fitting to join the tube ends.
- B. only by replacing the tubing section run (connection to connection) using the same size and material as the original.
- C. by cutting out the damaged section and soldering in a replacement section of tubing.

9-21 AMG036
Scratches or nicks on the straight portion of aluminum alloy tubing may be repaired if they are no deeper than
- A. 20 percent of the wall thickness.
- B. 1/32 inch or 20 percent of wall thickness, whichever is less.
- C. 10 percent of the wall thickness.

9-22 AMG036
A scratch or nick in aluminum tubing can be repaired, provided it does not
- A. appear in the heel of a bend.
- B. appear on the inside of a bend.
- C. exceed 10 percent of the tube OD on a straight section.

9-23 AMG036
Which maintenance record entry best describes the action taken for a 0.125-inch deep dent in a straight section of 1/2-inch aluminum alloy tubing?
- A. Dented section removed and replaced with identical new tubing flared to 45 degrees.
- B. Dent within acceptable limits, repair not necessary.
- C. Dented section removed and replaced with identical new tubing flared to 37 degrees.

9-24 AMG036
Which of the following defects are NOT acceptable for metal lines?
1. Cracked flare.
2. Seams.
3. Dents in the heel of a bend less than 20 percent of tube diameter.
4. Scratches/nicks on the inside of a bend less than 10 percent of wall thickness.
5. Dents in straight sections that are 20 percent of wall thickness.
- A. 1, 2, 3, 4, and 5
- B. 1, 2, and 3
- C. 1, 2, 3, and 5

FLUID LINES AND FITTINGS

ANSWERS

9-19 Answer C.
Never apply material to the faces of the fitting and flare as this destroys the metal to metal contact which is necessary to ensure a fluid proof seal.
[Ref: General Handbook H-8083-30A-ATB, Chapter 09 Page 15-16]

9-22 Answer A.
Scratches or nicks not deeper than 10 percent of the wall thickness in aluminum alloy tubing, which are not in the heel of a bend, may be repaired by burnishing with hand tools.
[Ref: General Handbook H-8083-30A-ATB, Chapter 09 Page 16]

9-20 Answer A.
A severely damaged line should be replaced. However, the line may be repaired by cutting out the damaged section and inserting a tube section of the same size and material. Flare both ends of the undamaged and replacement tube sections and make the connection by using standard unions, sleeves, and tube nuts. Aluminum 6061-T6, corrosion resistant steel 304-1/8h and Titanium 3AL-2.5V tubing can be repaired by swaged fittings.
[Ref: General Handbook H-8083-30A-ATB, Chapter 09 Page 16]

9-23 Answer C.
Ten percent of 0.5 is .05, the dent is greater than the allowable 10% and therefore the tubing must be replaced. Standard tube flares are 37°.
[Ref: General Handbook H-8083-30A-ATB, Chapter 09 Page 5-16]

9-21 Answer C.
Scratches or nicks not deeper than 10 percent of the wall thickness in aluminum alloy tubing, which are not in the heel of a bend, may be repaired by burnishing with hand tools.
[Ref: General Handbook H-8083-30A-ATB, Chapter 09 Page 16]

9-24 Answer C.
When installing or inspecting metal tubing the following defects are not allowed:
- Flare distorted into nut threads
- Sleeve cracked
- Flare cracked or split
- Flare out of round
- Inside of flare rough or scratched
- Threads of nut or union dirty, damaged, or broken
- Scratches or nicks deeper than 10 percent of the wall thickness
- Severe die marks, seams, or splits in the tube
- Dents greater than 20 percent of the tube diameter in the heel of a bend.

[Ref: General Handbook H-8083-30A-ATB, Chapter 09 Page 16]

9-25 AMG036

In a metal tubing installation;
- A. rigid straight line runs are preferable.
- B. tension is undesirable because pressurization will cause it to expand and shift.
- C. a tube may be pulled in line if the nut will start on the threaded coupling.

9-26 AMG036

The primary purpose of providing suitable bends in fluid and pneumatic metal tubing runs is to
- A. clear obstacles and make turns in aircraft structures.
- B. provide for access within aircraft structures.
- C. prevent excessive stress on the tubing.

9-27 AMG036

Which of the following hose materials are compatible with phosphate-ester base hydraulic fluids?
1. Butyl
2. Teflon
3. Buna-N
4. Neoprene
- A. 1 and 2
- B. 2 and 4
- C. 1 and 3

9-28 AMG036

Which of the following can be identified by the letters and numbers printed on aircraft hydraulic hose?
- A. The recommended expiration date.
- B. The hose size.
- C. Its compatible fluid types.

9-29 AMG036

Which is NOT an advantage of a Teflon hose?
1. An almost limitless shelf life.
2. Less resistance to viscous fluids.
3. May be used in very cold to very hot conditions.
4. Compatible will nearly all substances and fluids.
5. May be preformed to clear obstruction.
- A. 3, 4, and 5
- B. 1, 2, and 3
- C. All the above are advantages

9-30 AMG036

The term "cold flow" is generally associated with
- A. the effects of low temperature gasses or liquids flowing in the hose or tubing.
- B. impressions left in natural or synthetic rubber hose material.
- C. flexibility characteristics of various hose materials at low ambient temperatures.

FLUID LINES AND FITTINGS

ANSWERS

9-25 Answer B.
If the tube must be machine formed, definite bends must be made to avoid a straight assembly. Bends are also necessary to permit the tubing to expand or contract under temperature changes and to absorb vibration. In all cases, the new tube assembly should be formed prior to installation so it will not be necessary to pull or deflect the assembly into alignment by means of the coupling nuts.
[Ref: General Handbook H-8083-30A-ATB, Chapter 09 Page 15-16]

9-26 Answer C.
Bends are necessary to permit the tubing to expand or contract under temperature changes and to absorb vibration, which cause stress on the tubing.
[Ref: General Handbook H-8083-30A-ATB, Chapter 09 Page 16]

9-27 Answer A.
Butyl is a synthetic rubber compound made from petroleum raw materials. It is an excellent material to use with phosphate ester base hydraulic fluid (Skydrol). Do not use with petroleum products. Teflon™ is the DuPont trade name for tetrafluoroethylene resin. It has a broad operating temperature range (–65 °F to +450 °F). It is compatible with nearly every substance or agent used. Teflon™ hose is unaffected by any known fuel, petroleum, or synthetic based oils, alcohol, coolants, or solvents commonly used in aircraft. Buna-N and Neoprene are synthetic rubber and are resistant to petroleum based products but not phosphate ester base hydraulic fluid (Skydrol).
[Ref: General Handbook H-8083-30A-ATB, Chapter 09 Page 18]

9-28 Answer B.
Hydraulic hose is marked every 9 inches of length to identify its MIL type, its size, the quarter and year of manufacture, and a 5 digit code to identify its manufacturer.
[Ref: General Handbook H-8083-30A-ATB, Chapter 09 Page 19]

9-29 Answer C.
Teflon hoses typically come preformed and are braided with stainless steel wire for strength and protection. They offer all of the advantages listed above.
[Ref: General Handbook H-8083-30A-ATB, Chapter 09 Page 18]

9-30 Answer B.
The term "cold flow" describes the deep, permanent impressions in the hose produced by the pressure of hose clamps or supports.
[Ref: General Handbook H-8083-30A-ATB, Chapter 09 Page 19]

9-31 AMG037
Flexible fluid lines must be installed with?
  A. enough slack to allow maximum flexing during operation.
  B. slack equal to approximately 5% of their length.
  C. snuggly around its path to prevent entanglement with other lines or components.

9-32 AMG037
The maximum distance between end fittings to which a straight hose assembly is to be connected is 50 inches. The minimum hose length to make such a connection should be
  A. 54 1/2 inches.
  B. 51 inches.
  C. 52 1/2 inches.

9-33 AMG037
A certain amount of slack must be left in a flexible hose during installation because, when under pressure, it
  A. Expands in length and diameter.
  B. expands in length and contracts in diameter.
  C. contracts in length and expands in diameter

9-34 AMG036
When installing bonded clamps to support metal tubing;
  A. paint removal from tube is not recommended as it will increase corrosion.
  B. repaint clamp and tube after clamp installation to prevent corrosion.
  C. remove paint or anodizing from tube at clamp location.

9-35 AMG036
Which of the below statements is/are true?
  1. Bonded clamps are used for support when installing metal tubing.
  2. Unbonded clamps are used for support when installing wiring.
  A. Only #1 is true.
  B. Both #1 and #2 are true.
  C. Only #2 is true.

FLUID LINES AND FITTINGS

ANSWERS

9-31 Answer B.
Hose assemblies must not be installed in a manner that will cause a mechanical load on the hose. When installing flexible hose, provide slack or bend in the hose line from 5 to 8 percent of its total length to provide for changes in length that will occur when pressure is applied.
[Ref: General Handbook H-8083-30A-ATB, Chapter 09 Page 29]

9-32 Answer C.
Hose assemblies must not be installed in a manner that will cause a mechanical load on the hose. When installing flexible hose, provide slack or bend in the hose line from 5 to 8 percent of its total length to provide for changes in length that will occur when pressure is applied.
5% of 50 = 2.5
therefore, 50 inches + 2.5 inches = 52.5 inches.
[Ref: General Handbook H-8083-30A-ATB, Chapter 09 Page 20]

9-33 Answer C.
Flexible hose contracts in length and expands in diameter when pressurized.
[Ref: General Handbook H-8083-30A-ATB, Chapter 09 Page 20]

9-34 Answer C.
Bonded clamps are used to secure rigid fluid lines from electrical buildup. Thus, any paint or anodizing on that portion of the tube must be removed to provide an adequate electrical contact.
[Ref: General Handbook H-8083-30A-ATB, Chapter 09 Page 23]

9-35 Answer B.
Use bonded clamps to secure metal hydraulic, fuel, or oil lines in place. Unbonded clamps should be used only for securing wiring.
[Ref: General Handbook H-8083-30A-ATB, Chapter 09 Page 23]

ORAL EXAM

9-1(O).   What are the three most common types of metals used for rigid fluid line fabrication in aviation?

9-2(O).   Which metal is used for low to medium pressure hydraulic and pneumatic systems?

9-3(O).   Which metals are best suited for high-pressure hydraulic systems?

9-4(O).   How is metal tubing fluid line sized?

9-5(O).   Name at least three synthetic materials commonly used in the manufacture of flexible hose.

9-6(O).   Which synthetic rubber hosing is best for use with fuel?

9-7(O).   Which synthetic rubber hosing is best for use with phosphate ester base hydraulic fluid (Skydrol)?

9-8(O).   How do you determine the correct sizing for flexible hose?

9-9(O).   What is the color of an AN steel flared-tube fitting?

9-10(O).   What is an advantage of a double flare on aluminum tubing?

9-11(O).   How much slack must flexible lines have when installed?

9-12(O).   Why must a pressurized flexible hose be installed with slack?

9-13(O).   Why should you never overtighten a flareless tube fitting?

ANSWERS

ORAL EXAM

9-1(O).   Aluminum alloy, steel, and titanium.
            [Ref: General Handbook H-8083-30A-ATB, Chapter 09 Page 2]

9-2(O).   Aluminum alloy tubing.
            [Ref: General Handbook H-8083-30A-ATB, Chapter 09 Page 2]

9-3(O).   Corrosion resistant steel and titanium.
            [Ref: General Handbook H-8083-30A-ATB, Chapter 09 Page 2]

9-4(O).   Metal tubing is sized by outside diameter (o.d.), which is measured fractionally in sixteenths of an inch.
            [Ref: General Handbook H-8083-30A-ATB, Chapter 09 Page 2]

9-5(O).   Buna-N, neoprene, butyl, ethylene propylene diene rubber (EPDM) and Teflon™. While Teflon™ is in a category
            of its own, the others are synthetic rubber.
            [Ref: General Handbook H-8083-30A-ATB, Chapter 09 Page 17]

9-6(O).   Buna-N
            [Ref: General Handbook H-8083-30A-ATB, Chapter 09 Page 18]

9-7(O).   Butyl
            [Ref: General Handbook H-8083-30A-ATB, Chapter 09 Page 18]

9-8(O).   By a dash number, stenciled on the side of the hose, indicating the size of tubing with which it is compatible.
            When the dash number of the hose corresponds with the dash number of the tubing, the proper size hose is
            being used.
            [Ref: General Handbook H-8083-30A-ATB, Chapter 09 Page 19]

9-9(O).   All AN steel fittings are colored black.
            [Ref: General Handbook H-8083-30A-ATB, Chapter 09 Page 10]

9-10(O).   A double flare is smoother and more concentric than a single flare and therefore seals better. It is also more
            resistant to the shearing effect of torque.
            [Ref: General Handbook H-8083-30A-ATB, Chapter 09 Page 6]

9-11(O).   When installing flexible hose, provide slack or bend in the hose line from 5 to 8 percent of its length.
            [Ref: General Handbook H-8083-30A-ATB, Chapter 09 Page 20]

9-12(O).   Flexible hose contracts in length and expands in diameter when pressurized.
            [Ref: General Handbook H-8083-30A-ATB, Chapter 09 Page 20]

9-13(O).   Flareless tube fittings should never be overtightened as this may cause permanent damage to the sleeve
            and nut.
            [Ref: General Handbook H-8083-30A-ATB, Chapter 09 Page 15]

PRACTICAL EXAM

9-1(P). Given the appropriate materials and specifications, fabricate a rigid line to include tube fittings, bends, and tube flaring.

9-2(P). Given the appropriate materials and specifications, fabricate a flexible line with replaceable fittings on at least one end.

9-3(P). Given a section of rigid and/or flexible lines, inspect for and identify any defects.

9-4(P). Given an aircraft or mockup, remove and install a rigid and/or flexible line.

9-5(P). Given an aircraft or mockup, inspect an installed flexible and/or rigid line for correct installation. Write up any discrepancies found.

9-6(P). Given the appropriate materials and specifications, assemble a flareless fitting tube connection.

9-7(P). Given an aircraft or mockup, repair a damaged rigid line per industry standards.

9-8(P). Identify various sizes and types of aircraft fittings.

9-9(P). Given an aircraft or mockup, secure a rigid line using clamps per industry standards.

9-10(P). Given an aircraft or mockup, identify various fluid and/or air lines installed.

PAGE LEFT BLANK INTENTIONALLY

INSPECTION CONCEPTS AND TECHNIQUES

Preparation, Logs and Checklists, Publications, Required Inspections, Special Inspections, Composite and Weld Inspection, and Tools

10-1 AMG059
What record would indicate an approved return to service following a completed annual or 100 hour inspection?
   A. Airworthiness certificate
   B. Aircraft maintenance manual
   C. Aircraft log book

10-2 AMG062
Which publication would describe work required to correct an unsafe condition discovered in the design of an aircraft?
   A. Structural repair manual
   B. Manufacturer's maintenance manual
   C. Airworthiness directive

10-3 AMG097
An aircraft was not approved for return to service after an annual inspection and the owner wanted to fly the aircraft to another maintenance base. Which statement is correct?
   A. The owner must obtain a special flight permit.
   B. The owner may fly without restriction up to 10 hours.
   C. The owner may fly in the restricted category up to 10 hours.

10-4 AMG097
Which piece of information would NOT be found in a Type Certificate Data Sheet?
   A. CG range and datum locations
   B. Frequency and type of inspections required for the aircraft
   C. Control surface movement limitations

10-5 AMG062
The person ultimately responsible for determining whether an aircraft is in an airworthy condition is the
   A. pilot in command.
   B. aircraft's owner.
   C. A&P mechanic who signed off the current annual or 100 hour inspection.

10-6 AMG059
Which inspection schedule plan must be individually approved by an FAA Flight Standard District Office?
   A. 100 hour inspection schedule
   B. Annual inspection schedule
   C. Progressive inspection schedule

INSPECTION CONCEPTS AND TECHNIQUES

ANSWERS

10-1 Answer C.
The aircraft logbook is the register in which all significant events involving the aircraft are recorded including scheduled inspections, AD compliance, service bulletins, major and minor repairs, etc.
[Ref: General Handbook H-8083-30A-ATB, Chapter 10 Page 2]

10-2 Answer C.
Title 14 of the Code of Federal Regulations (14 CFR) Part 39, Airworthiness Directives, defines the authority and responsibility of the Administrator for requiring the necessary corrective action of unsafe conditions that may exist because of a design defect, maintenance, or other causes. The Airworthiness Directives (ADs) are published to notify aircraft owners and other interested persons of unsafe conditions and to prescribe the conditions under which the product may continue to be operated. Airworthiness Directives are Federal Aviation Regulations and must be complied with unless a specific exemption is granted.
[Ref: General Handbook H-8083-30A-ATB, Chapter 10 Page 5]

10-3 Answer A.
According to CFR Part 21, for an aircraft which is overdue on an inspection or maintenance, but deemed safe to operate, a special flight permit may be requested from FAA to transport the aircraft to a preferred repair station.
[Ref: General Handbook H-8083-30A-ATB, Chapter 10 Page 17]

10-4 Answer B.
For determining the overall condition of an aircraft, 14 CFR provides for the inspection of all civil aircraft at specific intervals, depending generally upon the type of operations in which they are engaged. Refer to the CFR for specific inspection requirements and rules for the performance of inspections.
[Ref: General Handbook H-8083-30A-ATB, Chapter 10 Page 12]

10-5 Answer A.
The pilot in command of a civil aircraft is responsible for determining whether that aircraft is in condition for safe flight. Additionally, it is the pilot's responsibility to review the airworthiness certificate, maintenance records, and other required paperwork to verify the aircraft is indeed airworthy.
[Ref: General Handbook H-8083-30A-ATB, Chapter 10 Page 12]

10-6 Answer C.
Each registered owner or operator of an aircraft desiring to use a progressive inspection program must submit a written request to the FAA Flight Standards District Office (FSDO) having jurisdiction over the area in which the applicant is located. Title 14 of the Code of Federal Regulations (14 CFR) part 91, §91.409(d) establishes procedures to be followed for progressive inspections.
[Ref: General Handbook H-8083-30A-ATB, Chapter 10 Page 12]

10-7 AMG088

An aircraft scheduled for a 100 hour inspection has flown 98 hours since the last inspection. It is currently located 4 hours from its primary maintenance facility. What must be done?

A. The inspection must be done at a facility within 2 hours flying time of its present location.

B. A special ferry permit must be obtained from the local FSDO to fly the aircraft beyond its 100 hour term.

C. It is close enough for government. Fly it home and do the inspection at your regular facility

10-8 AMG059

A turbine powered business jet typically undergoes what type of inspection schedule?

A. Progressive Inspections

B. A-D checks

C. 100 hour inspections

10-9 AMG074

An aircraft equipped with an Air Traffic Control transponder must have that transponder checked

A. as part of the normal aircraft inspection schedule.

B. within 24 calendar months of the previous transponder inspection.

C. within 12 calendar months of the previous transponder inspection.

10-10 AMG026

Which of the following ATA systems designation is correct?

A. ATA 21 regards air conditioning; and ATA 32 regards landing gear.

B. ATA 28 regards hydraulic power and ATA 33 regards ice and rain protection.

C. ATA 26 regards oxygen systems; and ATA 49 regards vacuum systems.

10-11 AMG059

An aircraft encountering severe turbulence in flight should undergo a

A. structural inspection before its next operation.

B. structural inspection only if personal injury occurred during the encounter.

C. standard annual, or 100 hour inspection before its next operation.

10-12 AMG059

When an aircraft is struck by lightning in flight, which components are the most likely to suffer damage?

A. Electrically conductive metallic components.

B. Non-electrically conductive composite and plastic components.

C. Aircraft electronic systems.

INSPECTION CONCEPTS AND TECHNIQUES

ANSWERS

10-7 Answer C.
When an aircraft is due for a 100 hour inspection, it may be flown up to 10 hours beyond the 100 hour limit, if necessary, to fly to a destination where the inspection is to be conducted.
[Ref: General Handbook H-8083-30A-ATB, Chapter 10 Page 12]

10-8 Answer B.
Continuous inspection programs are similar to progressive inspection programs, except they apply to large or turbine-powered aircraft and are therefore more complicated and include both routine and detailed inspections. However, the detailed inspections may include different levels of detail. A-checks are the least comprehensive and occur frequently. D-checks, on the other hand, are extremely comprehensive, involving major disassembly, removal, overhaul, and inspection of systems and components. D-checks might occur only three to six times during the service life of an aircraft.
[Ref: General Handbook H-8083-30A-ATB, Chapter 10 Page 12]

10-9 Answer B.
Aircraft having an air traffic control (ATC) transponder must have each transponder checked within the preceding 24 months. These checks must be conducted by appropriately certified individuals.
[Ref: General Handbook H-8083-30A-ATB, Chapter 10 Page 14]

10-10 Answer A.
Answer A is correct. Of the wrong answers; ATA 28 regards fuel systems, ATA 33 regards lights, ATA 26 regards fire protection, and ATA 47 regards auxiliary power systems.
[Ref: General Handbook H-8083-30A-ATB, Chapter 10 Page 15]

10-11 Answer A.
When an aircraft encounters a gust condition, the load on the wings may exceed the normal wing load supporting the aircraft weight. A special inspection should be performed after a flight through severe turbulence.
[Ref: General Handbook H-8083-30A-ATB, Chapter 10 Page 16]

10-12 Answer B.
When surges pass through good electrical conductors, damage is likely to be minimum or non-existent. However, with non-conductive components such as composite cowls, windows, or radomes, burning or more serious damage can occur. Look for burn marks or delamination damage to composite structures.
[Ref: General Handbook H-8083-30A-ATB, Chapter 10 Page 16]

10-13 AMG085
A Rockwell test of affected components would be useful during an inspection of an aircraft subject to _____.
A. a lightening strike.
B. flood damage.
C. fire damage.

10-16 AMG024
Liquid penetrant inspection methods may be used on which of the following?
1. Porous plastics
2. Ferrous metals
3. Nonferrous metals
4. Smooth primer-sealed wood
5. Nonporous plastics
A. 2, 3, and 4
B. 1, 2, and 3
C. 2, 3, and 5

10-14 AMG019
Which of the following methods may be suitable to detect cracks open to the surface in aluminum forgings and castings?
1. Dye or liquid penetrant inspection
2. Magnetic particle inspection
3. Metallic ring (coin tap) inspection
4. Eddy current inspection
5. Ultrasonic inspection
6. Visual inspection
A. 1, 4, 5, and 6
B. 1, 2, 4, 5, and 6
C. 1, 2, 3, 4, 5, and 6

10-17 AMG024
A part which is being prepared for dye penetrant inspection should be cleaned with
A. the prescribed cleaning solvent.
B. the penetrant developer.
C. water-base solvents only.

10-15 AMG024
Detection of a minute crack using dye penetrant inspection usually requires
A. the developer be applied to a flat surface.
B. a longer-than-normal penetrating time.
C. the surface to be highly polished.

10-18 AMG024
If dye penetrant inspection indications are not sharp and clear, the most probable cause is the part
A. was not correctly degaussed before the developer was applied.
B. has no appreciable damage.
C. was not thoroughly washed before the developer was applied.

INSPECTION CONCEPTS AND TECHNIQUES

ANSWERS

10-13 Answer C.
The heat from an onboard fire could affect the hardness ratings of ferrous metal components that have been affected. A Rockwell Hardness test can help determine if they remain airworthy.
[Ref: General Handbook H-8083-30A-ATB, Chapter 10 Page 17]

10-14 Answer A.
Dye or liquid penetrant inspection, eddy current inspection, ultrasonic inspection, and visual inspection are all suitable inspections for detecting cracks open to the surface in both aluminum forgings and castings. Visual inspection can be enhanced by looking at the suspect area with a bright light, a magnifying glass, and a mirror (when required). Some defects might be so obvious that further inspection methods are not required. Penetrant inspection is a nondestructive test for defects open to the surface in parts made of any nonporous material. Eddy current inspection can frequently be performed without removing the surface coatings such as primer, paint, and anodized films. It can be effective in detecting surface and subsurface corrosion, pots and heat treat condition. Ultrasonic detection equipment makes it possible to locate defects in all types of materials. Minute cracks, checks, and voids too small to be seen by x-ray can be located by ultrasonic inspection. Magnetic particle inspection is a method of detecting invisible cracks and other defects in ferromagnetic materials such as iron and steel. It is not applicable to nonmagnetic materials. Tap testing, also referred to as the ring test or coin test, is widely used as a quick evaluation of an accessible surface to detect the presence of delamination or debonding.
[Ref: General Handbook H-8083-30A-ATB, Chapter 10 Page 18]

10-15 Answer B.
When inspecting a component, the smaller the defect, the longer the penetrating time. Fine crack- like apertures require a longer penetrating time than defects such as pores. Be sure to follow the manufacturer's inspection instructions.
[Ref: General Handbook H-8083-30A-ATB, Chapter 10 Page 18-21]

10-16 Answer C.
Liquid penetrant inspection can be used on both ferrous and nonferrous metals, nonporous plastics, ceramics, molded rubber, and glass.
[Ref: General Handbook H-8083-30A-ATB, Chapter 8 Page 19]

10-17 Answer A.
Before performing a penetrant inspection, thoroughly clean the metal surface per the instructions.
[Ref: General Handbook H-8083-30A-ATB, Chapter 10 Page 20]

10-18 Answer C.
The defect must be clean and free of contaminating materials so that the penetrant is free to enter.
[Ref: General Handbook H-8083-30A-ATB, Chapter 10 Page 20]

10-19 AMG024
In performing a dye penetrant inspection, the developer
  A. seeps into a surface crack to indicate the presence of a defect.
  B. acts as a blotter to produce a visible indication.
  C. thoroughly cleans the surface prior to inspection.

10-20 AMG019
What nondestructive testing method requires little or no part preparation, is used to detect surface or near-surface defects in most metals, and may also be used to separate metals or alloys and their heat treat conditions?
  A. Eddy current inspection.
  B. Ultrasonic inspection.
  C. Magnetic particle inspection.

10-21 AMG024
Which non-destructive testing method is typically used to inspect aluminum components subjected to fire or extreme heat?
  A. Liquid penetrant inspection
  B. Eddy current inspection
  C. Ultrasonic inspection

10-22 AMG019
Which is NOT an advantage of the eddy current nondestructive inspection technique?
  A. Can often be performed without removing paint and primer.
  B. Can be used with almost all types of structural material.
  C. Can test a substance for both corrosion and heat treat condition.

10-23 AMG024
Which of these nondestructive testing methods is suitable for the inspection of most metals, plastics, and ceramics for surface and subsurface defects?
  A. Eddy current inspection
  B. Magnetic particle inspection
  C. Ultrasonic inspection

10-24 AMG024
Which type of ultrasonic testing would normally be used to measure the thickness of a material when the backside surface is inaccessible?
  A. Pulse echo
  B. Through transmission
  C. Resonance

INSPECTION CONCEPTS AND TECHNIQUES

ANSWERS

10-19 Answer B.
Visible penetrant-type developer, when applied to the surface of a part, will dry to a smooth, even, white coating. As the developer dries, bright red indications will appear where there are surface defects, acting like a blotter absorbing the penetrant that remained in the defects after removing the penetrant. If no red indications appear, there are no surface defects.
[Ref: General Handbook H-8083-30A-ATB, Chapter 10 Page 20]

10-20 Answer A.
Eddy current inspection can frequently be performed without removing the surface coatings such as primer, paint, and anodized films. It can be effective in detecting surface and subsurface corrosion, pots and heat treat condition.
[Ref: General Handbook H-8083-30A-ATB, Chapter 10 Page 21]

10-21 Answer B.
Inspection of aircraft structures that have been subjected to fire or intense heat can be relatively simple if visible damage is present. Visible damage requires repair or replacement. If there is no visible damage, the structural integrity of an aircraft may still have been compromised. Since most structural metallic components of an aircraft have undergone some sort of heat treatment process during manufacture, an exposure to high heat not encountered during normal operations could severely degrade the design strength of the structure. The strength and airworthiness of an aluminum structure that passes a visual inspection but is still suspect can be further determined by use of a conductivity tester which uses eddy current.
[Ref: General Handbook H-8083-30A-ATB, Chapter 10 Page 7-21]

10-22 Answer B.
Eddy current inspection can frequently be performed without removing the surface coatings such as primer, paint, and anodized films. It can be effective in detecting surface and subsurface corrosion, pots and heat treat condition. However, it can only detect faults in metal structures.
[Ref: General Handbook H-8083-30A-ATB, Chapter 10 Page 21]

10-23 Answer C.
Ultrasonic detection equipment makes it possible to locate defects in all types of materials. Magnetic particle inspection is suitable only with ferrous metals. Eddy current inspection is suitable only with materials that conduct electricity.
[Ref: General Handbook H-8083-30A-ATB, Chapter 10 Page 23-25]

10-24 Answer C.
The resonance method is used principally for thickness measurements when the two sides of the material being tested are smooth and parallel and the backside is inaccessible.
[Ref: General Handbook H-8083-30A-ATB, Chapter 10 Page 26]

10-25 AMG019
What is the purpose of a couplant used during ultrasonic inspections?
- A. Creates a reflective surface.
- B. Creates a sealed interface.
- C. Electrically excite the sonic pulse.

10-26 AMG019
What method of magnetic particle inspection is used most often to inspect aircraft parts for invisible cracks and other defects?
- A. Residual
- B. Inductance
- C. Continuous

10-27 AMG019
The pattern for an inclusion is a magnetic particle buildup forming
- A. a fernlike pattern.
- B. a single line.
- C. parallel lines.

10-28 AMG019
In magnetic particle inspection, a flaw that is perpendicular to the magnetic field flux lines generally causes
- A. a large disruption in the magnetic field.
- B. a minimal disruption in the magnetic field.
- C. no disruption in the magnetic field.

10-29 AMG019
Circular magnetization of a part can be used to detect which defects?
- A. Defects parallel to the long axis of the part.
- B. Defects perpendicular to the long axis of the part.
- C. Defects perpendicular to the concentric circles of magnetic force within the part.

10-30 AMG019
When checking an item with the magnetic particle inspection method, circular and longitudinal magnetization should be used to
- A. reveal all possible defects.
- B. evenly magnetize the entire part.
- C. ensure uniform current flow.

INSPECTION CONCEPTS AND TECHNIQUES

ANSWERS

10-25 Answer B.
Because ultrasonic energy does not travel through air, a layer of couplant is required between the transducer and specimen to fill any voids in between.
[Ref: General Handbook H-8083-30A-ATB, Chapter 10 Page 29]

10-26 Answer C.
The highly critical nature of aircraft parts and assemblies and the necessity for subsurface inspection in many applications have resulted in the continuous method being more widely used. The continuous procedure provides greater sensitivity than the residual procedure, particularly in locating subsurface discontinuities.
[Ref: General Handbook H-8083-30A-ATB, Chapter 10 Page 30]

10-27 Answer C.
Inclusions are foreign material formed by impurities in the metal during the metal processing stages. Inclusions interrupt the continuity of the metal because they prevent the joining or welding of adjacent faces of the metal. Indications of subsurface inclusions are usually broad and fuzzy. They are seldom continuous or of even width and density throughout their length. Larger inclusions, particularly those near or open to the surface, appear more clearly defined. Close examination will generally reveal a lack of definition and consists of several parallel lines rather than a single line. These characteristics will usually distinguish a heavy inclusion from a crack.
[Ref: General Handbook H-8083-30A-ATB, Chapter 10 Page 30]

10-28 Answer A.
To locate a defect in a part, it is essential the magnetic lines of force pass approximately perpendicular to the defect. It is therefore necessary to induce magnetic flux in more than one direction since defects are likely to exist at any angle to the major axis of the part.
[Ref: General Handbook H-8083-30A-ATB, Chapter 10 Page 31]

10-29 Answer A.
Circular magnetization is the induction of a magnetic field consisting of concentric circles of force about and within the part achieved by passing electric current through the part. This type of magnetization will locate defects running approximately parallel to the axis of the part.
[Ref: General Handbook H-8083-30A-ATB, Chapter 10 Page 32]

10-30 Answer A.
To locate a defect in a part, it is essential the magnetic lines of force pass approximately perpendicular to the defect. It is therefore necessary to induce magnetic flux in more than one direction since defects are likely to exist at any angle to the major axis of the part. This requires two separate magnetizing operations, referred to as circular magnetization and longitudinal magnetization.
[Ref: General Handbook H-8083-30A-ATB, Chapter 10 Page 32]

10-31 AMG019
Which type crack can be detected by magnetic particle inspection using either circular or longitudinal magnetization?
- A. 45 degree
- B. Longitudinal
- C. Transverse

10-34 AMG019
Under magnetic particle inspection, a part will be identified as having a fatigue crack under which condition?
- A. The discontinuity pattern is straight.
- B. The discontinuity is found in a non- stressed area of the part.
- C. The discontinuity is found in a highly stressed area of the part.

10-32 AMG019
What defects will be detected by magnetizing a part using continuous longitudinal magnetization with a cable?
- A. Defects perpendicular to the long axis of the part.
- B. Defects parallel to the long axis of the part.
- C. Defects parallel to the concentric circles of magnetic force within the part.

10-35 AMG019
What two types of indicating mediums are available for magnetic particle inspection?
- A. Wet and dry process materials.
- B. High retentivity and low permeability material.
- C. Iron and ferris oxides.

10-33 AMG019
Which statement is true regarding the residual method of magnetic particle inspection?
- A. Subsurface discontinuities are made readily apparent.
- B. It provides greater sensitivity than the continuous method of magnetic particle inspection.
- C. It is only used with steels that have been heat treated.

10-36 AMG019
One way a part may be demagnetized after magnetic particle inspection is by
- A. subjecting the part to high voltage, low amperage ac.
- B. slowly moving the part out of an ac magnetic field of sufficient strength.
- C. slowly moving the part into an ac magnetic field of sufficient strength.

INSPECTION CONCEPTS AND TECHNIQUES

ANSWERS

10-31 Answer A.
To locate a defect in a part, it is essential the magnetic lines of force pass approximately perpendicular to the defect. Circular magnetization will locate defects running approximately parallel to the axis of the part. In longitudinal magnetization, the magnetic field is produced in a direction parallel to the long axis of the part thus detecting defects at a 90° angle to axis. Defects at a 45° angle should therefore be detected by either method.
[Ref: General Handbook H-8083-30A-ATB, Chapter 10 Page 32]

10-32 Answer A.
In longitudinal magnetization, the magnetic field is produced in a direction parallel to the long axis of the part, thus detecting defects that are perpendicular to the axis of the part.
[Ref: General Handbook H-8083-30A-ATB, Chapter 10 Page 32]

10-33 Answer C.
The residual method of magnetic particle inspection is used only of heat treated steel. While the process is easier to perform, it is not as sensitive as the continuous method. All forms of magnetic particle inspections are most useful in detecting anomalies on or near the surface.
[Ref: General Handbook H-8083-30A-ATB, Chapter 10 Page 32]

10-34 Answer C.
Fatigue occurs in materials which are exposed to frequent reversals of loading or repeatedly applied loads if the fatigue limit is reached or exceeded.
Repeated vibration or bending will ultimately cause a minute crack to occur at the weakest point. As vibration or bending continues, the crack lengthens until the part completely fails. This is termed shock and fatigue failure. Although cracks generally run in a uniform direction, they are not straight and would not appear in a non-stressed (non-fatigued) area or part.
[Ref: General Handbook H-8083-30A-ATB, Chapter 10 Page 32]

10-35 Answer A.
The various types of indicating mediums available for magnetic particle inspection are divided into two general material types: wet and dry. The basic requirement for any indicating medium is that it produces acceptable indications of discontinuities.
[Ref: General Handbook H-8083-30A-ATB, Chapter 10 Page 34]

10-36 Answer B.
The simplest procedure for developing a reversing and gradually decreasing magnetizing force in a part involves the use of a solenoid coil energized by alternating current. As the part is moved away from the alternating field of the solenoid, the magnetism in the part gradually decreases.
[Ref: General Handbook H-8083-30A-ATB, Chapter 10 Page 35]

10-37 AMG019
The testing medium that is generally used in magnetic particle inspection utilizes a ferromagnetic material that has
  A. high permeability and low retentivity.
  B. low permeability and high retentivity.
  C. high permeability and high retentivity.

10-38 AMG019
Regarding the below statements.
  1. An aircraft part may be demagnetized by subjecting it to a magnetizing force from alternating current that is gradually reduced in strength.
  2. An aircraft part may be demagnetized by subjecting it to a magnetizing force from direct current that is alternately reversed in direction and gradually reduced in strength.
  A. Both #1 and #2 are true
  B. Only #1 is true
  C. Only #2 is true

10-39 AMG024
Which is an advantage of the radiographic inspection technique?
  A. Provides a very precise image of a defect.
  B. Results can be interpreted with a minimal amount of training.
  C. Can often be accomplished without disassembly of the part from the aircraft.

10-40 AMG024
Which of these factors are considered essential knowledge for x-ray exposure?
  1. Processing of the film
  2. Material thickness and density
  3. Exposure distance and angle
  4. Film characteristics
  A. 2 and 3 only
  B. 1 and 4 only
  C. All of the above

10-41 AMG024
A mechanic has completed a bonded honeycomb repair using the potted compound repair technique. What nondestructive testing method is used to determine the soundness of the repair after the repair has cured?
  A. Eddy current test
  B. Metallic ring test
  C. Ultrasonic test

10-42 AMG024
Which of the following are commonly used nondestructive testing methods on composite structures?
  A. Tap test, ultrasonic, and radiographic
  B. Tap test, eddy current, and dye penetrant
  C. Tap test, magnaglo, and flux density

INSPECTION CONCEPTS AND TECHNIQUES

ANSWERS

10-37 Answer A.
For acceptable operation, magnetic particle inspection must have an indicating medium that has high permeability and low retentivity. High permeability ensures that a minimum of magnetic energy will be required to attract the material to flux leakage caused by discontinuities. Low retentivity ensures that the mobility of the magnetic particles will not be hindered by the particles themselves becoming magnetized and attracting one another.
[Ref: General Handbook H-8083-30A-ATB, Chapter 10 Page 34]

10-38 Answer A.
Demagnetization may be accomplished in a number of different ways. A convenient procedure for aircraft parts involves subjecting the part to a magnetizing force that is continually reversing in direction and, at the same time, gradually decreasing in strength. As the decreasing magnetizing force is applied first in one direction and then the other, the magnetization of the part also decreases. How the magnetizing force is achieved is irrelevant.
[Ref: General Handbook H-8083-30A-ATB, Chapter 10 Page 34]

10-39 Answer C.
Radiographic inspection techniques are used to locate defects or flaws in airframe structures or engines with little or no disassembly.
[Ref: General Handbook H-8083-30A-ATB, Chapter 10 Page 35]

10-40 Answer C.
The factors of radiographic exposure are so interdependent that it is necessary to consider all factors for any particular radiographic exposure. These factors include, but are not limited to, material thickness and density, shape and size of the object, type of defect expected, characteristics of x-ray machine used, the exposure distance, the exposure angle, film characteristics, and types of intensifying screen, if used.
[Ref: General Handbook H-8083-30A-ATB, Chapter 10 Page 35-36]

10-41 Answer B.
Tap testing, also referred to as the ring test, coin test or metallic ring test, is widely used as a quick evaluation of any accessible surface to detect the presence of delamination or debonding.
[Ref: General Handbook H-8083-30A-ATB, Chapter 10 Page 37]

10-42 Answer A.
Common aviation nondestructive testing methods include ultrasonic, acoustic emission, and radiographic inspections.
[Ref: General Handbook H-8083-30A-ATB, Chapter 10 Page 37]

10-43 AMG098

Which is a characteristic of a good gas weld?
  A. The depth of penetration shall be sufficient to ensure fusion of the filler rod.
  B. The height of the weld bead should be 1/8 inch above the base metal.
  C. The weld should taper off smoothly into the base metal.

10-45 AMG098

Using Figure 10-1 below, identify the weld caused by an excessive amount of acetylene.
  A. 1
  B. 2
  C. 3

10-44 AMG098

On a fillet weld, the penetration requirement includes what percentage(s) of the base metal thickness?
  A. 100 percent
  B. 25 to 50 percent
  C. 60 to 80 percent

10-46 AMG098

Using Figure 10-1 below, select the illustration which depicts a cold weld.
  A. 1
  B. 2
  C. 4

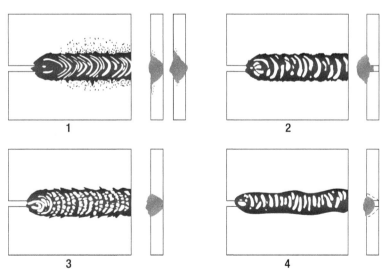

Figure 10-1. Examples of welds.

ANSWERS

10-43 Answer C.
A good weld is uniform in width with the ripples even and well feathered into the base metal, which shows no burn due to overheating.
[Ref: General Handbook H-8083-30A-ATB, Chapter 10 Page 39]

10-45 Answer C.
The puddle has a tendency to boil during the welding operation if an excessive amount of acetylene is used. This often leaves slight bumps along the center and craters at the finish of the weld.
[Ref: General Handbook H-8083-30A-ATB, Chapter 10 Page 39]

10-44 Answer B.
On a fillet weld, the penetration requirements are 25 to 50 percent of the thickness of the base metal.
[Ref: General Handbook H-8083-30A-ATB, Chapter 10 Page 39]

10-46 Answer B.
A weld that has improper penetration and cold laps caused by insufficient heat appears rough and irregular, and its edges are not feathered into the base metal.
[Ref: General Handbook H-8083-30A-ATB, Chapter 10 Page 40]

ORAL EXAM

10-1(O). Describe the characteristics of a good weld.

10-2(O). When inspecting a fillet weld, how much penetration is required of the base metal?

10-3(O). What two types of indicating mediums are available for magnetic particle inspection?

10-4(O). Magnetic particle inspections are used primarily for detecting what types of defects?

10-5(O). Liquid penetrant inspection methods can be used on what types of materials?

10-6(O). What tools are needed to aid in visual inspections?

10-7(O). Tap testing, also referred to as the ring test or coin test, is widely used to detect what types of defects and on what type of material?

PRACTICAL EXAM

NOTE: Additional application of your skills in inspection will be tested during the airframe and powerplant practical application tests. Be sure you understand the basics as outlined in this text.

10-1(P). Given an aircraft component or mock-up, perform a dye or fluorescent penetrant inspection and record your findings.

10-2(P). Given an aircraft component or mock-up, find a non-visible defect using eddy current or ultrasonic inspection equipment and record your findings.

10-3(P). Given an aircraft or mock-up, inspect hardware for defects and proper installation.

10-4(P). Given an aircraft or mock-up, visually inspect welds and record findings.

INSPECTION CONCEPTS AND TECHNIQUES

ORAL EXAM

10-1(O).   A good weld is uniform in width with the ripples even and well feathered into the base metal, which shows no burn due to overheating.
[Ref: General Handbook H-8083-30A-ATB, Chapter 10 Page 38-39]

10-2(O).   The penetration requirements are 25 to 50 percent of the thickness of the base metal.
[Ref: General Handbook H-8083-30A-ATB, Chapter 10 Page 39]

10-3(O).   Wet and dry process materials.
[Ref: General Handbook H-8083-30A-ATB, Chapter 10 Page 30-32]

10-4(O).   Defects located on or near the surface.
[Ref: General Handbook H-8083-30A-ATB, Chapter 10 Page 30]

10-5(O).   Ferrous and nonferrous metals and nonporous plastics.
[Ref: General Handbook H-8083-30A-ATB, Chapter 10 Page 19]

10-6(O).   A bright light, a magnifying glass, and a mirror (when required).
[Ref: General Handbook H-8083-30A-ATB, Chapter 10 Page 18]

10-7(O).   It detects the presence of delamination or debonding in composite material.
[Ref: General Handbook H-8083-30A-ATB, Chapter 10 Page 37]

HAND TOOLS AND MEASURING DEVICES

General Purpose Tools, Metal Cutting Tools, Drills, Taps and Dies, Layout and Measuring Tools

11-1 AMG020
What type of pliers are typically used for twisting safety wire?
A. Round nose pliers
B. Duckbill pliers
C. Needle nose pliers

11-2 AMG020
Which of the following is not an appropriate use of a center punch?
A. Removing rivets from holes
B. Transfer dimensions from a paper template to metal
C. Create an indentation to start a twist drill

11-3 AMG020
What wrench type is best used on the B-nut of a fuel or hydraulic line?
A. Crow foot
B. Flare nut
C. Hook spanner

11-4 AMG020
When choosing a hacksaw blade; which pitch of the blade's teeth is best for cutting cold-rolled or structural steel?
A. 14 pitch
B. 24 pitch
C. 32 pitch

11-5 AMG020
Which is true regarding the use of metal cutting hand snips?
A. Cutting with snips hardens the material at the edge line.
B. Cutting with snips leaves fractures along the edge line.
C. Cutting with snips removes small amounts of metal at the edge line.

11-6 AMG020
Which file type will provide the smoothest cut and finest finish?
A. Vixen file
B. Lead float file
C. Mill file

HAND TOOLS AND MEASURING DEVICES

ANSWERS

11-1 Answer B.
Duck-bill pliers resemble a "duck's bill" in that the jaws are thin, flat, and shaped like a duck's bill. They are used exclusively for twisting safety wire.
[Ref: General Handbook H-8083-30A-ATB, Chapter 11 Page 3]

11-2 Answer A.
Punches are used to locate centers for drawing circles, starting holes for drilling, punch holes in sheet metal, transfer location of holes in patterns, and to remove damaged rivets, pins or bolts.
[Ref: General Handbook H-8083-30A-ATB, Chapter 11 Page 4]

11-3 Answer B.
The flare nut wrench has the appearance of a box- end wrench that has been cut open on one end. This opening allows the wrench to be used on the B-nut of a fuel, hydraulic, or oxygen line.
[Ref: General Handbook H-8083-30A-ATB, Chapter 11 Page 6]

11-4 Answer A.
The courser of these blades with 14 teeth per inch is best for cutting solid steel bars. 24 teeth per inch is recommended for aluminum, and 32 teeth per inch is recommended for thin walled pipe or sheet metal.
[Ref: General Handbook H-8083-30A-ATB, Chapter 11 Page 9]

11-5 Answer B.
Minute fractures often occur along the cut line when using aviation hand snips. Therefore the cut should be made about 1/32" from the line and then the edge should be finished with a hand file to the line.
[Ref: General Handbook H-8083-30A-ATB, Chapter 11 Page 9]

11-6 Answer A.
Vixen (curved tooth files)—Curved tooth files are especially designed for rapid filing and smooth finish on soft metals and wood. The regular cut is adapted for tough work on cast iron, soft steel, copper, brass, aluminum, wood, slate, marble, fiber, rubber, and so forth. The fine cut gives excellent results on steel, cast iron, phosphor bronze, white brass, and all hard metals. The smooth cut is used where the amount of material to be removed is very slight, but where a superior finish is desired.
[Ref: General Handbook H-8083-30A-ATB, Chapter 11 Page 10]

11-7 AMG020
Which system provides the most accuracy in measuring drill
bit diameter?
   A. The numbering system; sizes 1-80.
   B. The lettering system; sizes A-Z.
   C. The fraction system by 64ths of an inch.

11-10 AMG020
Which tap type is used to cut full threads in a blind hole?
   A. A taper tap.
   B. A plug tap.
   C. A bottom tap.

11-8 AMG020
For drilling most materials, a bit with a lip angle of 59 degrees
is most common. However, for soft materials such as
Plexiglas, use a bit with a lip angle of
   A. 20 degrees.
   B. 45 degrees.
   C. 90 degrees.

11-11 AMG057
Which tool is used to find the center of a shaft or other
cylindrical work?
   A. Combination set
   B. Dial indicator
   C. Micrometer caliper

11-9 AMG020
A proper procedure to produce a precision hole exactly .125"
in diameter would be to drill
   A. once with a precision 4 flute 1/8" or #49 drill bit.
   B. a hole at .120" and then remove the final .005" with
      a reamer.
   C. a hole at .115" and then remove the final .010" with
      a reamer.

11-12 AMG057
If it is necessary to accurately measure the diameter of a
hole approximately 1/4" in diameter, the mechanic should
use a
   A. telescoping gauge and determine the size of the hole
      by taking a micrometer reading of the adjustable end of
      the telescoping gauge.
   B. 0-1 inch inside micrometer and read the measurement
      directly from the micrometer.
   C. small hole gauge and determine the size of the hole
      by taking a micrometer reading of the ball end of
      the gauge.

HAND TOOLS AND MEASURING DEVICES

ANSWERS

11-7 Answer A.
The number system of classification is the most accurate: N80 (0.0314 inch) to Number 1 (0.228 inch).
[Ref: General Handbook H-8083-30A-ATB, Chapter 11 Page 12]

11-8 Answer C.
For most drilling, a twist drill with a cutting angle of 118° (59° on either side of center) will be sufficient; however, when drilling soft metals, a cutting angle of 90° may be more efficient.
[Ref: General Handbook H-8083-30A-ATB, Chapter 11 Page 13]

11-9 Answer B.
Reamers are used to smooth and enlarge holes to exact size. A hole that is to be reamed to exact size must be drilled about 0.003 to 0.007 inch under size.
[Ref: General Handbook H-8083-30A-ATB, Chapter 11 Page 13]

11-10 Answer C.
The bottoming tap is not tapered. It is used to cut full threads to the bottom of a blind hole.
[Ref: General Handbook H-8083-30A-ATB, Chapter 11 Page 17]

11-11 Answer A.
The center head of a combination set is used to find the center of shafts or other cylindrical work.
[Ref: General Handbook H-8083-30A-ATB, Chapter 11 Page 18]

11-12 Answer C.
Small hole gauges were not discussed in the text. They are a measuring tool with a round expandable head on one end. The ball is split with the use of a wedge. Place the round head of the gauge into the hole, turn the handle to expand the ball until it touches the sides of the hole. Then with the micrometer measure the size of the ball, being very careful not to crush the ball in the micrometer. A telescoping gauge and an inside micrometer could possibly give a measurement of the diamotor but for very small holes they are not accurate. The small hole gauge would be the most accurate, it will also tell you if the hole has become out of round due to wear. See picture below for example of a small hole gauge.
[Ref: General Handbook H-8083-30A-ATB, Chapter 11 Page 21]

11-13 AMG057
What tool is generally used to set a divider to an exact dimension?
- A. Machinist scale
- B. Surface gauge
- C. Dial indicator

11-14 AMG057
What precision measuring tool is used for measuring crankpin and main bearing journals for out of round wear?
- A. Dial indicator
- B. Micrometer caliper
- C. Depth gauge

11-15 AMG057
What may be used to check the stem on a poppet type valve for stretch?
- A. Dial indicator
- B. Micrometer
- C. Telescoping gauge

11-16 AMG057
Identify the correct statement.
- A. An outside micrometer is limited to measuring diameters.
- B. Tools used on certified aircraft must be an approved type.
- C. Dividers do not provide a reading when used as a measuring device.

11-17 AMG057
Which number represents the vernier scale graduation of a micrometer?
- A. .01
- B. .001
- C. .0001

11-18 AMG057
The measurement reading on the illustrated micrometer below is
- A. 0.2851
- B. 0.2911
- C. 0.2901

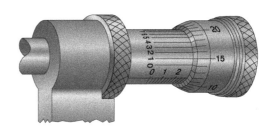

HAND TOOLS AND MEASURING DEVICES

ANSWERS

11-13 Answer A.
A machinist scale is the same thing as a rule. They are for transferring measurements from the rule to the work.
[Ref: General Handbook H-8083-30A-ATB, Chapter 11 Page 21]

11-16 Answer C.
They are used to scribe circles and arcs and for transferring measurements from the rule to the work. Micrometers can measure length and width as well as diameters, within its range. Not all tools have to be approved, many do have to be calibrated and some specialty tools need to be authorized.
[Ref: General Handbook H-8083-30A-ATB, Chapter 11 Page 21]

11-14 Answer B.
The micrometer caliper is the correct answer. Out- of-round describes the physical condition of a round object that has become oblong due to wear. Dial indicators are used to measure variations in a surface and used to determine runout (bend) in a shaft. Depth gauges are not used to measure diameters.
[Ref: General Handbook H-8083-30A-ATB, Chapter 11 Page 21]

11-17 Answer C.
Some micrometers are equipped with a vernier scale that makes it possible to directly read the fraction of a division that is indicated on the thimble scale. The vernier graduations divide the inch into 10 equal parts, each equal to 0.0001 inch.
[Ref: General Handbook H-8083-30A-ATB, Chapter 11 Page 23]

11-15 Answer B.
Stretch is measured in length. Of the three measuring tools listed, only a micrometer measures length.
[Ref: General Handbook H-8083-30A-ATB, Chapter 11 Page 21]

11-18 Answer A.
First read the barrel (A), remembering each division is .25. The thimble has been moved past the third notice giving us a reading of .275, then add in the amount reading on the thimble (B) which is .010 which now gives us .285, then add in the reading from the venier scale (C) which is .0001, which now gives us a measurement of 0.2851.
[Ref: General Handbook H-8083-30A-ATB, Chapter 11 Page 23]

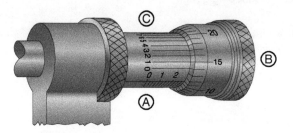

11-19 AMG057

What is the measurement reading on the vernier caliper scale below is

A. 1.411 inches
B. 1.436 inches
C. 1.700 inches

11-21 AMG057

The measurement reading on the micrometer in Figure 9-2 is

A. .2758
B. .2702
C. .2792

Figure 9-2. Micrometer.

11-20 AMG057

What does the micrometer in Figure 11-1 below read?

A. .2974
B. .3004
C. .3108

11-22 AMG057

Which tool can be used to measure the alignment or bend of a rotor shaft or for warp in a rotating component?

A. Dial indicator
B. Shaft gauge
C. Protractor

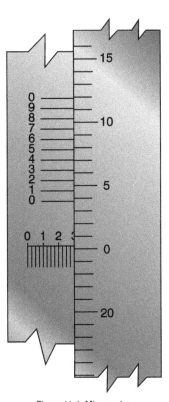

Figure 11-1. Micrometer.

ANSWERS

11-19 Answer B.
The zero on the vernier scale has moved beyond the 1 inch mark, it has also moved past the 4, and is past the first 0.025 mark, giving an initial measurement of 1.425 inches. Locate the mark on the vernier scale that lines up, in this case the 11. Add 0.011 to 1.425 and the final measurement is 1.1436.
[Ref: General Handbook H-8083-30A-ATB, Chapter 11 Page 24]

11-21 Answer C.
The thimble has moved past the 0.275 mark on the barrel, but has not reached the .005 mark on the thimble. Adding 0.275 and .004 equals 0.279. Locate the mark on the thimble that aligns with the vernier scale, which in this case is .0002. Adding 0.279 and 0.0002 gives a final measurement of 0.2792.
[Ref: General Handbook H-8083-30A-ATB, Chapter 11 Page 24]

11-20 Answer B.
The thimble has been moved past the 3 on the barrel, but only slightly. Locate the mark on the vernier scale that lines up, in this case the 4, which is equal to 0.0004. When 0.004 is added to .3 the final measurement will be 0.3004.
[Ref: General Handbook H-8083-30A-ATB, Chapter 11 Page 24]

11-22 Answer A.
A variation of the micrometer is the dial indicator, which measures variations in a surface. For example if a bend is suspected, the part can be rotated while resting between a pair of machined V-blocks. A dial indicator is then clamped to a fixed stand while the shaft is rotated. The amount of bend or misalignment of the shaft is displayed on the dial or LCD display as the needle fluctuates within thousandths of an inch.
[Ref: General Handbook H-8083-30A-ATB, Chapter 11 Page 25]

ORAL EXAM

11-1(O). What is a dial indicator and what is it used to measure?

11-2(O). The vernier micrometer caliper can be used to measure objects to what increment?

11-3(O). What measuring tool can be used to measure the inside of a hole?

11-4(O). What measuring tool can be used to measure the depth of blind holes?

PRACTICAL EXAM

Your ability to select and use the appropriate tools while on the job is tested throughout the various sections of your practical test. Be sure you are comfortable with using all the tools. If not, practice using them; it is the only way to become proficient.

Check with the examiner to confirm if you will need to supply your own tools for the test and be sure to come prepared.

You are required to be able to perform, read, and record a precision measurement using various tools, including but not limited to, a dial indicator, micrometer, or a vernier caliper.

11-1(P). Given a vernier caliper, measure the given object to the nearest ten-thousandths of an inch and record your findings.

11-2(P). Given a dial indicator, measure the run out of a given object and record your findings.

11-3(P). Given a micrometer, measure a given object and record your findings.

ORAL EXAM

11-1(O). A dial indicator is a type of micrometer that measures variations in a surface by using an accurately machined probe linked to a circular indicator whose movement indicates thousandths of an inch.
[Ref: General Handbook H-8083-30A-ATB, Chapter 11 Page 25]

11-2(O). The vernier micrometer caliper can measure to one ten-thousandths (0.0001) of an inch.
[Ref: General Handbook H-8083-30A-ATB, Chapter 11 Page 23]

11-3(O). Inside calipers can be used to measure the diameters of holes.
[Ref: General Handbook H-8083-30A-ATB, Chapter 11 Page 21]

11-4(O). The slide caliper, when fitted with a depth gauge.
[Ref: General Handbook H-8083-30A-ATB, Chapter 11 Page 25]

FUNDAMENTALS OF ELECTRICITY AND ELECTRONICS

Electricity and Electronics, General Composition of Matter, Magnetism Current, Instrumentation, Batteries, and Semiconductors

CHAPTER 12

QUESTIONS

12-1 AMG031
1.2 KV equals
A. 20 volts.
B. 2.0 volts.
C. .2 volt.

12-2 AMG020
Through which material will magnetic lines of force pass the most readily?
A. Copper.
B. Iron.
C. Aluminum.

12-3 AMG020
The potential difference between two conductors which are insulated from each other is measured in
A. volts.
B. amperes.
C. coulombs.

12-4 AMG031
Which term means .001 ampere?
A. Microampere
B. Kiloampere
C. Milliampere

12-5 AMG031
Which is the correct formula that defines Current?
A. amperes = charge / time
B. volts = joules / charge
C. power = volts / time

12-6 AMG031
How much current does a 30-volt, 1/2 horsepower motor that is 85-percent efficient draw from the bus?
(Note: 1 horsepower = 746 watts)
A. 14.6 amperes
B. 12.4 amperes
C. 14.1 amperes

FUNDAMENTALS OF ELECTRICITY AND ELECTRONICS

ANSWERS

12-1 Answer B.
"KV" is short for kilovolt. One kilovolt is equal to a 1000 volts, therefore two thousandths of a kilovolt is equal to 2.0 volts.
[Ref: General Handbook H-8083-30A-ATB, Chapter 12 Page 5]

12-4 Answer C.
"Milli" is the metric prefix representing one thousandth, therefore a milliampere is one thousandths of an ampere or .001 ampere.
[Ref: General Handbook H-8083-30A-ATB, Chapter 12 Page 17]

12-2 Answer B.
Permeability is the measure of the ease with which a magnetic flux can pass through a material. Of the three options, iron has the highest permeability.
[Ref: General Handbook H-8083-30A-ATB, Chapter 12 Page 11]

12-5 Answer A.
The unit of electrical current is Amperes. Thus answer A. $I = Q / t$ is correct were (I) is the symbol for current (amperes), (Q) represents charge in coulombs, and (t) represents time.
[Ref: General Handbook H-8083-30A-ATB, Chapter 12 Page 17]

12-3 Answer A.
A volt is the basic unit of electrical potential or electromotive force. Potential difference between two conductors is measured in volts.
[Ref: General Handbook H-8083-30A-ATB, Chapter 12 Page 16]

12-6 Answer A.
We are solving for current (I) and given power (P) and volts (E), then we must use the formula $I = P/E$. Note: One 1/2 horsepower working at 85 percent efficiency is 746 divided by 2 and then divided by .85.
$I = [(746)/2] / .85] / 30$ $I = (343 / .85) / 30$
$I = 438.8 / 30$
$I = 14.6$
[Ref: General Handbook H-8083-30A-ATB, Chapter 12 Page 22, Figure 12-43]

12-7 AMG031
The voltage drop in a circuit of known resistance is dependent on
   A. the voltage of the circuit.
   B. the resistance of the conductor and does not change with voltage or amperage.
   C. the amperage of the circuit.

12-8 AMG031
How much power is being furnished to the circuit depicted in Figure 12-1 below?
   A. 575 watts
   B. 2,875 watts
   C. 2,645 watts

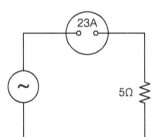
Figure 12-1.

12-9 AMG031
Which of these will cause the resistance of a conductor to decrease?
   A. Decrease the length or the cross-sectional area.
   B. Decrease the length or increase the cross sectional area.
   C. Increase the length or decrease the cross sectional area.

12-10 AMG031
If the cross-sectional area of a given conductor is increased to four times its original value, and the length and temperature remain constant, the resistance of the conductor will be
   A. one-fourth its original value.
   B. four times its original value.
   C. found by multiplying the original resistance by the percentage increase in cross-sectional area.

12-11 AMG031
Which of the below is the product of electrical resistance?
   A. coulombs
   B. heat
   C. ohms

12-12 AMG031
How much power must a 24-volt generator furnish to a system which contains the following loads?
(Note: 1 horsepower = 746 watts)
   A. 385 watts
   B. 402 watts
   C. 450 watts

UNIT	RATING
One Motor (75 percent efficient)	1/5 hp
Three Position Lights	20 watts each
One Heating Element	5 amp
One Anticollision Light	5 amp

FUNDAMENTALS OF ELECTRICITY AND ELECTRONICS

ANSWERS

12-7 Answer C.
The relationship between voltage, resistance, and current (measured in amps) is expressed in Ohm's Law (E = I(R)). If resistance is known, then the voltage (E) drop will be affected by or dependent upon the current (amperage) of the circuit.
[Ref: General Handbook H-8083-30A-ATB, Chapter 12 Page 18]

12-10 Answer A.
Since resistance varies inversely with the cross-sectional area of a conductor, increasing the cross-sectional area of the conductor will reduce the resistance by one-fourth.
[Ref: General Handbook H-8083-30A-ATB, Chapter 12 Page 20]

12-8 Answer C.
The circuit contains only resistance, therefore you can use the power formula P = I × E. However, we first have to determine the voltage. Using Ohm's Law (E = I × R) we can determine the voltage to be 115 volts (23 amps × 5 ohms). Power can now be determined as 2,645 watts (115 volts × 23 amps).
[Ref: General Handbook H-8083-30A-ATB, Chapter 12 Page 18]

12-11 Answer B.
When current flows through a resistive circuit, energy is dissipated in the form of heat. Ohms are the unit of resistance with a circuit. Coulombs are the unit of charge which is defined by amps × time.
[Ref: General Handbook H-8083-30A-ATB, Chapter 12 Page 22]

12-9 Answer B.
The resistance of a metallic conductor is directly proportional to its length, the longer the length of a given size of wire, the greater the resistance. The resistance of a metallic conductor is inversely proportional to the cross-sectional area. If the cross-sectional area of a conductor is doubled, the resistance to current flow will be reduced in half.
[Ref: General Handbook H-8083-30A-ATB, Chapter 12 Page 19]

12-12 Answer C.
To determine total power requirements, first calculate the power needed for each unit. 450 watts is the closest correct answer.
[Ref: General Handbook H-8083-30A-ATB, Chapter 12 Page 22]

12-13 AMG031

A 12-volt electric motor has 1,000 watts input and 1 horsepower output. Maintaining the same efficiency, how much input power does a 24-volt 1- horsepower electric motor require?
- A. 1,000 watts
- B. 2,000 watts
- C. 3,000 watts

12-14 AMG031

A 1-horsepower, 24-volt DC electric motor that is 80 percent efficient requires 932.5 watts. How much power will a 1-horsepower, 12-volt DC electric motor that is 75 percent efficient require?
- A. 832.5 watts
- B. 900.5 watts
- C. 994.6 watts

12-15 AMG031

Which requires the most electrical power during operation? (Note: 1 horsepower = 746 watts)
- A. A 12-volt motor requiring 8 amperes.
- B. Four 30-watt lamps in a 12-volt parallel circuit.
- C. Two lights requiring 3 amperes each in a 24-volt parallel system.

12-16 AMG031

Which requires the most electrical power? (Note: 1 horsepower = 746 watts)
- A. Four 30-watt lamps arranged in a 12-volt parallel circuit.
- B. A 1/5-horsepower, 24-volt motor which is 75 percent efficient.
- C. A 24-volt anti-collision light circuit consisting of two light assemblies, which require 3 amperes each during operation.

12-17 AMG031

Which symbol in Figure 12-2 represents a potentiometer?
- A. 2
- B. 3
- C. 4

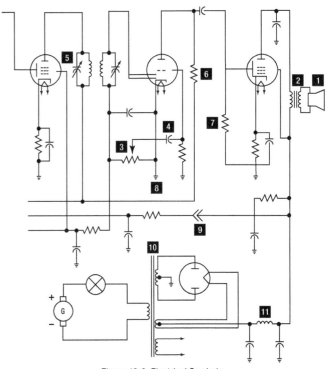

Figure 12-2. Electrical Symbols.

FUNDAMENTALS OF ELECTRICITY AND ELECTRONICS

ANSWERS

12-13 Answer A.
Maintaining the same efficiency, a 1 horsepower motor will require the same 1,000 watts of input, no matter the voltage.
[Ref: General Handbook H-8083-30A-ATB, Chapter 12 Page 22]

12-16 Answer B.
Calculate the power requirements of each answer to determine the correct answer.
4 × 30 watts = 120 watts
(746 × 1/5) / .75 = 199 watts
2 × (24 volts × 3 amps) = 144 watts
[Ref: General Handbook H-8083-30A-ATB, Chapter 12 Page 22]

12-14 Answer C.
Due to friction and heat loss, motors are not 100% efficient. Therefore, it will take more than 746 watts to maintain a 1 horsepower output. Calculate the watts needed by dividing 746 by 75%, which equals 994.6 watts. The voltage in this example is irrelevant.
[Ref: General Handbook H-8083-30A-ATB, Chapter 12 Page 22]

12-17 Answer B.
Symbol 3 is a variable resistor. Symbol 2 identifies a relay. Symbol 4 identifies a circuit breaker.
[Ref: General Handbook H-8083-30A-ATB, Chapter 12 Page 27-28]

12-15 Answer C.
Calculate the power requirements of each answer to determine the correct answer.
12 volt motor × 8 amps = 96 watts
4 lamps × 30 watts = 120 watts
2 × (3 amps x24 volts) = 144 watts
[Ref: General Handbook H-8083-30A-ATB, Chapter 12 Page 22]

FUNDAMENTALS OF ELECTRICITY AND ELECTRONICS

12-18 AMG031
Which of the components is a potentiometer in the Figure 12-2 below?
- A. 2
- B. 3
- C. 4

12-20 AMG031
Referring to Figure 12-3 below, what is the measured voltage of the series-parallel circuit between terminal A and B?
- A. 1.5 volts
- B. 3.0 volts
- C. 4.5 volts

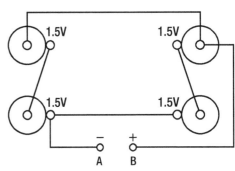

Figure 12-3. Battery circuit.

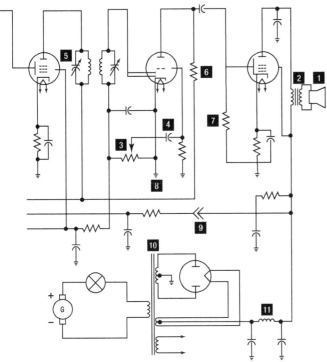

Figure 12-2. Electrical Symbols.

12-19 AMG031
If a thermal protector switch activates to prevent overheating damage to an electric motor, once the motor has cooled;

_____.

- A. The motor will reset by itself.
- B. The circuit can be reset from the flight deck.
- C. The circuit protector is replaced by a maintenance crew.

12-21 AMG031
What is the operating resistance of a 30-watt light bulb designed for a 28-volt system?
- A. 1.07 ohms
- B. 26 ohms
- C. 0.93 ohm

FUNDAMENTALS OF ELECTRICITY AND ELECTRONICS

ANSWERS

12-18 Answer B.
The component symbol labeled #3 represents a potentiometer.
[Ref: General Handbook H-8083-30A-ATB, Chapter 12 Page 28]

12-20 Answer B.
A voltage source is an energy source that provides a constant voltage to a load. Two or more of these sources in series will equal the algebraic sum of all the sources connected in series. Only two of the batteries are in series. Therefore, 1.5 V + 1.5 V = 3.0 V.
[Ref: General Handbook H-8083-30A-ATB, Chapter 12 Page 36]

12-19 Answer A.
A thermal protector switch contains a bimetallic strip that bends when it is heated, and so opening the circuit. Once the temperature reduces, the metal strip bends back and so again closes the circuit for continued operation.
[Ref: General Handbook H-8083-30A-ATB, Chapter 12 Page 30]

12-21 Answer B.
We can use a variation of Ohm's Law to calculate resistance: Resistance(R) = Voltage (E) / Current (I). Unfortunately, we do not know the current. However, using the power formula we can calculate current and then solve for resistance.
Using the formula I = P / E, we get I = 30 watts / 28 volts = 1.07 amps. Now solve for resistance: R = 28 volts / 1.07= 26.17 ohms. The closest correct answer is B.
[Ref: General Handbook H-8083-30A-ATB, Chapter 12 Page 38]

12-22 AMG031
A 14-ohm resistor is to be installed in a series circuit carrying .05 ampere. How much power will the resistor be required to dissipate?
- A. At least .70 milliwatt.
- B. At least 35 milliwatts.
- C. Less than .035 watt.

12-25 AMG031
Which statement is correct when made in reference to a parallel circuit?
- A. The current is equal in all portions of the circuit.
- B. The total current is equal to the sum of the currents through the individual branches of the circuit.
- C. The current in amperes can be found by dividing the EMF in volts by the sum of the resistors in ohms.

12-23 AMG031
Referring to Figure 12-4 below, find the voltage across the 8-ohm resistor.
- A. 8 volts
- B. 20.4 volts
- C. 24 volts

12-26 AMG031
How many amperes will a 28-volt generator be required to supply to a circuit containing five lamps in parallel, three of which have a resistance of 6 ohms each and two of which have a resistance of 5 ohms each?
- A. 1.11 amperes
- B. 15.30 amperes
- C. 25.23 amperes

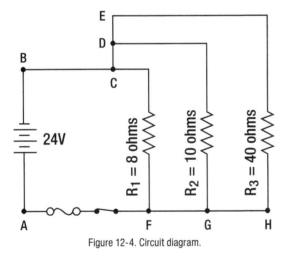

Figure 12-4. Circuit diagram.

12-24 AMG031
In a parallel circuit with four 6-ohms resistors across a 24-volt battery, what is the total voltage across resistor-three (VR3) in the circuit?
- A. 6 volts
- B. 18 volts
- C. 24 volts

12-27 AMG031
A 24-volt source is required to furnish 48 watts to a parallel circuit consisting of four resistors of equal value. What is the voltage drop across each resistor?
- A. 3 volts
- B. 12 volts
- C. 24 volts

FUNDAMENTALS OF ELECTRICITY AND ELECTRONICS

ANSWERS

12-22 Answer B.
To determine power, we need to know the current and voltage. Using Ohm's Law, first solve for voltage (E = I × R) or E = .05 amps × 14 ohms = 0.7 volts. Now we can solve for power: P = IE or .05 amps × .7 volts = .035 watts or 35 milliwatts.
[Ref: General Handbook H-8083-30A-ATB, Chapter 12 Page 39]

12-25 Answer B.
The total current of the circuit will be the sum of the current in all branches.
[Ref: General Handbook H-8083-30A-ATB, Chapter 12 Page 41]

12-23 Answer C.
No calculations are needed here. Remember, in a parallel circuit the voltage remains the same across each resistor.
[Ref: General Handbook H-8083-30A-ATB, Chapter 12 Page 40]

12-26 Answer C.
In this problem, determine the total resistance in a parallel circuit using the formula:
1/[(1/R1)+(1/R2)+(1/R3) +(1/R4) +(1/R5)] =
1/[1/6+1/6+1/6+1/5+1/5] = 1/[.167+.167+.167+.2+.2]=1/.901 =
1.11 ohms total resistance.
Now use Ohm's Law to determine the current required,
I = E/R = 28 volts/1.11 = 25.23 amps.
[Ref: General Handbook H-8083-30A-ATB, Chapter 12 Page 41]

12-24 Answer C.
In parallel circuits the voltage across any branch is equal to the voltage across all of the other branches.
[Ref: General Handbook H-8083-30A-ATB, Chapter 12 Page 40]

12-27 Answer C.
No calculations are needed to answer this questions. Kirchhoff's voltage law states that the algebraic sum of the applied voltage and the voltage drop around any closed circuit is zero. In simpler terms, the sum of all the voltage drops in a circuit must equal the sum of the voltage source(s) in the circuit.
[Ref: General Handbook H-8083-30A-ATB, Chapter 12 Page 42]

12-28 AMG031

A cabin entry light of 10 watts and a dome light of 20 watts are connected in parallel to a 30-volt source. If the voltage across the 10-watt light is measured, it will be

A. equal to the voltage across the 20-watt light.
B. half the voltage across the 20-watt light.
C. one-third of the input voltage.

12-30 AMG031

Referring to Figure 12-6 below, if resistor R_3 is disconnected at terminal D, what will the ohmmeter read?

A. Infinite resistance
B. 10 ohms
C. 20 ohms

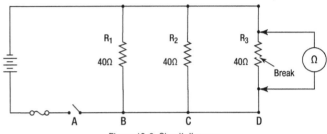

Figure 12-6. Circuit diagram.

12-29 AMG031

Referring to Figure 12-5 below, if resistor R_5 is disconnected at the junction of R_4 and R_3 as shown, what will the ohmmeter read?

A. 2.76 ohms
B. 3 ohms
C. 12 ohms

12-31 AMG031

With an ohmmeter connected into the circuit in Figure 12-7, what will the ohmmeter read?

A. 20 ohms
B. Infinite resistance
C. 10 ohms

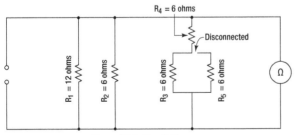

Figure 12-5. Circuit diagram.

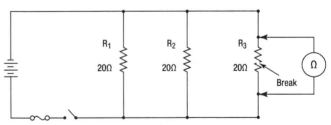

Figure 12-7. Circuit diagram.

FUNDAMENTALS OF ELECTRICITY AND ELECTRONICS

ANSWERS

12-28 Answer A.
In a parallel circuit, the voltage is constant across each path, while the current varies. The voltage across the 10 watt light will be equal to the voltage across the 20 watt light.
[Ref: General Handbook H-8083-30A-ATB, Chapter 12 Page 41]

12-30 Answer A.
When R3 is disconnected at Terminal D, the current flow is stopped and results in the ohmmeter registering an infinite resistance.
[Ref: General Handbook H-8083-30A-ATB, Chapter 12 Page 41]

12-29 Answer B.
When R5 is disconnected, the ohmmeter will register the resistance of the remaining resistors. Resisters 3 and 4 are in series and therefore their resistance is added together for a total resistance of 12 ohms. Resistors 1 and 2 are in parallel with resistors 3 and 4. To calculate the total resistance in a parallel circuit use the following formula:
$1/[(1/R1) + (1/R2) + (1/R3 \& 4)] = 1/[(1/12) + (1/6) + (1/12)] = 1/(.08 + .17 + .08) = 1/.33 = 3.03$ ohms.
The closest correct answer is B.
[Ref: General Handbook H-8083-30A-ATB, Chapter 12 Page 41]

12-31 Answer C.
The ohmmeter is only reading R1 and R2. To calculate the total resistance in a parallel circuit use the following formula:
$1/[(1/R1) + (1/R2)] = 1/[(1/20) + (1/20)] = 1/(.05 + .05) = 1/.1 = 10$ ohms
[Ref: General Handbook H-8083-30A-ATB, Chapter 12 Page 41]

12-32 AMG031

Find the total resistance of the circuit in Figure 12-8.

A. 22.0 ohms
B. 18.5 ohms
C. 21.2 ohms

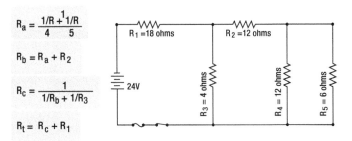

Figure 12-8. Circuit diagram.

12-33 AMG031

A 48-volt source is required to furnish 192 watts to a parallel circuit consisting of three resistors of equal value. What is the value of each resistor?

A. 36 ohms
B. 4 ohms
C. 12 ohms

12-34 AMG031

Which is correct concerning a parallel circuit?

A. Total resistance will be smaller than the smallest resistor.
B. Total resistance will decrease when one of the resistances is removed.
C. Total voltage drop is the same as the total resistance.

12-35 AMG031

A circuit has an applied voltage of 30 volts and a load consisting of a 10 ohm resistor in series with a 20 ohm resistor. What is the voltage drop across the 10 ohm resistor?

A. 10 volts
B. 20 volts
C. 30 volts

12-36 AMG031

Referring to Figure 12-9, determine the total current flow in the circuit.

A. 0.2 ampere
B. 0.8 ampere
C. 1.4 amperes

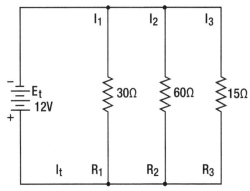

Figure 12-9. Circuit diagram.

12-37 AMG031

Which is correct in reference to electrical resistance?

A. Two electrical devices will have the same combined resistance either connected in series or connected in parallel.
B. If one of three bulbs in a parallel lighting circuit is removed, the total resistance of the circuit will increase.
C. A device that has a high resistance will use more power than one with a low resistance with the same applied voltage.

FUNDAMENTALS OF ELECTRICITY AND ELECTRONICS

ANSWERS

12-32 Answer C.

The formulas in the figure provide you with the means to solve this complex circuit problem. NOTE: When solving for total resistance of series- parallel circuits, begin calculations at the farthest point from the power source, working back towards the power source.

First solve for the parallel branches:
Ra = 1/(1/R4 + 1/R5) = 1/(1/12 + 1/6) = 1/.083 + .167 = 1/.25 = 4

Then determine the resistance in the series R2 and R4,5:
Rb = Ra + R2 = 4 + 12 = 16

Solve for the next parallel branches:
Rc = 1/(1/Rb + 1/R3) = 1/(1/16 + 1/4) = 1/.0625 + .25 = 1/.3125 = 3.2

Finally solve the last remaining series to determine the total resistance in this circuit:
Rt = Rc + R1 = 3.2 + 18 = 21.2 ohms
[Ref: General Handbook H-8083-30A-ATB, Chapter 12 Page 41]

12-33 Answer A.

To solve this problem you need to use the following formulas:
I = P / E to determine the current in the system.
I = 192 / 48 = 4 amps.
R = E / I to determine total resistance in the circuit.
R = 48/4 = 12 ohms.
The total resistance in the circuit is 12 ohms. Remember, in a parallel circuit the total resistance is less than any individual branch. To determine the resistance of each resistor use the following formula: r = Rt × n, where 'r' is the resistance of a resistor and 'n' is the number of resistor in the circuit.
R = 12 × 3 = 36 ohms
[Ref: General Handbook H-8083-30A-ATB, Chapter 12 Page 22, 37, 41]

12-34 Answer A.

Total resistance in a parallel circuit is smaller than the smallest resistor. This can be derived from the general formula for total resistance in a parallel circuit:
Rt = 1/[(1/R1) + (1/R2) + (1/R3)]
[Ref: General Handbook H-8083-30A-ATB, Chapter 12 Page 40-41]

12-35 Answer A.

For series circuits, current is the same throughout the circuit, but voltage drop varies with each resistor. First, determine the total resistance, which is sum of the two resisters (10+20=30 ohms). Next, determine the current by using Ohm's Law formula I=E/R = 30 volts/30 ohms = 1 amp. Finally to determine the voltage drop use the formula E1=IR1 = (1 amp)(10 ohms) = 10 volts.
[Ref: General Handbook H-8083-30A-ATB, Chapter 12 Page 41, 43]

12-36 Answer C.

Total current in a parallel circuit is equal to the sum of the current flowing through each branch in the circuit. Determine the current in each branch using the formula:
I = E/R (I1 = 12V/30 ohms = .4 amps.
I2 = 12V/60 ohms = .2 amps, and I3 = 12V/15 ohms = .8 amps). Add the currents from each branch for a total of 1.4 amps (.4 + .2 + .8).
[Ref: General Handbook H-8083-30A-ATB, Chapter 12 Page 43]

12-37 Answer B.

Total resistance in a parallel circuit is smaller than the smallest resistor; therefore, if you remove a resistor in a parallel circuit the total resistance will become larger.
[Ref: General Handbook H-8083-30A-ATB, Chapter 12 Page 43]

12-38 AMG031
If three resistors of 3 ohms, 5 ohms, and 22 ohms are connected in series in a 28-volt circuit, how much current will flow through the 3-ohm resistor?
A. 9.3 amperes
B. 1.05 amperes
C. 0.93 amperes

12-39 AMG031
The opposition offered by a coil to the flow of alternating current is called (disregard resistance)
A. impedance.
B. reluctance.
C. inductive reactance.

12-40 AMG031
Capacitors are sometimes used in DC circuits to
A. counteract inductive reactance at specific locations.
B. smooth out slight pulsations in current/voltage.
C. assist in stepping voltage and current up and/or down.

12-41 AMG031
The working voltage of a capacitor in an AC circuit should be
A. equal to the highest applied voltage.
B. at least 20 percent greater than the highest applied voltage.
C. at least 50 percent greater than the highest applied voltage.

12-42 AMG031
The amount of electricity a capacitor can store is directly proportional to the
A. distance between the plates and inversely proportional to the plate area.
B. plate area and is not affected by the distance between the plates.
C. plate area and inversely proportional to the distance between the plates.

12-43 AMG031
When different rated capacitors are connected in parallel in a circuit, the total capacitance is
(Note: CT = C1 + C2 + C3 ...)
A. less than the capacitance of the lowest rated capacitor.
B. equal to the capacitance of the highest rated capacitor.
C. equal to the sum of all the capacitances.

FUNDAMENTALS OF ELECTRICITY AND ELECTRONICS

ANSWERS

12-38 Answer C.
Using Kirchhoff's Voltage Law, voltage varies across each resister while the current remains the same in a series circuit. First determine the total resistance in this circuit (Rt = 3 ohms + 5 ohms + 22 ohms = 30 ohms), Then use the formula I = E/R to determine the current flowing across each resistor. I = 28V/30 ohms = 0.93 amperes
[Ref: General Handbook H-8083-30A-ATB, Chapter 12 Page 42]

12-39 Answer C.
Inductive reactance is the opposition to the flow of current.
[Ref: General Handbook H-8083-30A-ATB, Chapter 12 Page 44]

12-40 Answer B.
The function of capacitors is to smooth out DC pulsations.
[Ref: General Handbook H-8083-30A-ATB, Chapter 12 Page 76]

12-41 Answer C.
The capacitor should be selected so that its working voltage is at least 50 percent greater than the highest voltage to be applied.
[Ref: General Handbook H-8083-30A-ATB, Chapter 12 Page 52]

12-42 Answer C.
The capacitance of parallel plates is directly proportional to their area and inversely proportional to their spacing.
[Ref: General Handbook H-8083-30A-ATB, Chapter 12 Page 52]

12-43 Answer C.
We can derive from the formula that capacitors in a parallel circuit are equal to the sum of all the capacitances.
[Ref: General Handbook H-8083-30A-ATB, Chapter 12 Page 55]

12-44 AMG031
What is the total capacitance of a circuit containing three capacitors with capacitances of .25 microfarad, .03 microfarad, and .12 microfarad, respectively?
(Note: CT = C1 + C2 + C3 ...)
  A. .4 µF
  B. .04 pF
  C. .04 µF

12-45 AMG031
Transfer of electrical energy from one circuit to another without the aid of electrical connections
  A. is called induction.
  B. is called capacitance.
  C. is practical for use only with low voltages/amperages.

12-46 AMG031
When inductors are connected in series in a circuit, the total inductance is (where the magnetic fields of each inductor do not affect the others)
(Note: LT = L1 + L2 + L3 ...)
  A. less than the inductance of the lowest rated inductor.
  B. equal to the inductance of the highest rated inductor.
  C. equal to the sum of the individual inductances.

12-47 AMG031
Referring to the equation, when more than two inductors of different inductances are connected in parallel in a circuit, the total inductance is

$$L_T = \frac{1}{1/L_1 + 1/L_2 + 1/L_3...}$$

  A. less than the inductance of the lowest rated inductor.
  B. equal to the inductance of the highest rated inductor.
  C. equal to the sum of the individual inductances.

12-48 AMG031
An increase in which of the following factors will cause an increase in the inductive reactance of a circuit
  A. inductance and frequency.
  B. resistance and voltage.
  C. resistance and capacitive reactance.

12-49 AMG031
The term that describes the combined resistive forces in an AC circuit is
  A. resistance.
  B. reactance.
  C. impedance.

FUNDAMENTALS OF ELECTRICITY AND ELECTRONICS

ANSWERS

12-44 Answer A.
Use the formula to solve the problem.
CT = .25 µF + .03 µF + .12 µF = .4 µF
[Ref: General Handbook H-8083-30A-ATB, Chapter 12 Page 55]

12-45 Answer A.
Induction or induced current is produced when a conductor is cut or crossed by the changing lines of a magnetic flux. This transfer of energy is produced without the aid of electrical connections.
[Ref: General Handbook H-8083-30A-ATB, Chapter 12 Page 57]

12-46 Answer C.
We can derive this answer from the equation provided. In a series circuit total inductance (LT) is equal to the sum of the individual inductances.
[Ref: General Handbook H-8083-30A-ATB, Chapter 12 Page 59]

12-47 Answer A.
We can derive this answer from the equation provided. In a parallel circuit, total inductance (L_T) is less than the inductance of the lowest rated inductor.
[Ref: General Handbook H-8083-30A-ATB, Chapter 12 Page 60]

12-48 Answer A.
The inductive reactance of a component is directly proportional to the inductance of the component and the applied frequency to the circuit.
[Ref: General Handbook H-8083-30A-ATB, Chapter 12 Page 60]

12-49 Answer C.
Impedance is defined as the combined effects of resistance, inductive reactance, and capacitive reactance. Together, these effects make up the total opposition to current flow in an AC circuit.
[Ref: General Handbook H-8083-30A-ATB, Chapter 12 Page 61]

12-50 AMG031
What is the impedance of an AC series circuit consisting of an inductor with a reactance of 10 ohms, a capacitor with a reactance of 4 ohms, and a resistor with a resistance of 8 ohms?

$$Z = \sqrt{R^2 + (X_L - X_c)^2}$$

Z = Impedance
R = Resistance
X_L = Inductive Reactance
X_C = Capacitive Reactance

   A. 2.5 ohms
   B. 5.29 ohms
   C. 10 ohms

12-51 AMG031
The basis for transformer operation in the use of alternating current is mutual
   A. inductance.
   B. capacitance.
   C. reactance.

12-52 AMG031
When calculating power in a reactive or inductive AC circuit, the true power is
   A. more than the apparent power.
   B. less than the apparent power in a reactive circuit and more than the apparent power in an inductive circuit.
   C. less than the apparent power.

12-53 AMG031
What happens to the current in a voltage step-up transformer with a ratio of 1 to 4?
   A. The current is stepped down by a 1 to 4 ratio.
   B. The current is stepped up by a 1 to 4 ratio.
   C. The current does not change.

12-54 AMG031
Referring to Figure 12-10 below, how many instruments (voltmeters and ammeters) are installed correctly?
   A. All are installed correctly.
   B. 1
   C. 2

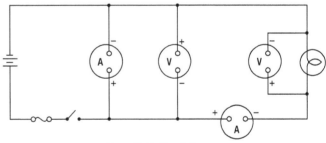

Figure 12-10. Circuit diagram.

12-55 AMG031
Troubleshooting an open circuit with a voltmeter as shown in the circuit in Figure 12-11 will
   A. permit current to illuminate the lamp.
   B. create a low resistance path and the current flow will be greater than normal.
   C. permit the battery voltage to appear on the voltmeter.

FUNDAMENTALS OF ELECTRICITY AND ELECTRONICS

ANSWERS

12-50 Answer C.
To find the impedance (Z), when a circuit contains resistance, inductance, and capacitance, use the following equation:

$$Z = \sqrt{R^2 + (X_L - X_c)^2}$$

$Z = \sqrt{[8^2 + (10-4)2]} = \sqrt{[64 + (6)2]} = \sqrt{[64 + 36]} = \sqrt{[100]} = 10$ ohms
[Ref: General Handbook H-8083-30A-ATB, Chapter 12 Page 63]

12-51 Answer A.
Basic transformers consist of two coils that are not electrically connected, but are arranged so that the magnetic field surrounding one coil cuts through the other coil. When an alternating voltage is applied to (across) one coil, the varying magnetic field set up around that coil creates an alternating voltage in the other coil by mutual induction.
[Ref: General Handbook H-8083-30A-ATB, Chapter 12 Page 66]

12-52 Answer C.
When there is capacitance or inductance in the circuit, the current and voltage are not exactly in phase and the true power is less than the apparent power.
[Ref: General Handbook H-8083-30A-ATB, Chapter 12 Page 66]

12-53 Answer A.
If a transformer steps up the voltage, it will step down the current by the same ratio. This should be evident if the power formula is considered. The power (I × E) of the output (secondary) electrical energy is the same as the input (primary) power minus the energy loss in the transforming process. In this example the current is stepped down by a 1 to 4 ratio.
[Ref: General Handbook H-8083-30A-ATB, Chapter 12 Page 67]

12-54 Answer C.
Refer to Figure 12-10 below. Always connect an ammeter in series with the element through which the current flow is to be measured. Item 1 is incorrect as it is parallel to the circuit, therefore Item 2 is correctly installed. When voltmeters are used, they are connected in parallel with a circuit. Observe that the polarity is correct before connecting the meter to the circuit or damage will occur by driving the movement backwards. Item 3 is incorrect because the polarity is reversed, therefore Item 4 is correctly installed.
[Ref: General Handbook H-8083-30A-ATB, Chapter 12 Page 71-72]

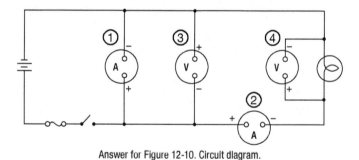

Answer for Figure 12-10. Circuit diagram.

12-55 Answer C.
When voltmeters are used, they are connected in parallel with a circuit. When a voltmeter is connected across two points in a circuit, current will be shunted, allowing the current to complete its circuit, however the use of a high resistance voltmeter will reduce the amount of current allowed to flow through the voltmeter to reduce the effects of shunting, but still allow the reading of the voltage in the circuit.
[Ref: General Handbook H-8083-30A-ATB, Chapter 12 Page 73]

12-56 AMG031
What is the correct way to connect a test voltmeter in a circuit is?
  A. In series with a unit.
  B. Between source voltage and the load.
  C. In parallel with a unit.

12-58 AMG031
Referring to Figure 12-12 below, the No.7 wire is used to
  A. Complete the PUSH-TO-TEST circuit.
  B. open the UP indicator light circuit when the landing gear is retracted.
  C. close the UP indicator light circuit when the landing gear is retracted.

12-57 AMG031
Referring to Figure 12-12 below, with the landing gear retracted, the red indicator light will not come on if an open occurs in wire
  A. number 7.
  B. number 17.
  C. number 19.

12-59 AMG031
Referring to Figure 12-12 below, when the landing gear is down, the green light will not come on if an open condition occurs in which wire?
  A. Number 6
  B. Number 7
  C. Number 17

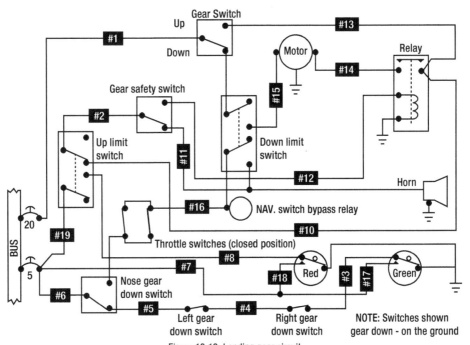

Figure 12-12. Landing gear circuit.

FUNDAMENTALS OF ELECTRICITY AND ELECTRONICS

ANSWERS

12-56 Answer C.
When voltmeters are used, they are connected in parallel with a circuit. Observe the polarity is correct before connecting the meter to the circuit.
[Ref: General Handbook H-8083-30A-ATB, Chapter 12 Page 72]

12-58 Answer A.
Wire #7 supplies power to both the red and green indicator lights push-to-test circuits. When the push-to-test button is pressed, the circuit is closed to ground. Push-to-test buttons verify the bulb is working.
[Ref: General Handbook H-8083-30A-ATB, Chapter 12 Page 89]

12-57 Answer C.
If an open condition should occur in wire #19 the red indicator light will not turn on. Wire #19 supplies power to red indicator light via the up limit switch and wire #8. Wire #7 supplies power to wire #18 for the red indicator light push-to-test circuit, and wire #17 for the green indicator light push-to-test circuit.
[Ref: General Handbook H-8083-30A-ATB, Chapter 12 Page 89]

12-59 Answer A.
If there is an open condition in wire #6, the green light will not come on when the landing gear is down. However, if there was an open condition in wire #5, #4, or #3 the light would not come on either. In the real world, additional troubleshooting would need to be completed to locate the wire with the open condition along this circuit.
[Ref: General Handbook H-8083-30A-ATB, Chapter 12 Page 89]

12-60 AMG031

The purpose of providing a space underneath the plates in a lead acid battery's cell container is to

- A. ensure the electrolyte quantity ratio to the number of plates and plate area is adequate.
- B. prevent sediment buildup from contacting the plates and causing a short circuit.
- C. allow for convection flow of the electrolyte to provide cooling of the plates.

12-61 AMG031

If electrolyte from a lead-acid battery is spilled in the battery compartment, which procedure should be followed?

- A. Apply boric acid solution to the affected area followed by a water rinse.
- B. Rinse the affected area thoroughly with clean water.
- C. Apply sodium bicarbonate solution to the affected area followed by a water rinse.

12-62 AMG031

Which statement regarding the hydrometer reading of a lead-acid storage battery electrolyte is true?

- A. The hydrometer reading does not require a temperature correction if the electrolyte temperature is 80 °F.
- B. A specific gravity correction should be subtracted from the hydro meter reading if the electrolyte temperature is above 20 °F.
- C. The hydrometer reading will give a true indication of the capacity of the battery regardless of the electrolyte temperature.

12-63 AMG031

What determines the amount of current which will flow through a battery while it is being charged by a constant voltage source?

- A. The total plate area of the battery.
- B. The state-of-charge of the battery.
- C. The ampere-hour capacity of the battery.

12-64 AMG031

A lead acid battery with 12 cells connected in series (no load voltage = 2.1 volts per cell) furnishes 10 amperes to a load of 2 ohms resistance. The internal resistance of the battery in this instance is

- A. 0.52 ohm.
- B. 2.52 ohms.
- C. 5.0 ohms.

12-65 AMG031

Which of the following statement(s) is/are generally true regarding the charging of several aircraft batteries together?

1. Batteries of different voltages (but similar capacities) can be connected in series with each other across the charger, and charged using the constant current method.
2. Batteries of different ampere-hour capacity and same voltage can be connected in parallel with each other across the charger, and charged using the constant voltage method.
3. Batteries of the same voltage and same ampere-hour capacity must be connected in series with each other across the charger, and charged using the constant current method.

- A. 3
- B. 2 and 3
- C. 1 and 2

FUNDAMENTALS OF ELECTRICITY AND ELECTRONICS

ANSWERS

12-60 Answer B.
This space permits the electrolyte to circulate freely around the plates and provides a path for sediment, causing shorting out of the plates, to settle to the bottom of the cell.
[Ref: General Handbook H-8083-30A-ATB, Chapter 12 Page 90]

12-61 Answer C.
If a spill occurs, wash out the compartment, neutralize with a sodium bicarbonate solution, rinse with water, and dry thoroughly.
[Ref: General Handbook H-8083-30A-ATB, Chapter 12 Page 93]

12-62 Answer A.
The specific gravity reading on a hydrometer will vary from the actual specific gravity as the temperature changes. No correction is necessary when the temperature is between 70 °F and 90 °F, since the variation is not great enough to consider. When temperatures are greater than 90 °F or less than 70 °F, it is necessary to apply a correction factor.
[Ref: General Handbook H-8083-30A-ATB, Chapter 12 Page 93]

12-63 Answer B.
The state of charge of a storage battery depends upon the condition of its active materials, primarily the plates. In the constant voltage method, a motor generator set with a constant, regulated voltage forces the current through the battery. In this method, the current at the start of the process is high but automatically tapers off.
[Ref: General Handbook H-8083-30A-ATB, Chapter 12 Page 93]

12-64 Answer A.
To determine the internal resistance, subtract the closed circuit voltage from the no load voltage and then divide by the closed circuit current.
No load voltage: 12 cells × 2.1 volts = 25.2 volts
Closed circuit voltage: 1- amps × 2 ohms = 20 volts
Closed circuit current: 10 amps (25.2 volts – 20 volts) ÷ 10 amps = .52. ohms
[Ref: General Handbook H-8083-30A-ATB, Chapter 12 Page 93]

12-65 Answer C.
In the constant current charging method, the current remains almost constant during the entire charging process. Multiple batteries may be charged at one time but must be placed in series so the current remains the same across all the batteries. This method requires a longer time to charge a battery fully and toward the end of the process, presents the danger of overcharging if care is not exercised. In the constant voltage method, a motor generator set with a constant, regulated voltage forces the current through the battery. The constant voltage method requires less time and supervision than does the constant current method. Multiple batteries can also be charged at the same time using the constant voltage charging method. The batteries must be placed in parallel with each other to maintain the same voltage within this recharging circuit.
[Ref: General Handbook H-8083-30A-ATB, Chapter 12 Page 94]

12-66 AMG031
When a charging current is applied to a nickel- cadmium battery, the cells emit gas?
  A. Toward the end of the charging cycle.
  B. Throughout the charging cycle.
  C. If the electrolyte level is too high.

12-67 AMG031
During inspection of a NiCad battery, at what point should the water level be checked and refilled if necessary?
  A. At least 3 hours after any significant discharge has occurred.
  B. When the battery is at a low charge state.
  C. When the battery is at a fully charged state.

12-68 AMG031
The electrolyte of a nickel-cadmium battery is highest when the battery is
  A. in a fully charged condition.
  B. in a discharged condition.
  C. under a no-load condition.

12-69 AMG031
The end-of-charge voltage of a 19-cell nickel-cadmium battery, measured while still on charge
  A. must be 1.2 to 1.3 volts per cell under normal operating temperature.
  B. must be 1.4 volts per cell averaged across the number of cells.
  C. depends upon its temperature and the method used for charging.

12-70 AMG031
Nickel-cadmium batteries, which are stored for a long period of time, will show a low liquid level because
  A. of the decrease in the specific gravity of the electrolyte.
  B. electrolyte evaporates through the vents.
  C. electrolyte becomes absorbed into the plates.

12-71 AMG031
How can the state-of-charge of a nickel-cadmium battery be determined?
  A. By measuring the specific gravity of the electrolyte.
  B. By a measured discharge.
  C. By the level of the electrolyte.

FUNDAMENTALS OF ELECTRICITY AND ELECTRONICS

ANSWERS

12-66 Answer A.
The cells of nickel-cadmium batteries emit gas towards the end of the charging cycle. This can also occur if the cells are overcharged.
[Ref: General Handbook H-8083-30A-ATB, Chapter 12 Page 94]

12-67 Answer C.
The level of electrolyte in a NiCad battery rises when it is being charged, and when fully charged it is at its higher state. Filling the battery from a low charge state will cause overflow when it later becomes fully charged.
[Ref: General Handbook H-8083-30A-ATB, Chapter 12 Page 93]

12-68 Answer A.
On recharge, the level of the electrolyte rises and, at full charge the electrolyte will be at its highest level.
[Ref: General Handbook H-8083-30A-ATB, Chapter 12 Page 95]

12-69 Answer C.
For nickel-cadmium batteries, the end-of-charge voltage is determined while the cell is on the charger and depends upon its temperature and the method used for charging.
[Ref: General Handbook H-8083-30A-ATB, Chapter 12 Page 95]

12-70 Answer C.
When stored for a long period of time, the water level in the battery evaporates and the electrolyte is absorbed into the plates, dropping the electrolyte level in the cells.
[Ref: General Handbook H-8083-30A-ATB, Chapter 12 Page 95]

12-71 Answer B.
This question is not specifically addressed in the text. Unlike lead-acid batteries, nickel-cadmium batteries cannot use a hydrometer to test for the state-of-charge. The only way to determine the state-of-charge for nickel-cadmium batteries is to fully discharge the battery, then recharge and measure the amount of charge put back in the battery.
[Ref: General Handbook H-8083-30A-ATB, Chapter 12 Page 95]

12-72 AMG031
Nickel-cadmium battery cases and drain surfaces, which have been affected by electrolyte, should be neutralized with a solution of
   A. boric acid solution.
   B. sodium bicarbonate.
   C. potassium hydroxide.

12-73 AMG031
Which of the following are commonly used as rectifiers in electrical circuits?
  1. Anodes
  2. Resistors
  3. Diodes
   A. 3, 1
   B. 3, 2
   C. 3

12-74 AMG031
Diodes are used in electrical power circuits primarily as
   A. cutout switches.
   B. rectifiers.
   C. relays.

12-75 AMG031
A typical application for zener diodes is as
   A. full-wave rectifiers.
   B. half-wave rectifiers.
   C. voltage regulators.

12-76 AMG031
Referring to Figure 12-13 below, if an open condition occurs at R_1, the light
  1. cannot be turned on.
  2. will not be affected.
  3. cannot be turned off.

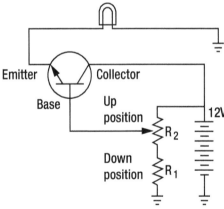

Figure 12-13. Transistorized circuit.

FUNDAMENTALS OF ELECTRICITY AND ELECTRONICS

ANSWERS

12-72 Answer A.
Boric acid solution. When replacing a lead-acid battery with a nickel-cadmium battery, the battery compartment must be clean, dry, and free of all traces of acid from the old battery. The compartment must be washed out and neutralized with boric acid solution, allowed to dry thoroughly, and then painted with an alkali resisting varnish.
[Ref: General Handbook H-8083-30A-ATB, Chapter 12 Page 94]

12-73 Answer C.
Diodes are commonly used as rectifiers within electrical circuits. Diodes can be described as electron check valves. They allow electrons to flow in only one direction. A rectifier is a device for converting alternating current to direct current, the diode only allows the flow of one of the alternation of the AC through the circuit.
[Ref: General Handbook H-8083-30A-ATB, Chapter 12 Page 105-107]

12-74 Answer B.
Diodes are commonly used as rectifiers within electrical circuits. Diodes can be described as electron check valves. They allow electrons to flow in only one direction. A rectifier is a device for converting alternating current to direct current, the diode only allows the flow of one alternation of the AC through the circuit.
[Ref: General Handbook H-8083-30A-ATB, Chapter 12 Page 107]

12-75 Answer C.
Within the normal operating range, the zener will function as a voltage regulator, waveform clipper, and other related functions.
[Ref: General Handbook H-8083-30A-ATB, Chapter 12 Page 106]

12-76 Answer C.
The schematic is a dimming circuit. The lamp is not meant to be completely turned off, the options range from full bright to full dim. If an open condition should occur at R_1 the light will not be able to be dimmed as the voltage drop will be reduced across R_2 and increase the brightness at all settings. The closest correct answer is C.
[Ref: General Handbook H-8083-30A-ATB, Chapter 12 Page 110]

12-77 AMG031
Referring to Figure 12-13 below, if R_2 sticks in the up position, the light will
1. be on full bright.
2. be very dim.
3. not illuminate.

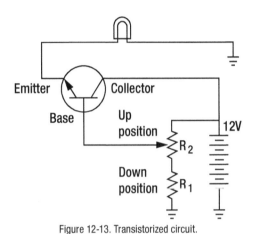

Figure 12-13. Transistorized circuit.

12-78 AMG031
Which statement concerning the logic gate depicted in Figure 12-13 above is true?
A. Any input being 1 will produce a 0 output.
B. Any input being 1 will produce a 1 output.
C. All inputs must be 1 to produce a 1 output.

12-79 AMG031
In a functional and operating circuit, the logic gate depicted in Figure 12-14 below will be 0
A. only when all inputs are 0.
B. when all inputs are 1.
C. when one or more inputs are 0.

12-80 AMG031
Which of the following logic gates illustrated in Figure 12-14 will provide an active high output only when all inputs are different?
A. XNOR
B. NOR
C. XOR

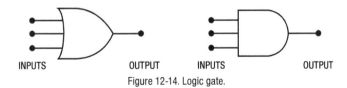

Figure 12-14. Logic gate.

FUNDAMENTALS OF ELECTRICITY AND ELECTRONICS

ANSWERS

12-77 Answer A.
The schematic is a dimming circuit. The up position is full bright. Therefore, if R_2 sticks in the up position, the light will be full bright and not be able to dim.
[Ref: General Handbook H-8083-30A-ATB, Chapter 12 Page 110]

12-79 Answer C.
This symbol represents a logic AND gate. It is telling us that when one or more inputs are 0 the output will be 0. In this logic AND gate all three inputs must have a value of 1 for the output to be 1.
[Ref: General Handbook H-8083-30A-ATB, Chapter 12 Page 125]

12-78 Answer B.
This symbol represents a logic OR gate. It is telling us that any input point with a value of 1 will result in an output of 1.
[Ref: General Handbook H-8083-30A-ATB, Chapter 12 Page 126]

12-80 Answer C.
Only the XOR or exclusive OR gate will provide a high (1) output only when the inputs are different.

The symbol for this is ⟐ and the truth table shows the inputs and outputs.
[Ref: General Handbook H-8083-30A-ATB, Chapter 12 Page 128]

A	B	C
0	0	0
0	1	1
1	0	1
1	1	0

ORAL EXAM

12-1(O).   Define capacitance.

12-2(O).   Name the two groups a capacitor can be classified.

12-3(O).   What is the basic unit of capacitance?

12-4(O).   Define inductance?

12-5(O).   What is the basic unit of inductance?

12-6(O).   Explain the relationship between mechanical and electrical power.

12-7(O).   In an AC circuit, does the capacitor cause the current to lead or lag the voltage? 10-8(O). In an AC circuit, does the inductor cause the current to lead or lag the voltage? 10-9(O). How is induction produced?

12-10(O). Name the basic unit of measurement for power.

12-11(O). State the formula for power.

12-12(O). State the three ways components can be arranged in a DC circuit?

12-13(O). State Ohm's Law in algebraic form and give the unit of measurement for each element.

12-14(O). Name the five sources of electrical energy.

12-15(O). Explain Kirchoff's voltage law.

2-16(O).   When measuring voltage, should the voltmeter be placed in series or parallel with the power source?

12-17(O). When measuring current, should an ammeter be placed in series or parallel with power source?

12-18(O). State the ingredients that makes up the electrolyte in a nickel-cadmium battery.

12-19(O). What instrument is used for measuring the specific gravity of the electrolyte in a lead-acid battery?

12-20(O). If the electrolyte of a lead-acid battery is spilled, what should be used to neutralize the acid?

12-21(O). If the electrolyte of a nickel-cadmium battery is spilled, what should be used to neutralize the acid?

12-22(O). What temperature range of the electrolyte in a lead-acid battery does not require a correction when measuring the specific gravity?

FUNDAMENTALS OF ELECTRICITY AND ELECTRONICS

ANSWERS

ORAL EXAM

12-1(O).   Capacitance is the property of an electric conductor that characterizes its ability to store an electric charge.
[Ref: General Handbook H-8083-30A-ATB, Chapter 12 Page 52, Glossary G-2]

12-2(O).   Fixed and variable.
[Ref: General Handbook H-8083-30A-ATB, Chapter 12 Page 53]

12-3(O).   The farad.
[Ref: General Handbook H-8083-30A-ATB, Chapter 12 Page 52]

12-4(O).   The ability of a coil or conductor to oppose a change in current flow.
[Ref: General Handbook H-8083-30A-ATB, Chapter 12 Page 58, Glossary G-5]

12-5(O).   The henry.
[Ref: General Handbook H-8083-30A-ATB, Chapter 12 Page 59]

12-6(O).   Mechanical power is measured in units of horsepower and electrical power is measured in watts. One horsepower is equivalent to 746 watts.
[Ref: General Handbook H-8083-30A-ATB, Chapter 12 Page 22]

12-7(O).   The current leads the applied voltage.
[Ref: General Handbook H-8083-30A-ATB, Chapter 12 Page 55]

12-8(O).   The current lags behind the applied voltage.
[Ref: General Handbook H-8083-30A-ATB, Chapter 12 Page 55]

12-9(O).   Induction or induced current is produced when a conductor is cut or crossed by the changing lines of a magnetic flux. This transfer of energy is produced without the aid of electrical connections.
[Ref: General Handbook H-8083-30A-ATB, Chapter 12 Page 57]

12-10(O).   The watt.
[Ref: General Handbook H-8083-30A-ATB, Chapter 12 Page 21, Glossary G-11]

12-11(O).   Power = Voltage times current (P=EI).
[Ref: General Handbook H-8083-30A-ATB, Chapter 12 Page 22]

12-12(O).   In series, in parallel, and in series-parallel.
[Ref: General Handbook H-8083-30A-ATB, Chapter 12 Page 34, 40, 42]

12-13(O).   E = I × R, where E is voltage and measured in volts, I is current and measured in amps, and R is resistance and measured in ohms.
[Ref: General Handbook H-8083-30A-ATB, Chapter 12 Page 17]

12-14(O).   Pressure, chemical, thermal, light, and magnetism.
[Ref: General Handbook H-8083-30A-ATB, Chapter 12 Page 23]

12-15(O).   The sum of all the voltage drops in a circuit must equal the sum of the voltage source(s) in the circuit.
[Ref: General Handbook H-8083-30A-ATB, Chapter 12 Page 41]

PRACTICAL EXAM

12-1(P).   Given an aircraft or mockup of a component with electrical power and the appropriate measuring equipment, measure the voltage in a specified circuit and record your findings.

12-2(P).   Given an aircraft or mockup of a component with electrical power and the appropriate measuring equipment, measure the current in a specified circuit and record your findings.

12-3(P).   Given an aircraft or mockup of a component with electrical power and the appropriate measuring equipment, measure the resistance in a specified circuit and record your findings.

12-4(P).   Given an aircraft or mockup of a component and the appropriate measuring equipment, determine the continuity of a specified circuit and record your findings.

12-5(P).   Given a listing of measurements, or those measurements gathered from readings you have taken and the appropriate publications, determine if the readings are within the acceptable range and record your findings.

12-6(P).   Given an electrical circuit diagram, answer written or oral questions about the diagram.

12-7(P).   Given a faulty electrical circuit on a aircraft or mockup, the required tools, and appropriate publications, troubleshoot the circuit and record your findings.

12-8(P).   Given the minimum required information, calculate voltage using Ohm's Law.

12-9(P).   Given the minimum required information, calculate current using Ohm's Law.

12-10(P).   Given the minimum required information, calculate resistance using Ohm's Law.

12-11(P).   Given an aircraft or mockup, inspect the battery and its associated electrical system and record your findings.

12-12(P).   Given an aircraft battery and a hydrometer determine the battery's state-of-charge and record your findings.

12-13(P).   Given an aircraft battery and the appropriate equipment, complete an electrical leak (cell imbalance) test and record your findings.

12-14(P).   Given an aircraft or mockup, the appropriate tools, and applicable publications, remove the battery.

12-15(P).   Given an aircraft or mockup, the appropriate tools, and applicable publications, install a battery.

12-16(P).   Given the appropriate equipment, set-up and connect a charger to one or more batteries for constant current charging.

12-17(P).   Given the appropriate equipment, set-up and connect a charger to one or more batteries for constant voltage charging.

FUNDAMENTALS OF ELECTRICITY AND ELECTRONICS

ANSWERS

ORAL EXAM

12-16(O). When voltmeters are used, they are connected in parallel with a circuit.
[Ref: General Handbook H-8083-30A-ATB, Chapter 12 Page 72]

12-17(O). An ammeter should be placed in series with the element through which the current flow is to be measured.
[Ref: General Handbook H-8083-30A-ATB, Chapter 12 Page 72]

12-18(O). The electrolyte is a potassium hydroxide (KOH) solution in distilled water.
[Ref: General Handbook H-8083-30A-ATB, Chapter 12 Page 93]

12-19(O). A hydrometer.
[Ref: General Handbook H-8083-30A-ATB, Chapter 12 Page 92]

12-20(O). Wash the area thoroughly with water and then apply bicarbonate of soda.
[Ref: General Handbook H-8083-30A-ATB, Chapter 12 Page 92]

12-21(O). In case of spillage on hands or clothes, neutralize the alkali immediately with vinegar or dilute boric acid solution (one pound per gallon of water); then rinse with clear water.
[Ref: General Handbook H-8083-30A-ATB, Chapter 12 Page 94]

12-22(O). The hydrometer reading does not require a temperature correction if the electrolyte temperature is 70 °F - 80 °F.
[Ref: General Handbook H-8083-30A-ATB, Chapter 12 Page 92]

MECHANIC PRIVILEGES AND LIMITATIONS

General Mechanic Certification, Specific Mechanic Certification, Inspection Authorization, and Ethics

QUESTIONS

As an AMT you are expected to be able to read, understand, and apply Federal Regulations to your everyday work. It is recommended that you read the actual regulations and confirm you understand how the answer to each question is interpreted from the regulation itself. These are not the only regulations you will be required to know and understand during your career, so it is highly recommended you understand how to read and interpret regulations. If you are having difficulties, ask for assistance from your instructor(s).

13-1 AMG082
A mechanic applicant is issued a temporary certificate after successful completion of the required tests to allow for what?
- A. Review of his/her application and supplementary documents.
- B. Background check/investigation that may be completed.
- C. Both A and b.

13-2 AMG082
What part of the FARs prescribes the requirements for issuing mechanic certificates and associated ratings and the general operating rules for the holders of these certificates and ratings?
- A. 14 CFR Part 43
- B. 14 CFR Part 56
- C. 14 CFR Part 65

13-3 AMG082
What is the maximum duration of a temporary airman certificate?
- A. 60 days
- B. 90 days
- C. 120 days

13-4 AMG082
Under Title 14 of the Code of Federal Regulations, what is the maximum penalty for falsification, alteration, or fraudulent reproduction of certificates, logbooks, reports, and records?
- A. Ineligibility to receive any certificate or rating for one year.
- B. Imprisonment for up to one year and up to a maximum $5,000 fine.
- C. Suspension or revocation of any certificate held.

13-5 AMG082
What is the normal duration of a mechanic certificate with airframe and/or powerplant ratings?
- A. Valid until the holder is relieved of duties for which the holder was employed and certificated.
- B. Valid until surrendered, suspended, or revoked.
- C. Valid until 24 months after the holder has last exercised the privileges of the certificate.

13-6 AMG082
What is the maximum penalty for cheating or other unauthorized conduct when taking an FAA mechanic test?
- A. Ineligibility to receive any certificate or rating for one year.
- B. Ineligibility to receive any certificate or rating for one year, and suspension or revocation of any certificate held.
- C. Ineligibility to receive any certificate or rating for one year, and suspension of any certificate held for 5 years.

MECHANIC PRIVILEGES AND LIMITATIONS

ANSWERS

NOTE: 14 CFR is the 14th Title of the Code of Federal Regulations, and include the Federal Aviation R egulations (FARs). FAR and 14 CFR are interchangeable and you will see both used throughout this text.

13-1 Answer A.
Temporary certificates are issued to allow the review of an individual's application and supplementary documents.
[Ref: General Handbook H-8083-30A-ATB, Chapter 13 Page 2]

13-4 Answer C.
The maximum penalty for falsification, alteration, or fraudulent reproduction of certificates, logbooks, reports, and records is the suspension or revocation of any certificate held.
[Ref: General Handbook H-8083-30A-ATB, Chapter 13 Page 3]

13-2 Answer C.
14 CFR Part 65 provides the requirements for issuing mechanic certificates as well as providing the general operating rules for the holders of those certificates and ratings.
[Ref: General Handbook H-8083-30A-ATB, Chapter 13 Page 2]

13-5 Answer B.
A certificate or rating issued under this part is effective until it is surrendered, suspended, or revoked, with the exception of repairman certificates.
[Ref: General Handbook H-8083-30A-ATB, Chapter 13 Page 2]

13-3 Answer C.
Temporary certificates are effective for a period of not more than 120 days.
[Ref: General Handbook H-8083-30A-ATB, Chapter 13 Page 2]

13-6 Answer B.
Cheating or other unauthorized conduct during testing will result in not being able to reapply for any certificate or rating for a period of 1 year. It is also grounds for the suspension of any currently held certificate(s).
[Ref: General Handbook H-8083-30A-ATB, Chapter 13 Page 2]

13-7 AMG082
How long does the holder of a certificate issued under 14 CFR part 65 have to notify the FAA after any change in permanent mailing address?
- A. 30 days
- B. 60 days
- C. 90 days

13-10 AMG082
An aircraft owner was provided a list of discrepancies on an aircraft that was not approved for return to service after an annual inspection. Which of the following statements is/are true concerning who may correct the discrepancies?
1. Only a mechanic with an inspection authorization
2. An appropriately rated mechanic
3. An appropriately rated repair station
- A. 1
- B. 2
- C. 2 & 3

13-8 AMG082
When may an otherwise qualified mechanic who does not read, write, speak, and understand the English language be eligible to apply for a mechanic certificate?
- A. When a special authorization has been issued by the supervising FAA Flight Standards District Office.
- B. When employed outside the United States by a U.S. air carrier.
- C. When employed outside the United States by a non-US manufacturer.

13-11 AMG082
According to 14 CFR Section 65.19, should an applicant fail to receive a passing grade on a knowledge exam, he/she may:
- A. Appeal the grade by demonstrating proficiency in an oral or practical exam.
- B. Retake the exam after 60 days.
- C. Retake the exam anytime following further instruction.

13-9 AMG082
Which of the following may a certificated airframe and powerplant mechanic perform on aircraft and approve for return to service?
1. 100 hour inspection.
2. An annual inspection, under specified circumstances.
3. A progressive inspection, under specified circumstances.
- A. 1 and 3
- B. 1, 2, and 3
- C. 1 and 2

13-12 AMG082
The 100 hour inspection required by the FARs for certain aircraft being operated for hire may be performed by
- A. persons working under the supervision of an appropriately rated mechanic.
- B. appropriately rated mechanics only if they have an inspection authorization.
- C. appropriately rated mechanics and approved by them for return to service.

MECHANIC PRIVILEGES AND LIMITATIONS

ANSWERS

13-7 Answer A.
You must notify the FAA of any permanent change of mailing address within 30 days.
[Ref: General Handbook H-8083-30A-ATB, Chapter 13 Page 3]

13-8 Answer B.
The requirement to read, write, speak, and understand the English language may be waived if the applicant is employed outside of the United States by a U.S. air carrier. His or her certificate will be endorsed "Valid only outside the United States".
[Ref: General Handbook H-8083-30A-ATB, Chapter 13 Page 4]

13-9 Answer A.
An airframe and powerplant mechanic can perform 100 hour inspections required by part 91 and approve and return the aircraft to service. Mechanics with an Inspection Authorization (IA) may also perform progressive inspections.
[Ref: General Handbook H-8083-30A-ATB, Chapter 13 Page 5]

13-10 Answer C.
A certificated mechanic with an airframe and/or powerplant ratings may perform the maintenance and return the aircraft to service. Certificated repair stations will have the appropriately rated personnel to perform maintenance and return aircraft to service as well.
[Ref: General Handbook H-8083-30A-ATB, Chapter 13 Page 4]

13-11 Answer C.
Following the failure of a written exam, the applicant may either retake the exam following 30 days or sooner with a signed statement by a certified technician that further instruction has been received.
[Ref: General Handbook H-8083-30A-ATB, Chapter 13 Page 3]

13-12 Answer C.
An appropriately rated mechanic may perform a 100 hour inspection and return the aircraft to service.
[Ref: General Handbook H-8083-30A-ATB, Chapter 13 Page 4]

13-13 AMG082

A person working under the supervision of a certificated mechanic with an airframe and powerplant rating is not authorized to perform

A. repair of a wing brace strut by welding.

B. a 100 hour inspection.

C. repair of an engine mount by riveting.

13-16 AMG082

Regarding the below statements;

1. Certificated mechanics with an airframe rating may perform a minor repair to an airspeed indicator providing they have the necessary tools and equipment available.

2. Certificated mechanics with a powerplant rating may perform a major repair to a propeller providing they have the necessary tools and equipment available.

A. Only 1 is true

B. Neither 1 nor 2 is true

C. Only 2 is true

13-14 AMG082

Certificated mechanics, under their general certificate privileges, may

A. perform minor repairs to instruments.

B. perform 100 hour inspection of instruments.

C. perform minor alterations to instruments.

13-17 AMG082

A certificated mechanic shall not exercise the privileges of the certificate and rating unless, within the preceding 24 months, the Administrator has found that the certificate holder is able to do the work or the certificate holder has

A. served as a mechanic under the certificate and rating for at least 18 months.

B. served as a mechanic under the certificate and rating for at least 12 months.

C. served as a mechanic under the certificate and rating for at least 6 months

13-15 AMG082

FAA certificated mechanics may

A. approve for return to service a major repair for which they are rated.

B. supervise and approve a 100 hour inspection.

C. approve for return to service a minor alteration they have performed appropriate to the rating(s) they hold.

13-18 AMG082

Which of the following is true regarding the privileges of an A&P mechanic?

A. He/she may perform minor and major repairs and approve the work for return to service.

B. He/she may perform minor repairs and approve the work for return to service.

C. He/she may perform minor and major repairs, but may not approve the work for return to service.

ANSWERS

13-13 Answer B.
Only a certificated mechanic has the authorization to conduct 100 hour inspections. The mechanic may supervise the maintenance, preventive maintenance, or alterations of others for which he/she is rated and he/she has done the work previously.
[Ref: General Handbook H-8083-30A-ATB, Chapter 13 Page 4]

13-16 Answer B.
Statement 1 is false because a certificated mechanic is not authorized to repair instruments. Statement 2 is false because a certificated mechanic is not authorized to perform major repairs to propellers.
[Ref: General Handbook H-8083-30A-ATB, Chapter 13 Page 4]

13-14 Answer B.
A certificated mechanic may perform 100 hour inspections on instruments. He or she is just not authorized to repair them if found to be unairworthy.
[Ref: General Handbook H-8083-30A-ATB, Chapter 13 Page 4]

13-17 Answer C.
A certificated mechanic may not exercise the privileges of his certificate and rating unless, within the preceding 24 months, the Administrator has found that he/she is able to do that work; or he/she has, for at least 6 months served as a mechanic under his certificate and rating.
[Ref: General Handbook H-8083-30A-ATB, Chapter 13 Page 5]

13-15 Answer C.
A certificated mechanic may return to service, any aircraft or appliance, or part thereof, for which he is rated, including minor alterations.
[Ref: General Handbook H-8083-30A-ATB, Chapter 13 Page 4]

13-18 Answer B.
He/she may perform an airframe minor repair or minor alteration, and approve the work for return to service.
[Ref: General Handbook H-8083-30A-ATB, Chapter 13 Page 4]

13-19 AMG082

An Airworthiness Directive requires that a propeller be altered. Certificated mechanics could

A. perform and approve the work for return to service if it is a minor alteration.

B. not perform the work because it is an alteration.

C. not perform the work because they are not allowed to perform and approve for return to service, repairs or alterations to propellers.

13-20 AMG082

Which of the following is a requirement to continue to hold an Inspection Authorization (IA) certificate?

A. You must have a fixed base of operations.

B. You must have exercised the privileges of the certificate within the last 60 days.

C. You must have performed an annual inspection in the past 90 days.

13-21 AMG082

Who has the authority to approve for return to service a powerplant or propeller or any part thereof after a 100 hour inspection?

A. A mechanic with a powerplant rating.

B. Any certificated repairman.

C. Personnel of any certificated repair station.

13-22 AMG082

Instrument repairs may be performed

A. by the instrument manufacturer only.

B. by an FAA-approved instrument repair station.

C. on airframe instruments by mechanics with an airframe rating.

13-23 AMG082

What experience requirements must be met prior to being able to apply for Inspection Authorization?

A. Held an A&P certificate for 3 years and active as a mechanic for previous 2 years.

B. Held an A&P certificate for 5 years and active as a mechanic for previous 3 years.

C. Held an A&P certificate for 3 Years and have logged at least 200 hours of service during previous year.

13-24 AMG082

Which of the following are privileges of holding an Inspection Authorization rating, beyond those permitted with only airframe and powerplant ratings?

1. Perform and approve return to service an annual or progressive inspection.

2. Perform and approve return to service a 100 hour inspection but not an annual inspection.

3. Service and approve return to service aircraft instruments.

4. Approve return to service of an aircraft part following a major repair.

   A. A. All of the above

   B. B. 1 and 4

   C. C. 1, 3, and 4

MECHANIC PRIVILEGES AND LIMITATIONS

ANSWERS

13-19 Answer A.
A certificated mechanic can perform minor alterations and approve the work for return to service.
[Ref: General Handbook H-8083-30A-ATB, Chapter 13 Page 4]

13-22 Answer B.
Per the general privileges and limitations of the certificate, a mechanic cannot perform any maintenance, repairs, or alterations to instruments. Only approved instrument repair stations can perform this work.
[Ref: General Handbook H-8083-30A-ATB, Chapter 13 Page 4]

13-20 Answer A.
An IA certificate is valid through its expiration date so long as the holder has a fixed base of operations including the required equipment and availability of inspection data. The performance of an annual inspection each 90 days is one option for renewing the certificate upon its natural expiration date.
[Ref: General Handbook H-8083-30A-ATB, Chapter 13 Page 6]

13-23 Answer A.
You may apply for an Inspection Authorization rating after you have held an A&P certificate for 3 years and have been active as a mechanic for the previous 2 years.
[Ref: General Handbook H-8083-30A-ATB, Chapter 13 Page 5]

13-21 Answer A.
A certificated mechanic with a powerplant rating may approve for return to service a powerplant or propeller after a 100 hour inspection.
[Ref: General Handbook H-8083-30A-ATB, Chapter 13 Page 5]

13-24 Answer B.
With the Inspection Authorization (IA) rating the mechanic may perform and return to service an annual or progressive inspection. He or she may also approve the return to service of an aircraft part following a major repair.
[Ref: General Handbook H-8083-30A-ATB, Chapter 13 Page 6]

ORAL EXAM

13-1(O). When qualifying for a mechanic certificate with both airframe and powerplant ratings, how many months of practical experience are needed to meet the eligibility requirements?

13-2(O). What certificate and ratings must a mechanic hold to be authorized to conduct an annual inspection on an aircraft and return it to service?

13-3(O). What certificate and ratings must a mechanic hold to be authorized to conduct a 100 hour inspection on an aircraft and return it to service?

13-4(O). If you should move, how long do you have to notify the FAA of your permanent change of address and how may you notify the FAA?

13-5(O). How old must you be before you are eligible for a mechanic's certificate?

13-6(O). How many months experience must you have within any 24-month period to continue to exercise your mechanic privileges?

PRACTICAL EXAM

You should be able to demonstrate the ability to understand mechanic privileges and limitations contained in 14 CFR Part 65 by locating and interpreting/explaining the essential information within the regulations. Although all Federal Aviation Regulations can be chosen during your exam, the following areas located within 14 CFR Part 65 should be reviewed.

A. Offenses involving alcohol or drugs. (§65.12)
B. Written tests: Cheating or other unauthorized conduct. (§65.18)
C. Applications, certificates, logbooks, reports, and records: falsification, reproduction, or alteration. (§65.20)
D. Refusal to submit to a drug or alcohol test. (§121.15)
E. §120.15 Refusal to submit to a drug or alcohol test by a Part 65 certificate holder.
    a. This section applies to all individuals who hold a certificate under part 65 of this chapter and who are subject to drug and alcohol testing under this part.
    b. Refusal by the holder of a certificate issued under part 65 of this chapter to take a drug or alcohol test required under the provisions of this part is grounds for:
        i. Denial of an application for any certificate or rating issued under part 65 of this chapter for a period of up to 1 year after the date of such refusal; and
        ii. (2) Suspension or revocation of any certificate or rating issued under part 65 of this chapter.
F. General privileges and limitations. (§65.81)
G. Recent experience requirements. (§65.83)
H. Airframe rating; additional privileges and/or Powerplant rating; additional privileges. (§65.85 and §65.87)
I. Display of certificate. (§65.89)

MECHANIC PRIVILEGES AND LIMITATIONS

ORAL EXAM

13-1(O).   30 months experience is needed to be eligible for application for a mechanic certificate with an airframe and powerplant ratings.
   [Ref: General Handbook H-8083-30A-ATB, Chapter 13 Page 4, and FAR 65.77]

13-2(O).   A mechanic certificate with both an airframe and powerplant rating and an Inspection Authorization.
   [Ref: General Handbook H-8083-30A-ATB, Chapter 13 Page 6, and FAR 65.95]

13-3(O).   A mechanic certificate with both an airframe and powerplant rating.
   [Ref: General Handbook H-8083-30A-ATB, Chapter 13 Page 5, FAR 65.85, and 65.87]

13-4(O).   Address changes must be made within 30 days of moving, either in writing or on-line.
   [Ref: General Handbook H-8083-30A-ATB, Chapter 13 Page 3, and FAR 65.21]

13-5(O).   You must be at least 18 years old.
   [Ref: General Handbook H-8083-30A-ATB, Chapter 13 Page 4, and FAR 65.71]

13-6(O).   6 months.
   [Ref: General Handbook H-8083-30A-ATB, Chapter 13 Page 5, and FAR 65.83]

HUMAN FACTORS

Psychology, Human Factors in Aviation, The Pear Model, Human Error, and The "Dirty Dozen"

Introduction to Human Factors
Human factors training has been implemented in many aviation maintenance organizations within the United States. Although not yet mandated to be included within the curriculum of FAA certificated part 147 aviation maintenance schools, its importance is spreading. This training is currently mandated by the European Aviation Safety Agency (EASA) and many other countries around the world within their part 147 schools.

In an effort to promote the importance of safety and work performance of the AMT through the study of human factors, the FAA has added a chapter specifically devoted to human factors in aviation maintenance. Be advised that even if your school does not offer formalized training on human factors, you will encounter questions regarding this subject in the certification testing to become an AMT. By reading and understanding the material presented in Chapter 14 of the Aviation Maintenance Technician Handbook – General (FAA-H-8083-30-ATB) you will be prepared for those questions relating to human factors.

14-1 AMA111
Anthropometrics is the study of
  A. ancient cultural artifacts.
  B. physical dimensions and abilities of the human body.
  C. how people behave in social settings.

14-2 AMA103
When we think of aviation safety in a contemporary way, human error is
  A. the starting point.
  B. the ending point.
  C. the intervention point.

14-3 AMA103
The branch of human factors that studies an AMTs ability to quickly solve problems is called?
  A. Cognitive science.
  B. Safety engineering.
  C. Clinical psychology.

14-4 AMA103
The concept that a system should continue to function even if one of its components fails describes the practice of
  A. industrial engineering.
  B. safety engineering.
  C. anthropometrics.

14-5 AMA105
The model that incorporates people's actions in relation to their workplace environment, physical abilities, and available resources is the
  A. SHEL Model.
  B. Dirty Dozen Model.
  C. PEAR Model.

14-6 AMA105
The environmental aspect of the PEAR model considers which of the following:
  1. Work place design
  2. Shared goals
  3. Company culture
  4. Lighting
  A. 2 of the above factors
  B. 3 of the above factors
  C. All of the above factors

HUMAN FACTORS

ANSWERS

14-1 Answer B.
Anthropometry is the study of the dimensions and abilities of the human body. It is a branch of anthropology that focuses on the comparative measurements of the human body and its parts. Anthropometry data contributes to various aspects of our lives from product design to ergonomics.
[Ref: General Handbook H-8083-30A-ATB, Chapter 14 Page 5]

14-2 Answer A.
Human factors should not be a consideration after an accident or incident, but should be identified and made visible before they produce damaging results.
[Ref: General Handbook H-8083-30A-ATB, Chapter 14 Pages 2 and 14]

14-3 Answer A.
Cognitive science is the interdisciplinary scientific study of how our brains process information. Problem solving is another way of expressing troubleshooting. Learning how good troubleshooters process information through perception, language, reasoning, and even emotion can help improve the problem solving capabilities of others.
[Ref: General Handbook H-8083-30A-ATB, Chapter 14 Page 6]

14-4 Answer B.
Safety engineering assures a life-critical system behaves as needed even if a component fails. Ideally, engineers study a system to study what happens when a fault occurs and develop redundancy or backup systems to prevent an overall failure.
[Ref: General Handbook H-8083-30A-ATB, Chapter 14 Page 6]

14-5 Answer C.
PEAR is an acronym formed from the words: People, Environment, Actions, and Resources. This model is used to describe human factors and the relationships between the various aspects of human interaction within our world.
[Ref: General Handbook H-8083-30A-ATB, Chapter 14 Page 10]

14-6 Answer C.
The PEAR model divides environmental factors into physical and organizational environments. The physical aspects encompasses aspects of physical comfort such as lighting, noise control, temperature, etc. The organizational aspects encompass psychological aspects such as teamwork, mutual respect, communication, etc.
[Ref: General Handbook H-8083-30A-ATB, Chapter 14 Page 11]

14-7 AMA107

Considering an incident in which an AMT falls off a poorly maintained ladder; which would be considered the latent error?

A. The AMT was inattentive when climbing the ladder.
B. The AMT did not inspect the ladder prior to use.
C. The broken ladder should have been previously replaced.

14-8 AMA107

A lack of communication is a contributing cause for accidents/incidents. Which of the following personal actions can you use to improve communication and mitigate or reduce these risks?

A. Ensure that the pressure being felt is not self-induced.
B. Discuss work to be done or what has been completed.
C. Stop and look rationally at the problem.

14-9 AMA107

Which of the following is the best way to insure that you have understood verbal instructions?

A. Immediately write down the instructions on paper for reference.
B. Repeat the instructions back to the speaker.
C. Immediately perform the directed task while you remember the instructions.

14-10 AMA107

Which of the following is caused by overconfidence in one's ability to perform a task?

A. Distraction
B. Fixation
C. Complacency

14-11 AMA107

Which of the following actions can help you avoid complacency?

A. Always expect to find faults or problems.
B. Documenting your work in greater detail.
C. Sharing the work with another team member.

14-12 AMA108

Getting applicable training, keeping your knowledge current, using current manuals, asking questions, and asking someone who knows, are all behaviors or safety nets to reduce errors caused by a

A. lack of resources.
B. lack of knowledge.
C. lack of communication.

HUMAN FACTORS

ANSWERS

14-7 Answer C.
A latent error constitutes previous issues which led to the event, in this case the company's failure to notice the damaged ladder or its reluctance to fix or replace it when first discovered. While each of the above factors contributed to the event, the first in the series of errors allowed the possibility of the others occurring.
[Ref: General Handbook H-8083-30A-ATB, Chapter 14 Page 14]

14-8 Answer B.
Discussing work to be done or what has been completed are personal actions can you use to improve communication and mitigate or reduce these risks. Communication is a key attribute to conducting proper maintenance and maintaining a safe work environment. Good communication is a skill that can be learned.
[Ref: General Handbook H-8083-30A-ATB, Chapter 14 Page 15]

14-9 Answer B.
After hearing verbal communication, repeating it back to the person is a sure way to know you have received and understand the message being sent. The text described the concept of call backs. This concept is used in medical operating rooms and by pilots communicating with Air Traffic Control. It is also a basic strategy recommended for all verbal communications when listening for understanding. By repeating or paraphrasing the conversation, the receiver of the message can assure the sender that the message was understood correctly. If not, the sender can repeat and/or rephrase the message for better understanding.
[Ref: General Handbook H-8083-30A-ATB, Chapter 14 Page 16]

14-10 Answer C.
Complacency occurs when we feel confident or secure in an existing situation. Complacency can impact task awareness and diminish the ability to detect potential danger or defects.
[Ref: General Handbook H-8083-30A-ATB, Chapter 14 Page 16]

14-11 Answer A.
To avoid complacency always expect to find faults or problems. AMT's are often tasked with repetitive inspections and more often than not, nothing is found to be deficient. These types of tasks that do not challenge our skills, are done so often they become automatic, and rarely find a failure can lead to complacency. By always expecting faults or problems, we can focus on the task. Tell yourself "today is the day I will find a discrepancy."
[Ref: General Handbook H-8083-30A-ATB, Chapter 14 Page 16]

14-12 Answer B.
Lack of Knowledge can be overcome by getting applicable training, keeping your knowledge current, using current manuals, asking questions, and asking someone who knows. An AMT must have a vast knowledge base of aircraft systems and technology. However, we cannot know and retain everything that is required to maintain the often numerous types of aircraft we work on. Even if you only work on one aircraft, the amount of reference material is too large to retain everything. Therefore the use of current manuals is mandatory. Staying current with technology will assist you in maintaining your proficiency in an ever changing technological industry. Also do not be afraid to ask questions, nobody knows everything.
[Ref: General Handbook H-8083-30A-ATB, Chapter 14 Page 16]

14-13 AMA107
A behavior or safety net to reduce errors caused by distractions is to
A. double inspect your work, either by yourself or someone else.
B. use a detailed checklist.
C. mark the uncompleted work.

14-14 AMA107
Teamwork best exists when _____.
A. Each member is aware of the job requirements of the others.
B. A supervisor delegates specific tasks to specific people.
C. Everyone works together towards a common objective.

14-15 AMA107
Which behavior or safety net can improve teamwork?
A. Performing team tasks without a full team
B. Assigning duties among team members, regardless of experience level.
C. Improved communication and coordination among team members.

14-16 AMA106
Which of the following are symptoms of fatigue?
1. Short-term memory loss
2. Hot or cold flashes
3. Tiredness
4. Failure to maintain situational overview
5. Hunger
6. Mood swings
A. 1, 3, 4, 6
B. 2, 4, 5, and 6
C. 2, 3, and 5

14-17 AMA106
Of those listed below, which is the best countermeasure to combat fatigue?
A. A vacation lasting several days
B. Getting extra sleep on days off
C. Sleeping at regular intervals

14-18 AMA108
If a specified tool or part is not available to complete an assigned task, and no equivalent tools or parts are authorized, you should
A. use the closest type of tool or part available.
B. modify the most similar tool or part available to get it as close to specifications as possible.
C. cease work until the actual tool or part can be obtained.

HUMAN FACTORS

ANSWERS

14-13 Answer B.
Use a detailed checklist to reduce errors caused by distractions. Distractions can be either mental or physical. Using a detailed checklist will help you know where you left a task. It is also recommended that your mark COMPLETED work as you complete the task(s) listed on the checklist.
[Ref: General Handbook H-8083-30A-ATB, Chapter 14 Page 16]

14-14 Answer C.
Teamwork exists when everyone works together toward a common objective. Teams need to have a common objective to be efficient. Good teamwork makes the work easier and improves moral. Good communication is also a key factor in improving teamwork.
[Ref: General Handbook H-8083-30A-ATB, Chapter 14 Page 18]

14-15 Answer C.
Communication is a key factor in improving teamwork. Tasks can be accomplished by teams that are reduced in numbers if coordination though communication is accomplished. (Note: Always maintain safety...if safety is compromised by not having a full team re-evaluate the work to be done.) Reconfirming duties before the work commences is accomplished through communication and coordination.
[Ref: General Handbook H-8083-30A-ATB, Chapter 14 Page 20]

14-16 Answer A.
Short-term memory loss, tiredness, failure to maintain situational overview (also referred to as situational awareness), and mood swings are all symptoms of fatigue. Fatigue may be displayed in any number of symptoms both physical and mental. These symptoms can include lack of energy, lack of motivation, difficulty concentrating, difficulty starting and completing tasks, dizziness, moodiness, and short-term memory loss.
[Ref: General Handbook H-8083-30A-ATB, Chapter 14 Page 21]

14-17 Answer C.
The best remedy for combating fatigue is quality sleep at regular intervals, even on days off. People on shift work or who regularly change shifts are often unable to readjust their body's circadian rhythm, making even long periods of sleep of little benefit due to the poor quality of sleep. A vacation period may often have the same result as shift changes by losing the regularity of your sleep schedule.
[Ref: General Handbook H-8083-30A-ATB, Chapter 14 Page 22]

14-18 Answer C.
A lack of resources can be frustrating when you are on a timeline. Aircraft need to be in-service to generate revenue and the pressure to get a job done without the required tools and/or parts can be high. Sadly, it is not a matter of 'if' you will experience this situation, but when. Good communication and assertiveness will help in maintaining your personal integrity. Remember, lives can be affected: yours, your co-workers and passengers (who include family and friends).
[Ref: General Handbook H-8083-30A-ATB, Chapter 14 Page 23]

14-19 AMA107
Which action can help a technician reduce the feelings of pressure to quickly complete a task?
   A. Ensure that the pressure is not self induced.
   B. Accept solutions to a problem to expedite completion.
   C. Use a detailed checklist to monitor your rate of completion.

14-22 AMA107
Which behavior or safety net can help reduce errors caused by stress?
   A. Discussing this situation with someone else to get their input and assistance.
   B. Eliminating all sources of stress before starting the job.
   C. Being sure the stress is outside of your control and there is nothing you can do about it.

14-20 AMA106
Not alerting others when something does not seem right, not speaking up when the actions of another concern you, or not reporting procedures are poorly written or impractical, are all actions of someone who lacks?
   A. Awareness.
   B. Assertiveness.
   C. Knowledge.

14-23 AMA105
Working in high temperature environments can cause?
   1. The body to overheat.
   2. An increase in perspiration.
   3. An increased heart rate.
   A. 1 and 2
   B. 2 and 3
   C. All of the above.

14-21 AMA106
Which behavior will give you the most credibility and provide the greatest safety net against a Lack of Assertiveness?
   A. Avoiding complex tasks.
   B. Never compromising your integrity.
   C. Having others check your work.

14-24 AMA107
Which answer is a safety net for Lack of Awareness?
   A. Check if work conflicts with an existing modification or repair.
   B. Get a good night's sleep before coming to work.
   C. Ask your spouse to review the work you performed.

HUMAN FACTORS

ANSWERS

14-19 Answer A.
To reduce the feelings of pressure ensure the pressure is not self-induced. Pressure in this context means you are being forced to act to meet a particular outcome that you would not normally chose, or you are being asked to complete tasks that create undue demands, such as reduced deadlines. However, as noted in the text, pressure can be self-induced. Therefore, ask yourself is the pressure coming from outside forces, e.g. your supervisor, departure schedules, or customers, or are you creating them needlessly by your own thoughts or actions to try to perform to an unrealistic standard.
[Ref: General Handbook H-8083-30A-ATB, Chapter 14 Page 24]

14-20 Answer B.
Assertiveness is the ability to express your feelings, opinions, beliefs, and needs in a positive, productive manner. This skill may not come naturally to you but it can be learned. Your self-esteem and ability to be assertive will improve by learning to be a better communicator, gaining knowledge in your field, and being a positive and hardworking member of your team. These skills will add credibility to any situation you might encounter and have to address that proves unsafe or non-compliant with regulations and/or policy and procedures.
[Ref: General Handbook H-8083-30A-ATB, Chapter 14 Page 25]

14-21 Answer B.
You maintain your personal integrity by adhering to a high level of work standards that you never compromise. This is also the best way to maintain your credibility as an AMT. By maintaining high standards, others will not bother to ask you to compromise them, and you will be setting the example for others. Remember, actions speak louder than words.
[Ref: General Handbook H-8083-30A-ATB, Chapter 14 Page 25]

14-22 Answer A.
One way to help address stress is to discuss it with someone, be it a trusted friend, co-worker, or professional counselor. Stress is the result of physical, psychological, or physiological factors affecting our well-being. Discussing the situation with someone can help us determine what the sources of the stress are, called stressors, and thereby allow us to take action to reduce the effects or eliminate it all together. Understand not all stressors can be eliminated, but the negative effects can be reduced if we know what is causing them. As mentioned earlier, pressure can also be self- induced. Pressure can be stressor, if we examine the causes of the pressure and determine if it self-induced we can then work on eliminating it.
[Ref: General Handbook H-8083-30A-ATB, Chapter 14 Page 28]

14-23 Answer C.
Temperature is a physical stressor. High temperature exposure can cause all of the physical reactions listed. Take caution when working in extreme heat, stay hydrated, use sunscreen and tinted eye protection, and rest periodically out of the direct sun.
[Ref: General Handbook H-8083-30A-ATB, Chapter 14 Page 28]

14-24 Answer A.
Checking to see if the work you are doing conflicts with an existing modification or repair is one safety net to help in improving your awareness. Be aware of who's around you and what's around you. Even be aware of what is behind the work you are doing, such as wiring that could be damaged from drilling.
[Ref: General Handbook H-8083-30A-ATB, Chapter 14 Page 29]

14-25 AMA107

"Lack of Awareness" is defined as

A. a failure to recognize all the consequences of an action or lack of foresight.

B. not understanding the technical procedures required for your task.

C. after repeating the same task multiple times, losing awareness of some of the minor details of a task.

14-27 AMA103

What percentage of aircraft accidents are deemed to be caused by human error?

A. 20%

B. 50%

C. 80%

14-26 AMA107

Most often, problems associated with a team's "normal way of doing things" can be best identified by the

A. most experienced member of the team.

B. team's supervisor.

C. newest member of the team.

14-28 AMA107

The "SHEL" model is another human factors tool. The goal is to determine not only what the problem is, but also

A. where and why the problem exists.

B. how to recognize when the problem is likely to occur again.

C. how many human and non-human factors contribute to the problem.

HUMAN FACTORS

ANSWERS

14-25 Answer A.
Lack of Awareness can be defined as a failure to recognize all the consequences of an action or lack of foresight. This is the definition provided in the text and what you will be tested on. However, the original definition provided by Gordon DuPont, who coined the Dirty Dozen, defines it as "a lack of alertness and vigilance in observing." Mr. DuPont does go on to state that this occurs when the AMT fails to take into consideration possible consequences of his or her actions or inactions through lack of planning. Staying alert to what is going on around you and asking "what if" questions when you have conflicting information or when things don't appear just right can help you to remain more aware of your surroundings. "C" is not a definition; it would be considered a probable cause for the loss of awareness. "B" refers to a lack of knowledge.
[Ref: General Handbook H-8083-30A-ATB, Chapter 14 Page 28]

14-26 Answer C.
New team members usually will ask why something is done the way it is, especially if it differs from written policies or procedures. In other cases, norms are passed from one employee to another as "tribal knowledge" and no written policy or procedure has been documented. Norms are not necessarily bad. Good norms contribute to safety and efficiency and should therefore be documented. Bad norms are usually unsafe and/or are short cuts that bypass acceptable procedures to meet time pressures on the job. Use communication, assertiveness, knowledge, and personal integrity to address and correct any bad norms you may observe.
[Ref: General Handbook H-8083-30A-ATB, Chapter 14 Page 28]

14-27 Answer C.
Historically 20% of aviation accidents are caused by mechanical failure and 80% are caused by human factors as discussed in the dirty dozen. However, even of those 20% deemed to be caused by mechanical failure, many can be also be traced down the line to human issues during the design, manufacturing, or assembly levels.
[Ref: General Handbook H-8083-30A-ATB, Chapter 14 Page 31]

14-28 Answer A.
The SHEL model is similar to the PEAR model. It can help us define Human Factors by showing the relationship between our world of procedures ("S" represents software), machines ("H: represents hardware), environment ("E" represents environment) and their relationship with humans ("L" represents live ware), and our world of procedures ("S" represents software), machines ("H" represents hardware), and "E" represents environment. When investigating accidents/incidents this model can be used to determine in which areas errors are taking place and to focus solutions within those areas to remove or mitigate future risks.
[Ref: General Handbook H-8083-30A-ATB, Chapter 14 Page 13]

ORAL EXAM

14-1(O).   Describe complacency and how it relates to job performance.

14-2(O).   What causes fatigue and what are some solutions?

14-3(O).   Under the PEAR model, there are physical and organizational environments; describe them both.

14-4(O).   Describe an active error and a latent error, give examples.

14-5(O).   To avoid errors due to Lack of Communication, what steps can be taken by the departing shift?

14-6(O).   If a Technician is not familiar with a particular airplane, what steps can he or she take to remedy the problem?

14-7(O).   There are two kinds of unintentional errors, what are they called? Describe them both.

14-8(O).   Norms can be both positive and negative. Define norms and describe both positive and negative norms.

14-9(O).   Give some examples of common maintenance errors.

HUMAN FACTORS

ANSWERS

ORAL EXAM

14-1(O).   As a technician gains knowledge, a sense of self satisfaction and false confidence may occur. Repetitive tasks may be overlooked or skipped. Inspection of items may not seem important and mistakes may be overlooked. The mind may wander during repetitive tasks, which may lead to mistakes.
[Ref: General Handbook H-8083-30-ATB Chapter 14, Page 16]

14-2(O).   The major causes of fatigue are lack of a good night's sleep, too much stress, working too many hours or working various shifts. It is important to get 8 to 9 hours of sleep, exercise daily and eat healthy meals. You need to be aware of your natural circadian rhythm and at your low points, schedule non complex tasks. Shift work degrades performance, morale, and safety; this affects physical health. The technician along with his/her company must regulate shift work and time off.
[Ref: General Handbook H-8083-30-ATB Chapter 14, Page 19]

14-3(O).   The physical environment includes the workspace in the hangar, shop and in the field. Items that effect the physical environment can include outside weather, workspace, lighting, sound and temperature in the physical workspace. The organizational environment is less tangible. Leadership and organizational structure define communication, shared values, mutual respect and stress the importance of safety in the workplace.
[Ref: General Handbook H-8083-30-ATB Chapter 14, Page 11]

14-4(O).   Active errors (also called unsafe acts) are specific activities that lead to and cause a specific, obvious event. They are the central cause of the accident; for example: the AMT did not have the correct part and knowingly installed an incorrect part. Latent errors are company issues that lead to an unsafe event that may or may not happen; for example: The purchasing manager did not order the correct part. This may lead to the technician intentionally installing the wrong part as above which would then become an active error or the technician delaying the job to wait for correct part.
[Ref: General Handbook H-8083-30-ATB Chapter 14, Page 14]

14-5(O).   Make sure there is an overlap in schedule allowing technicians to communicate face to face so that accurate information is exchanged. Make sure all steps were completed without any omissions. All steps in the procedure must be signed off by departing technician as the work is performed. Applicable logs must be detailed and reviewed and discussed.
[Ref: General Handbook H-8083-30-ATB Chapter 14, Page 16]

14-6(O)   Technician must be sure to use all data available; manuals, other technicians familiar with the airplane; and most importantly, be aware that there are differences that exist between airplanes. If resources are not available, a manufacturer's representative should be contacted. If none of these options exist, the repair should be delayed until resources are available.
[Ref: General Handbook H-8083-30-ATB Chapter 14, Page 16]

14-7(O).   Unintentional errors fall into two categories, slips and mistakes. Slips can be an error in your action – i.e. transposing numbers, forgetting to tighten a bolt or overlooking a stress fracture. Mistakes would be an error in judgment or insufficient knowledge; i.e. selecting the wrong part for a repair, using the wrong procedure, or deciding that the repair is not necessary. Both slips and mistakes are not intentional but mistakes that can have serious consequences.
[Ref: General Handbook H-8083-30-ATB Chapter 14, Page 14]

PRACTICAL EXAM

14-1(P).   Role Play - A repair is given a deadline that is not realistic. You are the mechanic on duty and the repairs are necessary without skipping steps in order to follow proper safety protocol. Handle the situation with your supervisor.

14-2(P).   Role Play - Your supervisor is slurring his words and seems slightly disoriented. Deal with the situation.

14-3(P).   You have completed your shift, but not all tasks were completed. Fill out a task card to be passed to the next shift.

ORAL EXAM

14-8(O). Norms can be both positive and negative. Define norms and describe both positive and negative norms.
Norms is short for Normal – The normal way we do something. Norms can be positive or negative. Positive norms are organizations with a risk adverse safety culture. Negative norms in a company would be making sure you meet the deadline, even if steps are skipped.
[Ref: General Handbook H-8083-30-ATB Chapter 14, Page 28]

14-9(O). Give some examples of Common Maintenance Errors.
1. Incorrect installation of components.
2. Fitting of wrong parts.
3. Electrical wiring discrepancies to include crossing connections.
4. Forgotten tools and parts.
5. Failure to lubricate.
6. Failure to secure access panels, fairings, or cowlings.
7. Fuel or oil caps and fuel panels not secured.
8. Failure to remove lock pins.
[Ref: General Handbook H-8083-30-ATB Chapter 14, Page 30]

A. BASIC ELECTRICITY

REFERENCES: FAA-H-8083-30

Objective. To determine that the applicant:

1. Exhibits knowledge in, as a minimum, two of the following elements;
   a. Sources and/or effects of capacitance in a circuit.
   b. Uses of capacitance in a circuit.
   c. Sources and/or effects of inductance in a circuit.
   d. Uses of inductance in a circuit.
   e. Operation of basic AC and/or DC electrical circuits.
   f. Ohm's law.
   g. Kirchoff's law(s).
   h. Procedures used in the measurement of voltage, current, and/or resistance.
   i. Determining power used in simple circuits.
   j. Troubleshooting, and/or repair or alteration using electrical circuit diagrams.
   k. Common types of defects that may occur in an installed battery system.
   l. Aircraft battery theory/operation.
   m. Servicing aircraft batteries.

2. Demonstrates skill to perform, as a minimum, one of the following elements;
   A1. Install wires in an electrical connector plug. (Level 3)
   A2. Measure voltage, resistance, current, or continuity in a circuit and determine the appropriateness of the measurement. (Level 3)
   A3. Calculate and measure aircraft electrical power requirements. (Level 2)
   A4. Calculate and measure total capacitance in an electrical circuit. (Level 2)
   A5. Read and interpret aircraft electrical circuit diagrams, including solid state devices and logic functions. (Level 3)
   A6. Determine or measure for open electrical circuits. (Level 3)
   A7. Interpret electrical system shorts. (Level 2)
   A8. Measure electrical system voltages. (Level 3)
   A9. Measure electrical system component resistance. (Level 3)
   A10. Compute voltage of electrical circuits. (Level 3)
   A11. Measure resistance, current, and/or voltage in an electrical circuit. (Level 3)
   A12. Calculate and measure total inductance in an electrical circuit. (Level 2)
   A13. Identify commonly used aircraft electrical symbols. (Level 2)
   A14. Interpret aircraft electrical circuit diagrams. (Level 2)
   A15. Service an aircraft battery. (Level 3)
   A16. Inspect an aircraft battery. (Level 3)
   A17. Remove and install an aircraft battery. (Level 3)
   A18. Inspect battery compartments. (Level 3)
   A19. Measure the voltage drop across a resistor. (Level 3)

B. AIRCRAFT DRAWINGS

REFERENCES: FAA-H-8083-30

Objective. To determine that the applicant:

1. Exhibits knowledge in, as a minimum, two of the following elements--
   a. Characteristics and/or uses of any of the various types of drawings/blueprints and/or system schematics.
   b. The meaning of any of the lines and symbols commonly used in aircraft sketches/drawings/blueprints.
   c. Using charts or graphs.
   d. Troubleshooting an aircraft system or component(s) using drawings/blueprints and/or system schematics.
   e. Inspection of an aircraft system or component(s) using drawings/blueprints and/or system schematics.

f. Repair or alteration of an aircraft system or component(s) using drawings/blueprints and/or schematics.
g. Use of drawings/blueprints in component fabrication.
h. Terms used in conjunction with aircraft drawings/blueprints and/or system schematics.

2. Demonstrates skill to perform, as a minimum, one of the following elements;
   B1. Identify lines and symbols. (Level 2)
   B2. Interpret dimensions. (Level 2)
   B3. Use installation diagrams and/or schematics. (Level 3)
   B4. Draw a sketch of a major repair or alteration. (Level 3)
   B5. Use blueprint information. (Level 3)
   B6. Use graphs and charts. (Level 3)
   B7. Identify blueprint changes. (Level 2)
   B8. Determine material requirements from a drawing. (Level 2)

C. WEIGHT AND BALANCE
REFERENCES: FAA-H-8083-30
Objective. To determine that the applicant:
1. Exhibits knowledge in, as a minimum, two of the following elements;
   a. The purpose(s) of weighing or reweighing.
   b. General preparations for weighing, with emphasis on aircraft preparation and/or weighing area considerations.
   c. The general location of airplane center of gravity (CG) in relation to the center of lift for most fixed main airfoils.
   d. Definitions of any of the following: datum, arm, moment (positive or negative), or moment index.
   e. The meaning and/or application of any terms/nomenclature associated with weight and balance other than those mentioned in element d above, including but not limited to any of the following: tare, ballast, and residual fuel/oil.
   f. Procedures for finding any of the following: datum, arm, moment (positive or negative), or moment index.
   g. Purpose and/or application of mean aerodynamic chord (MAC).
   h. Adverse loading considerations.

2. Demonstrates skill to perform, as a minimum, one of the following elements;
   C1. Compute the empty weight and empty weight CG of an aircraft. (Level 3)
   C2. Check aircraft weighing scales for calibration. (Level 2)
   C3. Establish new weight and balance data for an aircraft after an equipment change. (Level 3)
   C4. Compute forward and aft loaded CG. (Level 3)
   C5. Prepare an aircraft for weighing. (Level 2)
   C6. Determine a location for permanent ballast to bring an aircraft back into balance. (Level 2)
   C7. Make a maintenance record entry for a weight and balance change. (Level 3)
   C8. Compute the amount of fuel needed for minimum fuel for weight and balance computations. (Level 3)
   C9. Weigh an aircraft. (Level 3)
   C10. Record scale readings from a weighed aircraft. (Level 2)
   C11. Compute weight and balance CG for a helicopter. (Level 3)
   C12. Calculate the moment of an item of equipment. (Level 3)
   C13. Determine the distance between the forward and aft CG limits of a helicopter. (Level 3)
   C14. Identify tare items. (Level 3)
   C15. Locate weight and balance information. (Level 1)
   C16. Locate datum. (Level 1)
   C17. Locate the baggage compartment placarding requirements for an aircraft. (Level 1)
   C18. Revise an aircraft equipment list after equipment change. (Level 3)
   C19. Determine the weight and location of required ballast. (Level 2)
   C20. Calculate the change needed to correct an overweight or out of balance condition. (Level 3)

D. FLUID LINES AND FITTINGS

REFERENCES: AC 43.13-1B; FAA-H-8083-30

Objective. To determine that the applicant:

1. Exhibits knowledge in, as a minimum, two of the following elements;
   a. Tubing materials.
   b. Tubing materials application.
   c. Tubing sizes.
   d. Flexible hose material.
   e. Flexible hose materials application.
   f. Flexible hose sizes.
   g. Flexible hose identification.
   h. AN, MS, and/or AC plumbing fittings.
   i. Rigid line fabrication techniques/practices.
   j. Rigid line installation techniques/practices.
   k. Flexible hose fabrication techniques/practices.
   l. Flexible hose installation techniques/practices.

2. Demonstrates the skill to perform, as a minimum, one of the following elements;
   D1. Make a replacement fluid line (aluminum or stainless steel). (Level 3)
   D2. Form a bead on tubing. (Level 3)
   D3. Fabricate a flare on tubing. (Level 3)
   D4. Fabricate and install fittings on a flexible hose. (Level 3)
   D5. Identify defects in metal tubing. (Level 2)
   D6. Repair a section of tubing. (Level 3)
   D7. Install and secure a fluid line with clamps. (Level 3)
   D8. Identify fluid and air lines that may be installed on aircraft. (Level 2)
   D9. Identify different flexible fluid lines. (Level 2)
   D10. Determine fluid line routing. (Level 3)
   D11. Fabricate and install metal tubing. (Level 3)
   D12. Identify aircraft fittings. (Level 2)
   D13. Install a flareless-fitting-tube connection. (Level 3)

E. MATERIALS AND PROCESSES

REFERENCES: FAA-H-8083-30

Objective. To determine that the applicant:

1. Exhibits knowledge in, as a minimum, two of the following elements;
   a. Any of the metals commonly used in aircraft and their general application.
   b. Composites and other nonmetallic components and their general application.
   c. Heat-treated parts precautions, using DD or icebox rivets.
   d. Typical wood materials and fabric coverings.
   e. Visible characteristics of acceptable and/or unacceptable welds.
   f. Precision measurement and precision measurement tools.
   g. Using inspection techniques/methods, including any of the following: visual, metallic ring test, dye/fluorescent penetrant, magnetic particle, and/or eddy current.
   h. Identification, selection, installation, and/or use of aircraft hardware.
   i. Safetying of components and/or hardware.
   j. Finding information about material types for specific application(s).

2. Demonstrates skill to perform, as a minimum, one of the following elements;
   E1. Perform a visual inspection of various welds. (Level 2)
   E2. Perform magnetic particle inspection of a steel part. (Level 2)
   E3. Identify different kinds of aircraft materials and hardware by using manufacturer's markings. (Level 2)

E4.   Select and install aircraft bolts. (Level 3)
E5.   Perform dye penetrant inspection of an aircraft part. (Level 2)
E6.   Make precision measurements with an instrument that has a vernier micrometer scale. (Level 3)
E7.   Check the alignment of a shaft. (Level 3)
E8.   Safety wires a turnbuckle, using an approved method. (Level 3)
E9.   Identify aircraft control cable. (Level 3)
E10. Fabricate a cable assembly using a swaged end fitting. (Level 3)
E11. Select the correct aluminum alloy for a structural repair. (Level 2)
E12. Identify rivets by physical characteristics. (Level 2)
E13. Determine suitability of materials for aircraft repairs. (Level 2)
E14. Determine if certain materials can be welded. (Level 2)
E15. Distinguish between heat-treated and non heat-treated aluminum alloys. (Level 2)
E16. Determine required torque value of given item. (Level 3)
E17. Check for proper calibration of a micrometer. (Level 2)
E18. Identify proper installation procedures for a seal, backup ring, and/or gasket. (Level 2)

G. CLEANING AND CORROSION CONTROL

REFERENCES: FAA-H-8083-30

Objective. To determine that the applicant:

1. Exhibits knowledge in, as a minimum, two of the following elements;
    a. Aircraft preparation for washing, general aircraft cleaning (washing) procedures.
    b. Postcleaning (washing) procedures.
    c. Corrosion theory.
    d. Types/effects of corrosion.
    e. Conditions that cause corrosion.
    f. Corrosion prone areas in aircraft.
    g. Corrosion preventive maintenance procedures.
    h. Inspection for and identification of corrosion in any of its various forms.
    i. Corrosion removal and treatment procedures.
    j. Use of Material Safety Data Sheets (MSDS).

2. Demonstrates skill to perform, as a minimum, one of the following elements;
    G1.   Clean aluminum and/or magnesium parts with caustic cleaners. (Level 3)
    G2.   Identify approved cleaning agents. (Level 2)
    G3.   Clean assigned area of aircraft. (Level 3)
    G4.   Identify different types of corrosion. (Level 2)
    G5.   Remove corrosion from an aluminum alloy. (Level 3)
    G6.   Apply protective coating to a metallic material. (Level 3)
    G7.   Remove iron oxide. (Level 3)
    G8.   Remove grease or oil from an appropriate part or component. (Level 3)
    G9.   Mechanically remove paint from a corroded aircraft part and determine extent of corrosion. (Level 3)
    G10. Locate procedures for preparing aircraft parts for extended storage. (Level 1)
    G11. Clean and protect plastics and/or composite materials. (Level 3)
    G12. Apply a protective coating to a metal surface. (Level 3)

H. MATHEMATICS

REFERENCES: FAA-H-8083-30

Objective. To determine that the applicant:

1. Exhibits knowledge in, as a minimum, two of the following elements;
    a. Areas of various geometrical shapes.
    b. Volumes of various geometrical shapes.
    c. Definitions/descriptions of geometrical terms, including but not limited to any of the following: polygon, pi,

diameter, radius, and hypotenuse.
    d. Ratio problems, including one or more examples of where or how they may be used in relation to aircraft maintenance or system(s) operation.
    e. Proportion problems, including one or more examples of where or how they may be used in relation to aircraft maintenance or system(s) operation.
    f. Percentage problems, including one or more examples of where or how they may be used in relation to aircraft maintenance or system(s) operation.
    g. Algebraic operations, including one or more examples of where or how they may be used in relation to aircraft maintenance.
    h. Conditions or areas where metric conversion may be necessary.

2. Demonstrates skill to perform, as a minimum, one of the following elements;
    H1. Determine the square root of given numbers. (Level 2)
    H2. Locate the instructions for determining square root. (Level 1)
    H3. Locate formulas to determine area and/or volume. (Level 1)
    H4. Compute the volume of a cylinder. (Level 3)
    H5. Compute the area of a wing. (Level 3)
    H6. Calculate the volume of a baggage compartment. (Level 3)
    H7. Convert fractional numbers to decimal equivalents. (Level 3)
    H8. Compare two numerical values using ratios. (Level 3)
    H9. Compute compression ratio. (Level 3)
    H10. Add, subtract, multiply, and/or divide positive and negative numbers. (Level 3)
    H11. Compute the least common denominator of two or more fractions. (Level 3)
    H12. Compute the torque value change when using a torque wrench with an extension. (Level 3)

I. MAINTENANCE FORMS AND RECORDS
REFERENCES: 14 CFR Parts 1, 43, and 91; FAA-H-8083-30
Objective. To determine that the applicant:
1. Exhibits knowledge in, as a minimum, two of the following elements;
    a. Writing descriptions of work performed and approval for return to service after minor repairs or minor alterations.
    b. The content, form, and disposition of aircraft maintenance records reflecting approval for return to service after a 100-hour inspection.
    c. The content, form, and disposition of aircraft maintenance records reflecting disapproval for return to service after a 100-hour inspection.
    d. The recording content, form, and disposition requirements for certificated aviation mechanics (without an Inspection Authorization) that perform major repairs and/or major alterations.
    e. The inoperative instruments or equipment provisions of 14 CFR part 91.
    f. The definition/explanation of any of the terms used in relation to aircraft maintenance, such as overhaul(ed), rebuilt, time in service, maintenance, preventive maintenance, inspection, major alteration, major repair, minor alteration, and minor repair.

2. Demonstrates skill to perform, as a minimum, one of the following elements;
    I1. Inspect an aircraft and prepare a condition report. (Level 3)
    I2. Make a log book entry for a repair or alteration. (Level 3)
    I3. Write a 100-hour inspection aircraft record entry. (Level 3)
    I4. Write an AD compliance aircraft record entry. (Level 3)
    I5. Complete an FAA Form 337. (Level 3)
    I6. Determine aircraft airworthiness by examining maintenance record entries. (Level 3)
    I7. Examine a FAA Form 337 for potential errors. (Level 3)
    I8. Prepare a master AD list for a specific airframe, engine and/or propeller and determine applicability by make, model, and serial number. (Level 3)
    I9. Write an annual inspection aircraft record entry. (Level 3)

I10. Make a maintenance record entry for a propeller minor repair that was performed by an individual that is being supervised by an appropriately rated mechanic that will be approving the repair for return to service. (Level 3)

I11. Write a 100-hour inspection aircraft maintenance record entry for an aircraft not approved for return to service. (Level 3)

I12. Write a maintenance record entry for compliance with manufacturer's Service Bulletin, Service Instruction, or Service Letter. (Level 3)

I13. Create a current equipment list for an aircraft, listing all equipment installed. (Level 3)

I14. Make the required maintenance record entries for approval for return to service after a major repair or major alteration. (Level 3)

I15. Complete the proper part or component tag for a part of known condition. (Level 3)

I16. Make a maintenance record entry for the installation of a serviceable part. (Level 3)

I17. Prepare a list of discrepancies and unairworthy items following a 100-hour inspection. (Level 3)

J. BASIC PHYSICS

REFERENCES: FAA-H-8083-30

Objective. To determine that the applicant:

1. Exhibits knowledge in, as a minimum, two of the following elements;
   a. Any of the simple machines, how they function, and/or how mechanical advantage is applied in one or more specific examples.
   b. Sound resonance, how it can be a hazard to aircraft, and how sound may be used to aid in inspecting aircraft
   c. The relationship between fluid density and specific gravity.
   d. The characteristic of specific gravity of fluids and how it may be applied to aircraft maintenance.
   e. The general effects of pressure and temperature on gases and liquids and how the qualities of compressibility and/or incompressibility of gases and liquids are generally applied to aircraft systems.
   f. Density altitude and the effects of temperature, and/or pressure, and/or humidity on aircraft and/or engine performance.
   g. Heat, how it is manifested in matter, and how heat transfer is accomplished through conduction, and/or convection, and/or radiation.
   h. Coefficient of linear (thermal) expansion as related to aircraft materials.
   i. Aircraft structures and theory of flight/physics of lift.
   j. The operation of aerodynamic factors in the flight of airplanes and/or helicopters.
   k. The relationship between force, area, and pressure.
   l. The five forces or stresses affecting aircraft structures.
   m. The two forms of energy and how they apply to aircraft and/or aircraft systems.

2. Demonstrates skill to perform, as a minimum, one of the following elements;
   J1. Convert temperature from one scale to another, for example °F to °C or from °C to °F. (Level 2)
   J2. Determine density altitude. (Level 2)
   J3. Determine pressure altitude. (Level 2)
   J4. Calculate force, area, or pressure in a specific application. (Level 3)
   J5. Demonstrate the mechanical advantage of various types of levers. (Level 3)
   J6. Design an inclined plane on paper, indicating the mechanical advantage. (Level 2)
   J7. Identify changes in pressure and velocity as a fluid passes through a venturi. (Level 2)
   J8. Design a mechanical pulley system. (Level 2)
   J9. Determine density of a solid object with a specific gravity of less than one. (Level 2)
   J10. Determine horsepower for a given weight, distance, and time. (Level 2)
   J11. Calculate expansion due to temperature change. (Level 3)

K. MAINTENANCE PUBLICATIONS

REFERENCE: FAA-H-8083-30

Objective. To determine that the applicant:

1. Exhibits knowledge in, as a minimum, two of the following elements;
   a. How a mechanic makes use of Type Certificate Data Sheets (TCDSs) and/or Aircraft Specifications in conducting maintenance or inspections.
   b. Aircraft maintenance manuals and associated publications including any of the following types of publications and how they are used: service bulletin, maintenance manual, overhaul manual, structural repair manual, or instructions for continued airworthiness.
   c. The requirements of 14 CFR Parts 43.13, 43.15, or 43.16 in the performance of maintenance.
   d. Airworthiness Directives (AD), including purpose and/or AD categories and/or ADs issued to other than aircraft.
   e. In what form individuals may receive FAA published AD summaries and/or how they may be obtained.
   f. The AD identification numbering system.
   g. FAA Advisory Circulars (ACs) including any of the following: significance of the AC numbering system, one or more examples of ACs issued to provide information in designated subject areas, one or more examples of ACs issued to show a method acceptable to the FAA complying with the CFRs.
   h. The intent or function of the Aviation Maintenance Alerts.
   i. The Air Transport Association (ATA) Specification 100.

2. Demonstrates skill to perform, as a minimum, one of the following elements;
   K1. Locate applicable FAA aircraft specifications and/or FAA type certificate data sheet for assigned aircraft or component. (Level 1)
   K2. Locate the CG range of assigned aircraft using aircraft specifications and type certificate data sheets. (Level 1)
   K3. Locate aircraft flight control travel limits. (Level 1)
   K4. Locate manufacturer's service instructions. (Level 1)
   K5. Determine applicability of an AD. (Level 3)
   K6. Inspect aircraft for compliance with applicable ADs. (Level 3)
   K7. Check a technical standard order (TSO) part for the proper TSO marking. (Level 3)
   K8. Use a manufacturer's illustrated parts catalog to locate a specific part number. (Level 3)
   K9. Locate supplemental type certificates (STCs) applicable to a specific aircraft. (Level 2)
   K10. Determine the conformity of aircraft instrument range markings and/or placarding. (Level 3)
   K11. Determine approved tires for installation on a given aircraft. (Level 3) FAA-S-8081-26A 24
   K12. Determine the ATA code for a specific item. (Level 3)
   K13. Determine maximum allowable weight of a specific aircraft. (Level 3)

L. AVIATION MECHANIC PRIVILEGES AND LIMITATIONS

REFERENCES: 14 CFR part 65; AC 65-30A; FAA-H-8083-30

Objective: To determine that the applicant:

1. Exhibits knowledge in, as a minimum, two of the following elements;
   a. Required evidence of eligibility experience satisfactory to the Administrator.
   b. Length of experience required for eligibility.
   c. Practical experience required for eligibility.
   d. The privileges of a mechanic in relation to 100 hour and annual inspections.
   e. Change of address reporting requirements.
   f. Minimum age requirements.
   g. Recent experience requirements to exercise privileges of a certificate.
   h. Who is authorized to perform maintenance/inspection, preventive maintenance, rebuilding, or alteration and/or approve for return to service afterwards.
   i. Causes for revocation or suspension.
   j. Criteria for determining major and minor repair or alteration.

2. Demonstrates skill to perform, as a minimum, one of the following elements;

L1. Determine if a given repair is major or minor. (Level 3)

L2. Determine if a given alteration is major or minor. (Level 3)

L3. Locate address change notification procedures. (Level 1)

L4. List airframe mechanic privileges and limitations. (Level 2)

L5. List powerplant mechanic privileges and limitations. (Level 2)

L6. Locate mechanic privileges and limitations. (Level 1)

L7. List the authorities to which an A&P mechanic must show his/her A&P certificate on demand. (Level 2)

L8. Locate the 14 CFR reference that gives the privileges that a certified mechanic airframe or powerplant have. (Level 1)

L9. List types of inspections that a certificated mechanic with airframe and powerplant ratings may perform and the 14 CFR reference for each one. (Level 2)

L10. Determine references used in performing preventive maintenance. (Level 2)

L11. List the maintenance functions that a certificated mechanic may not supervise. (Level 2)